THE CONSULTANT'S GUIDE TO NEWSLETTER PROFITS

THE CONSULTANT'S GUIDE TO NEWSLETTER PROFITS

HERMAN R. HOLTZ

DOW JONES-IRWIN
Homewood, Illinois   60430

We recognize that certain terms in this book are trademarks, and we have made every effort to print these throughout the text with the capitalization and punctuation used by the holder of the trademark.

This publication is designed to provide accurate and authoritative information in regard to the subject matter covered. It is sold with the understanding that the publisher is not engaged in rendering legal, accounting, or other professional service. If legal advice or other expert assistance is required, the services of a competent professional person should be sought.

This book was set in Palatino by Impressions, Inc.
The editors were Waivah Clement and Jane Lightell.
The production manager was Bette Ittersagen.
BookCrafters was the printer and binder.

From a Declaration of Principles jointly adopted by a Committee of the American Bar Association and a Committee of Publishers.

ISBN 0-87094-956-X

Library of Congress Catalog Card No. 87–70724

Printed in the United States of America

1 2 3 4 5 6 7 8 9 0 BC 4 3 2 1 0 9 8 7

There is a simple and compelling reason for you, as an independent consultant, to publish a newsletter: It is probably the easiest and most effective way to attack the two most pressing problems you must solve to succeed as an independent consultant. First, and probably foremost, you must market your services effectively—win clients, to put it more plainly. Second, but not truly less important, you must somehow smooth out to at least some extent that corduroy road of peaks and valleys of activity and income that is so typical in consulting independently. A successful newsletter of your own can do both these things for you, while it helps you immeasurably in building your image and making your presence as a consultant both known and felt. At the same time, your newsletter can serve as a practical alternative to some other marketing measures many consultants dislike undertaking.

The pervasive problem in building a successful practice as an independent consultant is inevitably marketing. There are many difficulties in marketing consulting services successfully. Over some years of writing about, lecturing on, and discussing the subject of independent consulting with a large number of practitioners, I have found virtually universal agreement on that; few independent consultants are fortunate enough to win instant success or even to find it easy to market their services. In fact, many independent consultants are attracted to the profession and the venture by the chance fortune of having someone urge them to accept an initial assignment (as in my own case). Unfortunately, that often lures the new entrepreneur by creating the illusion that winning clients is easy, and there is no need to even think about the next assignment until the initial one is completed. Ultimately, however, reality shatters this illusion.

Consulting is a profession. For example, we consultants do not have customers; we have clients. As professionals we must conduct ourselves always with great dignity and discretion, always mindful of the need to maintain a proper professional image. Winning clients and assignments—being entrusted with assignments by clients—requires you to have an image that inspires confidence. Without that kind of image, how could you inspire a client to gamble on your sound judgment and experience enough to accept your counsel?

Viewed in this light, it is not difficult to understand why conventional advertising and sales promotion are not very effective in winning clients in this field. Aside from the fact that marketing in any field is rarely a simple matter, it is especially complicated in the selling of professional services for this and many other reasons. Those traditional marketing methods—advertising, knocking on doors, and conventional sales promotion—are at best rarely more than marginally effective in our field, or in selling any other professional service, for that matter. And even if they were reasonably effective in winning clients, these methods usually make exorbitant and unacceptable demands on the time that you, as an independent consultant, can afford to allot to other than directly productive hours, your *billable* time.

You can invest substantially in conventional advertising and sales promotion, having brochures and other literature printed, conducting mailing campaigns, running print advertisements, engaging in public relations activities, and otherwise doing the usual things in advertising and sales promotion, as a great many independent consultants do. Ultimately, these will work to at least some limited extent, if for no better reason than that in time they make your name reasonably familiar to potential clients. Ultimately, word of mouth makes its own contribution to success in marketing, too. And so, over the course of time and in the most classic pattern of marketing and building a clientele, your practice grows—if you can afford to wait and are able to survive that long. But many consultants cannot afford to wait for several years to build their clientele up to a level that produces an adequate income. That difficulty alone accounts for much of the high casualty and turnover rate among those who venture to establish independent practices, and admittedly the casualty rate is high indeed. Probably no single factor causes more defection of consultants from the ranks of independent practitioners than does the basic difficulty and frustration of winning clients and assignments on a consistent basis.

Further complicating matters is the erratic nature, at best, of results from successful marketing. Even when you have begun to win clients and assignments and you think you have turned the corner, you suddenly discover that it is still a feast-or-famine proposition, with constantly fluctuating peaks and valleys of business. The peaks are in themselves the cause of another kind of frustration, inasmuch as they often compel the independent consultant to refuse assignments, perhaps alienating and losing established clients and potential clients. But of course the valleys—the idle time, with its interruption of income—are a far more serious problem. This is the chief and most direct cause for so many independent consultants becoming discouraged and once again seeking the protection and security of a salaried position with a large organization.

Another problem I have observed with many independent consultants is their reluctance to devote time and energy to marketing, partly because they have a sensation that they are cheapening themselves by advertising and actually *asking* for business, but more because they shrink from some of the kinds of things consultants must do to build their images, such as public speaking and writing for publication in major periodicals. The newsletter offers alternatives to these activities—you do not have to do all the writing for your own newsletter if you choose not to—and your newsletter can serve in place of the personal speaking appearances many successful consultants find necessary or, at least, most helpful.

Building an independent practice can be quite a rough road. Publishing a newsletter is an excellent means to help you solve the problems of the seminal years, with numerous advantages over other alternatives as the answer to your most pressing problems. For one thing, it's a medium that is totally under your own control. For another, it is an excellent route to and method of gaining image-building and visibility in other media. And for still another, it has great potential as a major income producer both directly and indirectly.

But there is yet more to publishing your own newsletter than creating a great medium for marketing your consulting services and creating another source of income to help level the peaks and valleys. A newsletter is a natural fit for a consulting practice. It becomes an integral part of the practice, a consulting medium in itself. And even that is not all of it. There is more, much more. Publishing a newsletter of your own has a great many benefits and attractions that I can convey to you only with the help of all the pages that follow these introductory ones. In fact, it's a great adventure, as you will soon learn. But there are a few caveats.

Bear in mind that you publish a newsletter to do something for yourself, not to bring to the world the benefits of your wisdom or otherwise launch an ego trip. Your newsletter is a practical professional and business measure, and it must be treated as such, for the world does not need another newsletter to add to the 30,000 or more already in existence. And even that is probably a most conservative estimate, in fact, for both consultant/author Jeffrey Lant, writing in his book *Tricks of the Trade* (JLA Associates, Boston, MA, 1986) and Howard Penn Hudson in his book *Publishing Newsletters* put the number of newsletters published at 100,000. That is entirely possible, in my opinion, for newsletter publishing is a popular activity—even a hobby, for some—and one increasingly easy to engage in today with the ease of our modern methods of composition and printing. Certainly, there are newsletters of small size and quite limited circulation within thousands of organizations, as well as the tens of thousands of newsletters offered commercially to the public at large.

You will surely come to agree that newsletter publishing and consulting are not a force-fit, nor are the additional income and vehicle for marketing your services the sole benefits a newsletter produces for you. Quite the contrary, you will find your newsletter opening doors, the existence of which you did not even suspect. You will find your horizons widening far beyond your original concepts. And you will find, later in these pages, benefits and opportunities that I will not reveal here. They will have far greater impact and usefulness if you discover them at the right time, after proper preparation. I will tell you this, however: More than one entrepreneur who launched a newsletter to support an enterprise discovered later that the newsletter achieved a success, both directly and indirectly, that thoroughly eclipsed the original enterprise and became the entrepreneur's principal venture in itself.

Herman R. Holtz

CONTENTS

LIST OF FIGURES

Figure

CHAPTER ONE

A Brief Orientation to Newsletters

THE ORIGIN OF THE MODERN NEWSLETTER

No precise date or event marks the origin of the world's first newsletter. Perhaps it was a clay tablet with cuneiform marks or runes. Or perhaps it consisted of hieroglyphics on an ancient parchment. The antecedents of the modern newsletter have been traced back to the 16th century. Although the first newspaper to appear in America, in 1704, was named *The Boston News Letter*, what is considered the first modern newsletter appeared in the early years of this century. The classic model for the modern newsletter was the famed *Kiplinger Washington Letter*, published by Willard Kiplinger in 1923. It is still in existence, having grown and divided, cell-like, into several publications including the well-known *Changing Times*, and is published by what is now a multititle publishing house that grew from that modest beginning.

The major expansion of the modern newsletter industry came about after World War II, at least partly as the result of the technological revolution in typesetting and printing. With the rapid development of photo-offset lithographic printing, it was no longer necessary to set metal type and go through the laborious, costly, and time-consuming processes of picking metal type from California cases and preparing chases or using linotypes and other machines to turn out heavy metal plates for the printing press. It was suddenly possible to make a simple and inexpensive lightweight metal plate, hardly more than heavy foil, that would print anything that could be photographed: typewritten or handwritten material, material that had been printed earlier, and—with a bit of special processing—ordinary photographs of people and scenes of

1

all kinds. ("Pasteup" composition was being born!) Before very long, even those inexpensive metal plates were not essential any more. Cheaper plastic and paper printing plates had been developed, which would serve for many printing needs.

This meant that ordinary typewriters, especially the new, improved machines, could be used to compose and "typeset" informal publications. In fact, even old, manual typewriters were used for years to compose some highly successful newsletters, such as Bernard Gallagher's *The Gallagher Report*. The manual typewriter composition became itself a mark of merit, indicating that the newsletter was so timely that there had not been time to waste on formal or more cosmetic composition. And to this day, although it has now become possible through more recent technological breakthroughs to enjoy the appearance of formal type at modest cost, many still prefer the appearance of typewritten composition because it suggests greater spontaneity.

A very few years ago a new factor entered the picture: the personal computer and its most popular application, word processing. It was and still is to a large extent greatly misunderstood by many as a kind of automated typing system, which is probably the least important aspect of word processing. Nevertheless, it gained popularity quite swiftly and as the cost of personal computers plunged, the smallest offices soon had one or more of these new high-tech systems at work.

As better printers were developed, especially the new laser printers, the industry turned to an application called *desktop publishing*, enabling the personal computer user to do both the creative writing and the graphic arts functions. This is the latest influence lending impetus to the development of newsletters by making it even easier to turn out a highly professional product without special skills.

Thus, just about anyone can publish a newsletter today, and it is apparent that many thousands of people are well aware of that. At least 30,000 newsletters are being published today, by the best estimate I can find, but with some curious results: While there are a number of major newsletter publishers conducting multimillion dollar operations, there are so many thousands of individuals publishing little newsletters from offices in their own homes that they constitute a virtual cottage industry.

For many newsletter publishers, multipublication tycoons and tiny entrepreneurs alike, the newsletter is a business unto itself, with the income it produces or promises to produce its own reason for existence. For many others the newsletter is an adjunct to another enterprise, the purpose of which is closely related to the other enterprise.

A FEW STATISTICS

Gerre Jones, writing in his excellent manual on newsletter publications *Newsletters, Hot Marketing Tool* (Glyph Publishing Company, P.O. Box 32387, Washington, DC, 1982), reports on a study made by the McArdle Printing Company of several hundred newsletters published in the Washington area. With 448 newsletter editors and publishers responding, McArdle reported the following statistics:

> 86.8 percent used an 8½- × 11-inch physical format.
> Circulation or quantities printed ran from 50 to 250,000.
> 40 percent said that their "usual" issue was four pages.
> Only one fourth of the respondents said that their issues always had the same number of pages. (The others, presumably, varied in number of pages.)
> 11.7 percent were weekly publications.
> 6.5 percent were biweekly.
> 2.3 percent were twice-monthly.
> 44.1 percent were monthly.
> 12.4 percent were bimonthly.
> 23 percent were other than the above. ("Other" can mean quarterly, semiannual, annual, or occasional.)
> Approximately two thirds were composed by typewriter, about one third by photocomposition (equivalent in quality to metal type) and a few by metal type.
> 62 percent printed their newsletters in one color, 35 percent used two colors, the remainder used more than two colors.
> About 60 percent used white paper, the remainder used paper of other colors.
> About 60 percent mailed their newsletters in envelopes, the others mailed them without envelopes as self-mailers.

These statistics are most significant inasmuch as they illustrate the great diversity that exists in newsletter publishing and the many options and choices open to you should you decide to produce one of your own. As we proceed we will review and discuss many of these options, examining the pros and cons of each as they affect or are affected by your own objectives—your reasons for considering the publication of a newsletter of your own.

WHAT IS A NEWSLETTER?

Marvin Arth and Helen Ashmore, writing in the foreword to their widely acclaimed guidebook on the subject (*The Newsletter Editor's Desk Book*, 3rd ed., Parkway Press, Shawnee Mission, KS, 1984), define the newsletter as a "private newspaper," bringing specific information to a specific audience (or highly specialized information to a highly specialized audience).

The authors go on to stress the enormous diversity in all factors, as already mentioned here. In fact, the diversity is even greater than that suggested by the McArdle survey. Some of those publications included under the general designation of newsletters consist of a single sheet while others are voluminous enough to qualify as magazines. Some are virtual tabloids of 11- × 15-inch format, printed on newsprint like daily newspapers or produced on heavy, glossy stock, while still others are in a miniature 5- × 8-inch format. Some range widely over an entire industry, while others are extraordinarily specialized. Some are intended for a large readership and are modestly priced (or even free of charge), while others are destined for a relative handful of readers who must pay a high price. Some are mailed in envelopes, whereas others are self-mailers without envelopes. There are, in fact, many parameters along which comparisons can be made and differences noted. Here are a few more parameters for you to consider in planning your own newsletter. Note that space considerations are a dominant factor in most of these alternatives:

Illustrations (drawings, cartoons, and photographs): There is not much room to spare in the average newsletter, but some do carry such material.
Paid advertising: Same problem of little available space, but a few newsletter publishers do accept advertising, and may

expand newsletter size specifically to accommodate advertising.

Breadth of coverage: Newsletters are normally relatively specialized in the subject matter they cover, but some are broader than others.

Writing style: Space consideration dictates a terse—even telegraphic—style for many, but a few allow themselves a leisurely style.

A Generalized Description

This diversity makes it difficult to define a newsletter by any of the characteristics of the newsletter itself—size, frequency of publication, price, number printed, or other such feature. Nor can it be characterized easily in terms of who publishes newsletters, as you have seen, nor by any other denominator. Still, most newsletters fall within the bounds of the following general specifications:

Most are 8½ × 11 inches in physical page size.

Most are from 4 to 16 pages, with probably the vast majority from 4 to 8 pages.

There are many twice-monthly, bimonthly, and quarterly newsletters, but the most popular publication schedule is monthly.

Most are focused fairly sharply on a subject, an industry, or a given group of readers.

Some Examples

This latter point, the focus on a specific group or class of readers, is probably the feature or characteristic that most distinguishes and identifies—*explains*—the newsletter and its reason for existence. Here are a few newsletter titles that illustrate that point. Note, however, that while some titles identify an objective, subject, or audience quite sharply, others are much more general and some are even rather vague:

Consulting Opportunities Journal
Consultants News
Business Opportunities Digest
Direct Marketing News

Government Marketing News
The Advice Business
Tax Planning Ideas
Desktop Publishing
Micro Moonlighter
Buyer's and Seller's Exchange
Contracting Opportunities Digest
The Gallagher Report
The President's Letter

Subscription Rates

Some newsletters are quite costly, some modestly priced, some free to qualified subscribers, and some free to anyone who wants them. In many cases, such as those of the *Gallagher Report* and *The Information Report*, the newsletter was begun as a free publication to support the marketing of something (in this case, the services of an investment broker/counselor). The growing popularity of his publication encouraged Bernard Gallagher to begin asking subscribers for a $5 annual fee, later for much more, as the publisher found newsletter publishing more lucrative than his original business and turned to it as his main enterprise. *The Information Report* was launched by Matthew Lesko to help market the services of his new firm, Washington Researchers, and Lesko too began to charge for the newsletter later, after it and his firm were established.

Willard Kiplinger originally charged $10 for his *Kiplinger Washington Letter*, but even in 1923 that was not enough to cover costs and yield a profit, so he began to experiment to find the "right" price. It proved to be $18 at that time, although it rose considerably in later years, of course.

There is no such thing as a typical or average price for newsletters. The price varies with many factors—frequency of publication, size, number of subscribers, exclusivity of information, demand, and other imponderables such as the *perceived* value of the information and/or the authority of the publisher/editor. For example, a newsletter published and written by someone celebrated as an accepted authority in the field might have a perceived value that relates to or derives from that individual's reputation as a celebrated expert, far more than from any factor or quality inherent in the newsletter itself.

Readership

The bond or common factor among the readers of a newsletter may relate to their careers, business interests, personal interests, membership, or many other factors. Consider the following newsletter titles in terms of the readership the titles themselves suggest rather clearly:

> *Mailer's World*
> *Marketing Executive's Digest*
> *Backpacker Footnotes*
> *Alfa Owner*
> *Car Dealer Insider*
> *Building Owner and Manager*
> *Maintenance Supervisor's Bulletin*
> *Newsletter for Independent Business Owners*

On the other hand, association newsletters are obviously designed to be distributed to the members, usually included as an item paid for with their general membership dues, but with titles that do not reflect their parentage to the nonmember:

> *ITA News Digest* (International Tape Association)
> *RTNDA Communications* (Radio Television News Directors Association)
> *Spectra* (Speech Communication Association)
> *ACU Bulletin* (Association of Computer Users)
> *M-U-M (Magic-Unity-Might)* (Society of American Magicians)

WHAT SHOULD *YOU* DO?

For you, depending on your primary purpose in publishing your own newsletter, your readership will be your clients, your prospective clients, anyone likely to be interested in the subject matter of your newsletter, or all of these. That is, if you publish a newsletter entirely for marketing purposes, you have no reason to be interested in any but prospective clients, since you are giving the newsletter away without charge and all copies distributed to other than prospective clients represent a loss to you. But if you publish the newsletter as a profit center in itself—charge a subscription fee—you will want to include everyone so as to maximize the income from the newsletter.

There are pros and cons for each choice, of course. You can get much wider circulation with a free newsletter. With the printing of large quantities, the per copy cost will decline sharply. You can publish on an irregular schedule as an "occasional" publication. You have no obligation to your readers; you can suspend publication or discontinue it entirely whenever you wish. With a free publication you can do pretty much as you please.

On the other hand, if you charge for subscriptions you will get an income from the newsletter—and this can build to quite a substantial income in itself—while it will still serve you for marketing. And you will still be able to gain wide distribution, if you choose to, because you can still give copies away as free sample issues, offer free subscriptions, award many complimentary subscriptions (a common practice), and otherwise have it both ways.

Of course, you can do as Gallagher, Lesko, and others have done: Give the newsletter away initially, then start charging subscription fees later, after the newsletter is firmly established.

ABOUT NEWSLETTER SUBJECT MATTER

Whatever your primary purpose is in publishing a newsletter—and I unhesitatingly recommend that you use it as both a marketing tool and an income source, immediate or potential—you will have to decide on its content as almost a first order of business. What kinds of information will you publish (and the corollary: Where will you get your material)? But first you will have to decide on your broad purpose: to inform? persuade? advise? solicit? promote?

While the very term *newsletter* promises news coverage, how much "hard news" (news that is "hot" and fresh) is possible in a publication that is (usually) published only once a month and has room for only the equivalent of a single page of the daily big-city newspaper? Obviously, the very word *news* has a different meaning here. It refers to information about such things as people changing jobs or being promoted, new products being marketed, a list of new penny stocks, and other such data that has importance for only a limited number of people. In fact, even this kind of news is only one of many kinds of subject matter coverage by newsletters. Here are a few of the general categories:

News, generally in abstracted or condensed form, drawn from

a wide variety of other publications and relevant to the
interests of your readership.

Insider information not reported generally—news behind the
news or otherwise unpublished information.

Analysis of the news: what it means in terms of the readers'
interests.

New ideas, tips.

Advice generally on a subject, such as investment, good health,
or marketing.

Guest articles and/or editorials.

Interviews.

Reporting information of such specialized interest that it is not
generally covered in or by other publications.

A potpourri of much or even all of these.

The *Bottom Line* is an example of abstracted and condensed information. A large portion of its coverage consists of direct quotes from many other publications.

Mail Order Connection, published by copywriter/consultant Galen Stilson and his wife, Jean Stilson, presents such items as reviews of relevant books and service articles by other marketing consultants. (The publishers run a mail-order bookstore, too, as do many other newsletter publishers.)

Consulting Intelligence, monthly newsletter of the American Consultants League, is such a potpourri as that mentioned. It includes service articles, book reviews, comments from and responses to readers, and association news.

Talk With Us, a monthly one-sheet newsletter of U.S. Sprint Communications Company, is distributed free of charge to subscribers and others as a service to subscribers and a marketing device generally. It contains brief items on telephone communications and Sprint services.

In the end, despite all the variations and diversity in newsletter publishing, you are going to publish a newsletter for direct profit—as an adjunct to or a logical extension of or medium for your consulting—for promotion of your consulting practice, or for both, and all decisions ought to be based entirely on the successful pursuit and achievement of whichever are the objectives. From this point on let us explore and discuss how to best achieve those objectives.

CHAPTER TWO

Why Should You Publish a Newsletter?

THE FIRST AND MOST IMPORTANT REASON

As you almost surely have gathered by now, there are two compelling reasons for a consultant to publish a newsletter. Foremost of the two is the need for an effective medium for marketing your services. The marketing of professional services in general is not easy, and the marketing of your services as an independent consultant is, for many reasons, often an extreme case of even that difficult proposition. Fortunately, the well-designed and wisely employed newsletter is a powerful tool for that use, and many consultants have been able to ease their marketing problems considerably through the utilization of a newsletter of their own.

Despite the urgency of the need to solve the marketing problem generally, the other reason for creating a newsletter—to develop a supporting profit center—is certainly not an unimportant one. In fact, it has many ramifications in its potential to produce income and support the development of a profitable practice, while it is a strong right arm in carrying out the most basic mission of building a clientele for your consulting practice. But first let us consider the marketing problem and how the publication of your own newsletter helps solve it.

Why Conventional Marketing Rarely Works for Consultants

There are two fundamental reasons for the failure of conventional marketing tactics—commercial advertising, for example—to be effective in marketing your consulting services:

1. The average consulting assignment is a "big tag" sale, usually one of several thousand dollars, at least, and often of many thousands of dollars. Even sizable companies do not often spend thousands of dollars casually. Most clients require more than a sales letter, a brochure, or a newspaper advertisement to persuade them to spend thousands of dollars with someone they know only via those media.

2. In many, if not most, cases the client will have more at risk than the money represented by the consultant's fees. The risk often includes making the consultant privy to important and confidential information and may also include gambling some of the organization's assets, important decisions, or even major commitments on the basis of the consultant's judgment and recommendations. The consultant's fees may be the smallest part of the risk. (My own clients, for example, often risk major marketing efforts and thousands of dollars of staff time on my judgment and recommendations.)

Even that does not reveal the whole problem. Remember that while an organization may retain you and pay your fees, that retention is made on the recommendation or decision of some executive in the organization. (In fact, it is often that executive, rather than the organization, who is really your client!) That individual is gambling his or her personal reputation on you and your performance, and that risk also enters into the decision. Many executives are keenly aware of the platitude that "nobody was ever fired for buying from IBM," and are understandably often reluctant to gamble on an unknown quantity when an alternative that appears "safer" is available.

In light of these considerations—understanding the odds, which are not usually in your favor—it is easily understandable that to market your services effectively you must turn to marketing methods that aid prospective clients in developing faith in you—in your integrity and professionalism, as well as in your technical skills and good judgment. For it is that confidence and trust in you that is the indispensable ingredient in marketing your services. And that is, of course, especially the case in the early months and years, while you are struggling to become established and build your reputation. (However, it is also an ongoing need even for those who have built their practices.)

Some of the Typical Influences

There are many influences that instill enough confidence in clients to encourage them to retain independent consultants. These are usually "low key" influences, relatively subtle, but often quite effective. For example, the training manager of a very large, multidivisional corporation was seeking someone to conduct training seminars in a specialized marketing area. Failing to get the tangible help he wanted from a large organization of professional trainers to which he belonged, he hit on the idea of visiting some very large bookstores in quest of authors on the subject of that specialized marketing area. He then invited those authors—there were not many of them—to respond to his request for proposals and selected one for contract award.

On the other hand, a consultant who speaks often as a guest speaker at seminars and business meetings of various kinds—sometimes for an honorarium, sometimes for a regular full fee, but often without fee of any kind—finds a quite encouraging number of those appearances result in consulting assignments. She finds it worthwhile to make these appearances, even when she is not paid to do so.

A consultant who was having trouble winning even a first assignment after launching his practice began to contribute articles to several association newsletters and magazines, where his byline and squib made it clear that he was an independent consultant. Before long his telephone began to ring, and he began to win assignments.

THE SPECIFIC OBJECTIVES

Note that it is the prestigious activities of writing and lecturing that lend an aura of professionalism, dependability, and competence to the independent practitioner. The consultant doing these things is advertising, of course, but only in an indirect and discreet way, by making professional appearances and engaging in other highly professional activities.

What a consultant achieves through these activities is both visibility—becoming known to those who are prospects for the consultant's services—and a professional *image*. Image is a necessity for the independent consultant just as it is for organizations. Your image will form and grow, in time, no matter what you do. But unless you are quite different in your needs from most independent consultants, you can't afford the time that would take; you must do something to accelerate the image-building process through these indirect marketing activities—for these most definitely are marketing activities.

You will find that activities of this nature are practiced commonly. The most successful consultants are almost always those who make themselves prominent: They make many public appearances at business meetings, seminars, conventions, conferences, panel discussions, and other activities relevant to their specialties; and/or they write extensively about their work—books, articles, and papers of many kinds, including, of course, their own newsletters.

Admittedly, not everyone is at ease on the platform or likes to speak publicly. In fact, one rather well-known individual, long regarded as a paragon of inspirational messages, is most reluctant to face a live audience and virtually never does so. Instead, he does his speaking into a studio microphone, from whence it emerges and reaches his audience, finally, in the form of commercial audiotape cassettes.

Fortunately, if you happen to be among the many with a distaste for the lectern, it is not necessary to be a public speaker. You can accomplish your goals of developing the necessary public image and gaining visibility through writing and publishing your own newsletter. In fact, in some respects the newsletter offers advantages over public speaking for achieving a high degree of visibility because you can normally reach a great many more people with a newsletter than you can with public speeches.

Gerre Jones, author of a number of books and publisher of his own successful newsletter *Professional Marketing Report* suggests that a newsletter is an effective marketing medium once a rapport with the reader is established. He points out, however, that the newsletter is a medium for *soft sell* methods, not a hard sell, which would betray the newsletter as cynically self-serving.

Much the same idea is reflected in "Keeping Prospects Warm With Newsletters" (*Business Marketing,* October 1986). Author of the article Tom Jenkins also notes that the newsletter must use soft-sell methods. He quotes an editor of a newsletter published by a major construction engineering firm, who pointed out that the newsletter "doesn't get business immediately," but acts to break ground for follow-up sales activity.

The authors of *The Newsletter Editor's Desk Book* (Parkway Press, Shawnee Mission, KS, 1984), Marvin Arth and Helen Ashmore, point to the newsletter's usefulness as a public relations tool that can be used effectively to convey an image. They point out, however, that the publisher must know precisely what image he or she wishes to present (a most valid observation) if the publication is to produce the desired result.

Despite these obvious advantages of publishing your own newsletter, there are other less obvious ones.

A FEW OTHER ADVANTAGES

Before probing into the several ancillary advantages of publishing your newsletter, some other matters need to be examined. The first one is a cogent one, at the heart of consulting, and quite often controversial: Just what is consulting?

Probably the best way—perhaps the only way—to answer that properly is to ask these questions: Why do clients hire consultants? Just what do they want and expect to get?

Probably in most cases the client wants more than advice from the consultant. Most clients want both advice and the direct application of the consultant's special knowledge and skills to the solution of the client's problem. For in the end the client's need represents a problem indeed to the client, and it is invariably the search for help in solving a problem that impels an individual or an organization to become a client. However, there are many cases where the client really wants only information or counsel.

The client who wants only information or advice is understandably reluctant to hire a consultant who will almost surely cost at least one half a day's fee—probably $300 to $500. This is one situation in which the newsletter can serve a useful purpose for both you and your clients. You can, in fact, actually render consulting services via the printed page, thereby deriving income otherwise unavailable to you, while your client is well served also in getting the benefits of your knowledge and skills at a most reasonable cost.

In short, publishing a newsletter, when properly handled, is very much a legitimate and integral element of your consulting practice, not an outboard attachment. You serve a special class of clients—

those who could not justify the cost of your services on a face-to-face basis. But many of your subcribers will become face-to-face clients eventually, especially if you employ tactics to encourage such outcomes, just as many of your regular consulting clients will become subscribers to your newsletter.

Gaining the Marketing Advantage of the Newsletter

In consideration of your need to build up and support your image as a professional consultant you will do well to regard and treat your readers as clients, rather than as mere subscribers. They usually have more than passing or casual interest in what you have to say. In most cases, they need your newsletter and expect it to counsel and advise them, something that goes a large step beyond informing them. In fact, if your newsletter is to be maximally effective as a marketing tool, you must seek out those who have such needs by deliberately designing your newsletter to do that, for the desire to get help in solving problems or satisfying needs is the basic motivation that leads to sales.

It is therefore very much in your interest to provide wise and helpful counsel in the pages of your newsletter. It is that kind of material that is also most useful in building your image as a consultant. It is through reading sage advice that you have published in your newsletter (not trade gossip and trivia) that your reader-clients begin to acquire respect for and confidence in you as a consultant—as someone who can *help*. Don't lose sight of the objective of building your image as a consultant, not as a journalist.

This is not to say that your coverage must be entirely of that nature. It is necessary to strike a balance of material and provide items of more general interest, to diversify your coverage enough to broaden the appeal of your newsletter. But if the main objective of your newsletter is support of your consulting practice per se, as distinct from becoming a totally independent enterprise, the focus of your newsletter must be on the subjects most directly relevant to your consulting work. And—never lose sight of this—even after you have built a suitable image and established a satisfactory practice, your newsletter must continue to sustain and support your image as a professional consultant. There is no more important ingredient in the consulting success formula than your personal image and reputation.

Oddly enough, the rationale presented here notwithstanding, the growing familiarity with your presence and persona, via your newsletter, itself contributes heavily to a developing confidence in you, as long as you do not do anything overt to damage that. It is in our nature that we are distrustful of the new and strange for no better reason than that it is new and unfamiliar. Ergo, familiarity tends to have the opposite effect of building or at least contributing to trust. It is therefore important that once launched, your newsletter must continue to appear with great regularity and consistency—to become an old, familiar friend, automatically welcome—and it must continue consistently to provide good coverage that avoids extremes and comforts readers.

Gaining the Income Advantage

Whether you launch your newsletter primarily to support your marketing or for broader reasons, a newsletter that is a commercial or economic success can contribute substantially to your income and thus contribute to your overall success in three ways: (1) it can contribute directly to the marketing of your basic consulting services and building of your practice generally, as discussed here; (2) it can provide income and thus make you somewhat less dependent on face-to-face consulting assignments; and (3) it can buy you time by helping you survive during that lean period when you are slowly building your practice.

Is There a Paradox Here?

There is an apparent anomaly here that you may have detected: To be commercially successful—to be profitable and produce income—a newsletter must have a substantial circulation. But the same may be said for its success as a marketing tool, as that also depends on and is almost directly in proportion to the number of readers it reaches. But, admittedly, it takes quite a long time to build up a substantial circulation. As in the case of most ventures, even the break-even point is not always reached for one to three years after launching a new enterprise. Therefore, those launching a newsletter as a marketing aid tend to give it away free of charge, as though it were a brochure, thus enabling them to get a wide distribution and readership.

Is it possible, then, to have it both ways—to use a newsletter as both an effective marketing tool and a significant source of income?

Two Possible Solutions

There are two ways to attack this problem and solve it. One way has been suggested already, as exemplified by the history of newsletter publishers Bernard Gallagher and Matthew Lesko, among others. Their newsletters began life as free ones, distributed as widely as possible without charge, and the publishers began to charge subscription fees only later, as success in attaining their goals made this possible and practicable. (Recall that in one case his success was so great that the publisher abandoned his original enterprise in favor of his newsletter-publishing business.)

The other approach is to make a charge of some sort for subscriptions to your newsletter, but also give away as many subscriptions without charge as you can manage. These can be trial subscriptions, sample newsletters, subscriptions given as premiums, and/or free subscriptions given under a variety of newsletter-marketing plans (many of which will be discussed later in these pages).

It is necessary to create such marketing and distribution plans to justify giving away free subscriptions while you are also charging others for their subscriptions. But it is possible to have your cake and eat it too—to gain the widespread distribution of a free newsletter while building it up as an income producer, in effect combining the two ideas.

Still Other Benefits Possible

Even the several alternatives already presented do not represent all the possible beneficial uses to which your newsletter can be put. In fact, there are many newsletters that do not produce substantial income directly(through subscription fees or advertising) and do not have as their primary purpose the marketing of consulting services or building of a consulting practice, but are still the means of producing substantial income. They are published as marketing aids, but used to market other products, such as books, special reports, seminars, training courses, and other such items. One newsletter publisher in Washington produces a newsletter in the health services field and produces one hardcover book each year that he publishes himself and sells to his newsletter readers. The income from those annual book sales supports him, his newsletter editor, and his book author, and pays his other expenses, justifying the entire venture. Some others, such as Jim Kennedy (*Consultants News*) and Dottie Walters (*Sharing Ideas!*) run mail-order bookstores, carrying books relevant to their fields. (*Sharing Ideas!* is a periodical for both consultants and professional public speakers, especially the latter.)

Not the least of the benefits, however, is the economy furnished by the role of your own newsletter as your basic promotional material for a wide variety of purposes. In addition to its general missions of building your professional image and making your existence—the existence of your consulting service—known as widely as possible, it can serve as a brochure and as the central focus of your direct mail package. The economy referred to, however, is not an economy in dollars—although that is not insignificant—but, more importantly, an economy in your time and energy. Too, it furnishes a consistent focal point and orientation for all your promotional efforts, in itself an important consideration because repetition, regularity, and consistency are important factors in all promotion, just as persistence is an indispensable success ingredient in most efforts.

There is another somewhat subtle effect that is something of a phenomenon observed by many newsletter publishers: Many newsletter subscribers tend to regard themselves as "members" of your newsletter, instead of subscribers to it. Perhaps this is a manifestation of a well-known human need to "belong," to be closely associated with others, resisting the feeling of being an outsider. In any case, many publishers of newsletters get letters from subscribers who explain that they "belong" to or are "members of" the newsletter in introducing themselves.

You can turn this to advantage by encouraging readers to feel that they "belong." That is something that builds reader loyalty, a most valuable asset. You can suggest that belonging or membership through various subtle devices. Furnishing readers with "membership" certificates suitable for framing, pins, seals, logos, and other such distinctive devices is one way to achieve this encouragement. Another is to run a column of "insider tips" and/or other such data marked as special for readers of your newsletter.

But there are many other ways to achieve this, some of them even productive of added income.

I experimented with this some years ago, while publishing a newsletter I called *Buyer's & Seller's Exchange*. It worked so well that I created a "BSE Associates" offer, which (for a premium subscription price) included the newsletter subscription and several other things, including several special reports and free telephone or by-mail consultation. I found that fully one half of my subscribers eventually paid the premium to become members of BSE Associates, with at least one half of the new subscribers, given the choice, opting for the enhanced subscription. (One of the surprises I got from this, however, was that while the offer of free telephone or mail consultation was a major inducement and motivator in persuading prospects to sign up, relatively few ever took advantage of the service. But perhaps, in the light of other experiences, that should not have been too great a surprise.)

It is entirely feasible to create an "inner circle" of some sort, admitting members with or without premium payments and extra services. You might simply run a kind of "honor roll" of subscribers, who qualify for that list by having been your clients for regular consulting services, having contributed an article or worthy idea to your newsletter, or otherwise done something meriting special recognition. Some publishers run little contests for "best letter of the month," "best idea," or other such contribution, with a book or free subscription/extension of subscription as a prize award.

The sense of belonging, with its attendant loyalty, is one of the several factors that make your subscriber list a true premium list of prospects for your regular consulting services, as well as whatever else you may wish to sell. But it is the newsletter itself that is the best vehicle or medium for presenting your offers. Whereas your readers might cast aside a separate mailing piece as one of no interest, despite knowing that it comes from you, they will open and read the newsletter. You can thus be reasonably sure of succeeding in reaching most of your prospects with your offers, whether they are made as integral parts of the newsletter copy—by far the most preferable way—or via enclosures mailed with your newsletter.

The summation must be, in all fairness, that publishing your own newsletter offers you a great many advantages in marketing your services and in generating additional profits from several ancillary sources. But again in all fairness, there are burdens connected with publishing a newsletter, and we ought to look at those, too.

BUT THERE IS ANOTHER SIDE . . .

Despite all the advantages that accrue to you as a newsletter publisher, there is a downside too, as there always is, and the arguments *pro* ought to be balanced with the inevitable *con* of the subject. Newsletter publishing is a great way to build up your general consulting practice, but . . .

For one thing, publishing a newsletter normally means committing yourself to meeting a schedule. A month may seem like a leisurely period in which to get together a simple four- or even eight-page publication. And perhaps it would be if that is all you had to do in the 30 days intervening between issues. But you have many other things to do, of course, and the newsletter is an extra set of duties which in no way lessens your other professional and personal obligations—to your regular clients, to the administration of your enterprise, to your family, and even to yourself. (You have to have a personal existence, too.)

The month speeds by: It seems as though you have hardly managed, perhaps through the agency of a considerable expenditure of midnight oil, to get the latest issue to bed and, finally, into the mail, when deadline dates are again threatening you. How is it possible for time to shrink so, to vanish so rapidly? Never mind; it happens . . . every month. You have hardly recovered from last month's deadline battle when you must once again find suitable copy for the tyrannical demands of eight empty page forms. Yes, "tyrannical" is the proper word, for the newsletter turns into a merciless tyrant quite easily, consuming your days and nights with its relentless demand for fresh and newsworthy copy.

That isn't all of it. There is an obligation of dollars. The bills for printing and mailing arrive on your desk with alarmingly shrinking lapses of apparent time between occurrences, too. You have barely sent off checks to satisfy the vendors who made last month's issue a reality when you are confronted with a new set of invoices. You begin to appreciate the concept of the quarterly newsletter and even of the occasional newsletter and wonder what made you optimistic enough to launch yours on a monthly schedule.

Nor is that all. You get at least an occasional letter of complaint from a reader whose issue arrived late or didn't arrive at all, from one who is violently opposed to something appearing in an issue of several months ago, and from one who demands cancellation and refund.

Still, on balance, newsletter publishing is usually a "plus" operation for an independent consultant, despite the normal downside factors and the pitfalls that await unwary consultants who are would-be newsletter publishers. It is my firm intention to not only make you aware of these traps but to counsel and guide you away from them and onto surefooted routes to successful newsletter publishing.

CHAPTER THREE

Choosing the Vehicle

READERS AS A SPECIAL INTEREST GROUP

It is hardly necessary to point out that the newsletter, by its very nature, cannot bring readers information of mere-hours-before recency as the daily press and electronic news media can. "News" in a newsletter is information that would not normally appear in those latter media because it is of interest to only a relatively small and special group. It is, in fact, very similar in nature to the special interest group (SIG) idea practiced by large organizations and on many of today's electronic bulletin boards.

Electronic bulletin boards are computers acting as a central exchange of messages among subscribers who can post and read messages, both person to person and as contributions to general discussions or "conferences." Anyone with a small computer and a special device called a *modem* can use a telephone connection to read and write messages from and to a central computer that is the bulletin board. The messages they read and write will be displayed on their own computer screens.

Lively discussions spring up, but it soon becomes apparent that the subjects range widely, so the "sysop" (system operator who runs the central computer that acts as the bulletin board) soon sets up more than one message center or conference. One bulletin board to which I subscribe includes one SIG for writers, another for statisticians, another for computer programmers, and several others.

The idea of SIGs really developed in associations. A large organization of people in the training business, for example, might pursue either of two courses: It might be highly specialized, in terms of interest, or it might be generalized, with many SIGs. For example, there was a time when the then new idea of "programmed instruction" was in vogue, and it spawned the "NSPI" or National Society for Programmed Instruction. Only those interested in programmed instruction would want to be members of that organization. In fact, the entire organization was a special interest group. But as interest in programmed instruction waned, the group became more generalized in its interests, and NSPI came to stand for National Society for Performance and Instruction!

On the other hand, a general interest training organization such as the American Society for Training and Development (ASTD) might include members from all areas of training activity, but would almost surely develop special interest groups, such as those who develop training programs, those who develop tests, those who instruct, and those who develop only audiovisual programs. But an organization of those with audiovisual interests might include SIGs of trainers using audiovisual materials, sellers of audiovisual equipment and supplies, developers of movies, and other special audiovisual applications.

The newsletter of an organization reflects its interest, of course, and so may be relatively general—the entire field of training, for example—or rather specialized, as in using audiovisuals in training. (And in fact, some large associations have more than one newsletter, just as many newsletter publishers publish more than one newsletter, even when all are in the same industry or professional field.)

The same philosophy applies to the newsletter you publish. Obviously, it will bear some relationship to the kind of services you render and the field in which you specialize, but beyond that you will have to decide how broad (general) or how narrow (specialized) your coverage will be. But your choices are not simple ones; you have many options and they are options on more than one level.

THE BASIC CHOICES

Your newsletter may or may not be focused primarily on news as such, although you will probably include some news—not the "hard news" of the daily newspaper or broadcast news program, but still information about events, most of them having taken place since the prior issue. In general terms, your newsletter will probably fall into one of the following categories:

News.
Insider.
Analytical/ideas.
Advice/ideas/how-to.
Hybrid.

Each of these merits individual discussion.

The News Newsletter

The following are a few examples of the type of items normally found in the "news" newsletter.

New technological developments, inventions, scientific findings.
New or improved equipment, materials, and supplies available.
New methods and procedures, new ideas.
Mergers, acquisitions, divestitures, dissolutions, bankruptcies.
New companies, new start-ups, new plants, plant closings.
Personnel changes, promotions, awards, retirements, obituaries.
Relevant legislation, legislative activity.
Special events—conventions, conferences, symposia, exhibits.

Obviously, this kind of coverage is open-ended and may include both the news item itself—notice of the event—and sidebar stories or coverage of a related subject, such as a story on the professional career of some prominent individual who has died, been given an award, retired, or is otherwise newsworthy. In most fields there is an abundance of such information available. Here are the titles of just a few newsletters of this type. (The titles themselves suggest this type of coverage.)

Bridal Marketing News
News for Investors
Telephone News
ITA News Digest
Small Business News

The Insider Newsletter

There are newsletters that specialize in offering what is represented as special, insider information, information that is supposedly not readily available except via the very special methods, knowledge, "contacts," and "connections" of the publisher. Frequently, the items that appear in such newsletters are of the "story behind the news" variety, where the publisher has done some investigative reporting. Newsletters that offer investment counsel, especially that of recommendations for dealing in securities, often tend to be of this nature. Witness the following titles:

> *The COINfidential Report*
> *Consensus of Insiders*
> *Insider Indicator*
> *The Insiders*
> *Inside R&D*

The Analytical/Ideas Newsletter

Investment newsletters are often of both the analytical and the advice types, but so are a few others, especially those in scientific, technological, tax, legislative, social programs, and investment fields. Concomitant with the analytical bent, however, is that of ideas, and readers of analytical newsletters tend to expect that the analytical reports will include ideas based on the analyses. Here are some newsletter titles that reveal the analytical/ideas orientation:

> *Strategy Week*
> *The Mail Order Analyst*
> *Mail Order Connection*
> *R&D Management Digest*
> *"Insider's" Tax Loophole Digest*

The Advice/Ideas/How-To Newsletter

A great many newsletters are designed primarily to provide readers with guidance and advice—actually how-to, which is truly a consulting function. They are quite common in certain fields, notably investment, mail order, management, and small business generally. Very much as in the case of analytical newsletters, those offering advice tend to also offer many ideas and how-to-do-it instructions, and readers tend to expect to find these in each issue. As in the case of others, advice/ideas/how-to newsletters often reveal their nature in their titles by including the word *idea:*

> *The Copley Mail Order Advisor*
> *Idea Source Guide*
> *Personnel Advisory Bulletin*
> *Datacomm Advisor*
> *Digest of Investment Advice*

The Hybrid Newsletter

Probably most newsletters are hybrids to at least some extent, for few conform purely to the several categories suggested, which are intended to reflect their principal characteristics. However, many newsletters make no pretensions to any great degree of specialization but are unabashedly general in covering their fields.

The coverage is clearly indicated in Howard Penn Hudson's *The Newsletter Yearbook Directory,* a guide he issues periodically, where he footnotes most of the newsletter listings with notes describing what kinds of contributions the newsletter publisher is interested in receiving. Here are some of the notations revealing the coverage:

> Industry news.
> Personnel changes.
> Financial news.
> Product news.
> Features.

PROS AND CONS OF VARIOUS TYPES

The insider newsletter has great appeal if it is truly insider information. True inside information is usually worth a great deal to those who know how to profit from it. (And, presumably, you will suggest ways of profiting from it, however subtle the suggestions.) However, it must be truly insider information and information worth having; the mere claim of being insider information will soon wear out if not supported by fact, and inside information that has no value to anyone is not an asset either.

It takes a great deal more effort and can be prohibitively time-consuming to collect this kind of information exclusively for your newsletter, especially on a regular basis. It means almost constant contact with your sources, following up news items and even rumors frequently—investigative reporting—working hard to verify information, and otherwise putting forth great effort to maintain the flow of worthwhile insider information for every issue.

One consultant who launched such a newsletter was highly successful for a time. Ultimately, though, he either found it difficult to sustain the flow of information or he became "fat, dumb, and happy" with his success and began to take his subscribers for granted by recycling much of his old material, with predictable results in the loss of many subscribers.

In many respects, the analytical/ideas newsletter is similar to the insider newsletter. It also involves following up a great many bits of information to gather the entire set of facts and verify them, to collate a great deal of information from various sources and draw conclusions therefrom, and to interpret the information for your readers. But even then you are not done: It is in the nature of this kind of newsletter that readers will expect you to round out the analyses with specific ideas and suggestions, so that the analytical newsletter is also an ideas newsletter, something that befits a newsletter published by a consultant. However, bear in mind that with each issue you are putting your reputation as a consultant on the line in a very special way: The validity of your analyses and conclusions are (and will surely be so regarded as) a direct reflection of your consulting skills, and you will be judged thereby. It is almost certain, too, that not everyone will agree with your various analyses and conclusions, so that you are in that sense exposing yourself to possible hazard. However, this feature has great appeal and can make your newsletter quite valuable, but you must devote enough time to it to produce well thought-out analyses and uncover a steady stream of new information and ideas for each issue.

The advice/ideas/how-to newsletter is closely allied to the insider and analytical/ideas newsletters, and is even more closely tied to the ideas feature. Like the analytical/ideas newsletter, it is particularly appropriate to the consulting field. But where people subscribe to the analytical newsletter primarily to improve their understanding of events in their field of interest, they subscribe to advice newsletters to get guidance from someone who is authoritative and in a position to offer good counsel. So again you are in a somewhat exposed position, for at least some readers will act on your counsel and adopt your ideas, but without assuming any responsibility for outcomes. That is, if an outcome is less than favorable for some subscriber, you will be condemned by that subscriber, no matter the reason for the poor outcome (including the reader's failure to apply your advice properly).

Few newsletters are purely advice, analytical, news, or otherwise precisely of the type described here, of course. The characterizations suggested describe the dominant nature of the newsletter's slant. However, many newsletters are true hybrids of two or more of the characteristics described.

The hybrid newsletter is probably the easiest one to maintain because it allows you the greatest latitude in coverage and, therefore, in sources of information. Presumably it also has the widest appeal, with its "something for everyone" nature. At the same time, it is the least specialized of newsletters and lacks the lure of the highly specialized newsletter that implies being "on the inside" and "belonging" by the mere fact of being highly specialized and thus directed to a relatively select class of subscribers.

Probably, as in the case of your consulting practice itself, only experience will reveal the best course to you. That is, no matter which of these kinds of newsletters you opt for, as you gain experience with it you will probably redirect your efforts. Experience will teach you what your subscribers find most attractive and valuable, and you will also discover what is most practical for you to do in creating and shaping your newsletter. The possibility is excellent that your newsletter will eventually be a far different product than you planned, designed, and launched at the outset. This was my own experience when I published my first newsletter, *Government Marketing News*. It was experience that led to changing it considerably, as well as renaming it. (It had originally been *The GMNI Report*.) Experience—much of it disappointing experience— and testing (it is the testing from which you really learn) taught me that my readers were far more interested in learning how to design and develop effective proposals than they were in any other aspect of marketing to the government. It would not have been a bad idea to make another name change to reflect that new orientation when I finally discovered that, had I not already changed the name once. (I feared the appearance of instability that might result from yet another name change in only two years and so resisted the great temptation to assign a more appropriate title, such as "Guide for Writing the Winning Proposal.")

FACTORS AFFECTING YOUR CHOICE

The choice you make is probably not going to be entirely arbitrary because there are certain outside factors that will influence your decisions. For example, if you are a security specialist and your consulting service is designed to help clients improve the physical security of their plants with alarms and other devices, that almost mandates that you cover new developments, new devices, and new legislation affecting that field—unless your objective in publishing a newsletter is only indirectly related to your main consulting specialty. The latter is a possibility, of course, because we often change our courses as we gain experience in what does and does not work for us in the marketplace or we discover opportunities we did not know about and develop new interests.

Hubert Bermont, for example, began his consulting career as a consultant to book publishers and to those who wished to publish books, but he later diversified into publishing his own line of books for independent consultants, The Consultant's Library. Steve Lanning was himself a marketing consultant when he decided to launch his newsletter, *Consulting Opportunities Journal*, which soon occupied his full time and energies. And management consultant Jeffrey Lant is more public speaker, author, and publisher than consultant today, busily producing and marketing his own rapidly growing library of how-to-succeed books for consultants and other independent entrepreneurs.

There are several sets of factors that will affect your initial choice, including at least these:

> Your specific objective in publishing a newsletter.
> Your technical or professional field.
> Your personal preferences.
> The nature of your practice.

Your Specific Objective(s)

You should have both a general goal and a specific objective—or even a set of objectives—in deciding definitely to publish a newsletter. Your general goal probably ought to be one of those two identified earlier: the creation of an effective marketing tool or the creation of another profit center. You can, of course, hybridize those two goals as a single, bifurcated goal, but that tends to weaken your perspective and blur your focus. It is best to keep your goal singular and focused as sharply as possible as you establish objectives and make plans. At the minimum, if you are strongly convinced that you must pursue both goals, decide which is your *primary* and more important goal, so that you can make reasoned and sensible decisions geared to it. For example, if the creation of a sound marketing device is your primary goal, your specific and initial objectives (which may change later) might include one or more of the following:

> Building your credentials as an analyst.
> Demonstrating that you are a source of valuable ideas.
> Showing your mastery of the field.
> Getting your name in front of a great many prospective clients.
> Building a prospect list.

On the other hand, if you are aiming primarily to develop a profit center, your objectives might include one or more of the following:

> Finding ancillary products to sell.
> Finding the optimum subscription price.
> Finding the coverage most valuable to subscribers.

Of course, your decisions on designing your newsletter and its coverage are going to be affected by these considerations; as you are going to try to create the newsletter that helps most in meeting them. You are therefore going to try to match up the various possibilities with your goals and objectives. Coverage of industry news, for example, helps you gain a little prominence, perhaps, but it does not contribute much to your professional image as a consultant. Advice and analytical coverage are far more likely to demonstrate your professional abilities to readers who are prospective clients. On the other hand, you may have to experiment and test a bit, as I did, to discover what coverage most interests your readers and influences their decisions to subscribe to your newsletter or, for that matter, to retain you as a consultant. It seems rather clear to me, as a result of my own experiences with several newsletters and other direct mail ventures, that while you may make reasonable assumptions and be guided by what appear to be well-established premises, in the end everything must be tested to prove or disprove your premises, as well as your conclusions. The reasonableness of an assumption is not proof of validity by any means, and experience all too often invalidates what seemed to be the irrefutable logic on which you based your decisions.

First the Subject-Matter Linkage

The first order of business is deciding on subject matter. If you are using a newsletter to support the marketing of your consulting services, you must make the subject matter such that it supports your goal—that it builds your image as a highly competent professional in your chosen field. If you are a marketing consultant, your newsletter ought to be about marketing and structured to support your image as a consultant expert who can help clients solve problems of marketing and improve their marketing generally. But if your major goal is the creation of an ancillary profit-making venture, it may or may not matter to you whether the subject of your newsletter is closely related to your consulting specialty. However, unless you have some specific desire or reason to embark on a journey into information and guidance in an entirely new and different field, why not stick as closely as possible to that with which you are already associated and in which, presumably, you are most expert? Certainly it simplifies matters quite a lot. For one thing, it makes your setting up of sources for information input quite a lot simpler, since you are (presumably) already aware of and in touch with many such sources. In fact, if you take advantage of the resources you already have as a result of your consulting work and earlier years' experience, you will have a considerably easier (and probably less expensive) time of it in many ways than you would if you decided to tackle a new and totally different field with your newsletter.

Remember, too, that the marketing efforts of your consulting services and of your newsletter can be *mutually* supporting. You can employ your newsletter to help market your consulting services, but the inverse is also true: Your consulting practice can help your newsletter to succeed. Both clients and potential clients are excellent prospects as newsletter subscribers. In fact, you are likely to be surprised at the linkages in the mutual marketing of your consulting services and your newsletter. When I marketed seminars I enclosed other appeals with the seminar solicitations. Many who did not sign up for the seminars responded to my other enclosed appeals to subscribe to my newsletter and to buy my manuals and special reports, delivering multiple benefits from each mailing.

Obviously, the subject of your newsletter must be closely linked to that of your services to enable you to market both to the same prospects in simultaneous appeals. This alone is a most important consideration. And the boon of being able to address the same prospects for both newsletter subscriptions and consulting services is not the only advantage. The successful marketing of a newsletter—certainly of some kinds of newsletters, such as analytical and advice or how-to newsletters—also depends in large part on your credentials as a sage in the field. In the matter of establishing those credentials, the two are mutually supporting; each helps to validate the other.

And still another advantage to be gained by focusing the newsletter on the same set of prospect/client interests is the creation of customer and prospect lists for future services and products that can be sold via the newsletter. (As noted earlier, for many newsletter publishers this is the major benefit.)

Now this does not mean that you must necessarily deal with office systems in your newsletter even if you are an office systems consultant. You may choose a somewhat different subject, perhaps a subset or a special aspect of office systems. What is important is that the subject should appeal to both newsletter prospects and prospective consulting clients, if you wish to gain the maximum benefits and advantages of mutual marketing support between the two.

Of course, this does not mean that you may not find success even with a totally different subject. We have already witnessed consultants veering off successfully into byways and new careers. But most who change their focus must develop entirely new and separate campaigns to market their new ventures. (In my own case I began to write books for commercial publishers on the same subjects in which I consult and lecture, and even now, with many books in other fields, I still maintain some subject-matter linkage between my consulting specialties and most of my books.)

Samples of Your Work

In their promotional literature a number of how-to writers and lecturers on the subject of independent consulting promise to reveal the great secret of how to avoid giving your services away. They refer, generally, to the common problem of "having your brains picked" by those who seek to gain free access to your consulting wisdom through casual questions asked during chance meetings or during your sales presentations.

Their rationale appears reasonable enough: Can you afford to give away that commodity which you normally sell—information and advice, in this case? In principle the answer is crystal clear: Of course not. In practice, however, the entire question is somewhat trivial for several reasons. The following questions illustrate the point:

1. How can you possibly avoid venturing some preliminary opinions or rough estimates when discussing a potential assignment with a prospective client?

2. How can you write a proposal in pursuit of a contract without discussing the requirement and offering some ideas?

3. How can you address a group, lecturing, participating in a panel discussion, or guesting in a seminar, without explaining some of your work frankly and freely?

4. How much, in the final analysis, could you possibly give away in casual conversation or even in formal presentations when you have not really studied the client's problem or become familiar with any of the surrounding circumstances?

In fact, if you are unwilling to give away frequent small samples of your work—for that is what all the foregoing examples refer to—you are not going to demonstrate your abilities and build your image. If you evade direct questions and change the subject when asked to discuss your work or preview a prospective client's problem, what effect do you think that has on the probability of winning a contract with the prospective client?

The fact is that a well thought-out newsletter, especially one intended to offer maximum image-building and marketing support for your practice, ought to include many samples of your services. You must, after all, convince prospective clients that you *can* help them, and no claims, no hyperbole, and no loud protestations of excellence, are even marginally as effective as a demonstration. The refusal to offer such samples ensures that you will give nothing away, *especially not reasons to do business with you.*

On the other hand, if you intend your newsletter to be a significant profit center, to be itself a commercial and economic success, you have even greater reasons to be forthcoming in what you provide readers. There is no reason for readers to pay your subscription fees—and almost without exception newsletters are quite expensive, as compared with most periodicals—if they gain no direct benefits from your newsletter.

The Newsletter as Group Consultation

Bear in mind that the reader has, in fact, paid for those "samples" in subscribing to your newsletter. Many consultant's newsletters are a form of group consultation in which subscribers get answers to their questions, sometimes in a "Letters to the Editor" column or in a "Questions and Answers" column. Incorporating such columns and services in your newsletter does not take money out of your pocket: You are not giving anything away, for your readers have paid for the information and advice with their subscription fees. Nor are you losing consulting contracts, for no reader would retain you for hours or even days of your time to get that information and those answers that you supply in your newsletter in a few words. The type of "consulting" you do in the pages of your newsletter is in no way competitive with nor even comparable to the personal services you supply as a consultant. It is an addition and supplement to the latter services and produces income you would not otherwise have enjoyed.

Choices Based on Newsletter Features

As you have probably concluded by now, it is difficult to decide arbitrarily that your newsletter will be of this type or that type. The more you study and ponder this, the more you incline to the hybrid with its versatility and flexibility. In fact, one excellent way to decide what your newsletter will be is to review not the basic types of newsletters but the types of features available to you and decide which best suit your goals and objectives. Here, for example, are the most commonly found features in newsletters:

● News Stories.   These range over a spectrum, including but not necessarily restricted to such items as those enumerated earlier—personnel changes, new legislation, new products/services, and other such information.

● Editorials.   These may be your own opinions and/or those of guest writers invited by you to comment on matters relevant to your field. They are especially useful if you can induce prominent people in your field to write guest editorials for your newsletter. They might also be a useful device as a "sound-off" contest, with the best sound-off letters from readers run as guest editorials.

● Tips and Ideas Column.   Not all of these items need come out of your own head. Solicit ideas from readers to be exchanged with other readers, and try to pick items up from other sources as well.

● Interviews.   These can be very desirable features when well done, especially if you can persuade prominent people and recognized experts in your field to agree to be interviewed for your newsletter.

● Case Histories.   Summary reviews of some of your consulting assignments, where the central problems are common ones, are helpful to many readers. Be careful to get the client's permission, if the client is to be identified. Otherwise, disguise the client's identity thoroughly or don't use at all.

● Service articles.   Almost always well received by readers, service articles are how-to-do-it, how-it-works, what-it-means, why-it-works, short cuts, and similar pieces.

● Cartoons.   Good relief, but most newsletter publishers begrudge the space, which is always in short supply in a newsletter.

● Photographs.   Same problem and observation as that for cartoons.

● Humorous Fillers.   Good relief that takes up little space and, in fact, serves usefully to fill up leftover blank spaces.

● Letters to the Editor.   Space is a problem here too, but it is possible to abbreviate and summarize letters or to furnish brief responses without reproducing the letter.

● Questions and Answers.   This is a specialized Letters to the Editor column, in which the editor answers specific questions that are relevant. Because space is a problem, many editors answer only those questions posed by more than one reader or which appear to reflect common problems.

● Charts and Graphs.   These are excellent presentation devices. If appropriate and well done they can actually conserve space because they convey meaning much more efficiently than can words.
● Self-Scored Quizzes.   Good device, if scores are interpreted. Many people like to score themselves.
● Announcements.   Newsletters usually include announcements and schedules of upcoming events such as conventions, trade shows, and meetings of various kinds.
● Reviews.   Many newsletters include reviews of books, audiovisual programs, audiotapes, videotapes, articles, and other relevant publications.

AN EXAMPLE

Professional Marketing Report, the monthly newsletter of Gerre Jones Associates, Inc., is an excellent example of many of these features. (See Figure 3–1.) The issue described here is 16 pages, although other issues have been 8 pages. (It is not unusual for newsletters to vary from one issue to another, depending on circumstances.) Among the regular features are various service articles, book reviews, article reviews, and news items—whatever, in fact, the editor believes will be helpful to readers. The editor also allows space for illustrations—charts, graphs, and other line illustrations—when needed. This is a thoroughly professional product, produced with obvious care and pride, and is an excellent model to emulate. (The name and address for Glyph Publishing Company are listed in Appendix B.)

Mail Order Connection (MOC) is also a thoroughly professional product, but quite different than the *Professional Marketing Report*. *Mail Order Connection* (see Figure 3–2) is the eight-page, monthly newsletter of direct mail copywriter/consultant Galen Stilson, managing editor, with Jean Stilson as associate editor. He also has a number of consulting editors, several of whom contribute regularly to *MOC. MOC* is primarily a how-to/service-article newsletter, with frequent book reviews. (Note the contents listed in the nameplate under "THIS ISSUE . . .") *MOC* is an excellent example of a newsletter that offers group consulting, inasmuch as it is devoted primarily to tips, ideas, how-to-do-it pieces, and other service articles for the mail order field. Too, it is obviously designed to assist the publisher in vending his services as a copy-

FIGURE 3–1: Front Page of *Professional Marketing Report*

PROFESSIONAL MARKETING REPORT

Volume 11, Number 1   **October 1986**

Appraising the Marketing Effort

This article, adapted from a two-part series in *PMR* for September and October 1980, is another in a limited series of "golden oldies" to be reprinted during this tenth anniversary year of the newsletter. The material is based on a presentation made to the 1980 SMPS convention in Washington, D.C.

For a formal marketing program to be successful, four primary questions must be answered:

1. Where are we now? (the situational analysis)
2. Where do we want to go? (your objectives)
3. How do we get there? (programming and tasking)
4. How do we know we're there? (performance measurement and evaluation)

Our focus here will be on number 4, concerning the measurement and analysis of marketing efforts.

MARKETING PROGRAM CONTROL

In *Marketing Research: An Applied Approach* authors Thomas Kinnear and James Taylor make this cogent point:

Modern marketing management requires a control mechanism to monitor the effectiveness of the marketing program and to detect changes in the situational factors. Control involves:

1. Setting standards of performance in order to reach objectives.
2. Measuring actual performance against these standards.
3. Taking action to correct deviations in performance.

In short, your marketing plan (and program) must include

- performance standards
- a system to measure performance against those standards
- and a method for achieving corrections when performance fails to meet standards

William Stanton, in *Fundamentals of Marketing*, sets out the evaluation process as a three-stage task for management:

1. Find out what happened. Get the facts, then compare actual results with budgeted goals to determine the extent of the variations.
2. Find out *why* it happened. Which specific factors in the marketing program accounted for the failures?
3. Decide what to *do* about it. Plan the next period's program and activities so as to improve on unsatisfactory results and to capitalize on favorable ones.

The interrelation of the four steps in the marketing process—an interrelation that should be reflected in the marketing plan—is illustrated in Figure 1.

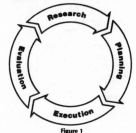

Figure 1

One marketer—perhaps a little embittered and overly cynical—suggests that the process diagram in Figure 1 resembles a dog chasing his own tail.

MARKETING MEASUREMENT MATRIX

With those marketing basics out of the way, we're ready for what I call the *Marketing 9.9.*

A hit film of several years ago had the ultrabrief title of *10.* It starred, among others, Bo Derek and Dudley Moore. In the movie Bo Derek represented a "10" in Moore's female numerical rating scale. (1 is the lowest; 10 is the ultimate, if you are unfamiliar with such scales.)

With that movie title and theme in mind, and with apologies to Harvard professor Theodore Levitt, we can devise a simple marketing measurement matrix for design professionals to use in grading both performance

writer and consultant. And, you may note, his consulting editors are all independent entrepreneurs in associated and relevant enterprises. Their names and credentials lend authority and credibility to the publication. Hence the prominent listing of the names

FIGURE 3–2: Front Page of *Mail Order Connection*

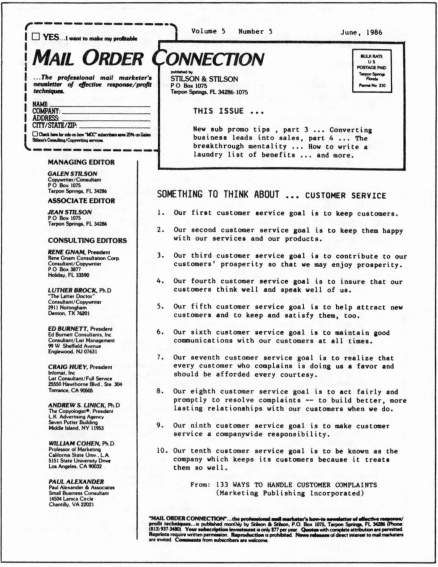

and credentials on the front page as a permanent feature of the page form. (This kind of listing is found on letterheads quite often, especially in the case of associations, and so is not unprecedented, although the names of associate or contributing editors are usually listed on an inner page in what is called the "masthead" of the periodical.)

In general, Galen Stilson's newsletter is a composite of many ideas and words from a number of people—that is a distinguishing feature—whereas Gerre Jones's newsletter is much more a distillation of his own thoughts, ideas, and personal research each month, which he obviously has prepared with a great deal of labor and care. This again is a choice you can make, for both are workable ideas, as the two newsletters demonstrate: One reflects the editor/publisher directly and is under his or her total control in all respects, but requires a great deal of work to prepare each month; the other is far less burdensome for the editor/publisher to prepare each month, but is not totally his or her product nor totally under his or her control as far as content is concerned and may sometimes present problems of editorial balance or conflicts with editorial policy for that reason. (Once again you see the inevitable trade-offs to be faced in making decisions.)

SOME MISCELLANEOUS CONSIDERATIONS

As we proceed through these pages together you will find that these and the other choices discussed earlier are not the only ones you will be called on to make; there are many others. Even some of the more mechanical choices, such as typewriter or computer printer composition versus formal typesetting, have deeper editorial ramifications than are readily apparent. There are the matters of readability and psychological effects of each—and these are what often drive the decisions—but there is another, less obvious one: Typeset copy normally is more efficient in its use of space than are the alternatives (especially if a condensed type is used), and this allows significantly more material to be included in any given number of pages, an advantage for both you and the subscriber.

But there is a more basic choice you can make, as exemplified in small part by the two newsletters discussed here: There are many newsletters which are almost entirely distillations and/or reproductions of material from other sources, usually abstracts or condensations of essential information recently published elsewhere (in both periodicals and books). These are designed to be read by people too busy to read a large number of publications every week or every month. It is a digest type of newsletter that offers to select and report the essence of as many as 50 other publications regularly. These newsletters serve a useful purpose, of course, reporting what others are saying and writing about whatever is the subject of interest—sales, energy, or other. Virtually all newsletters do some of this, but some, such as *Boardroom Reports,* focus primarily on such reporting (although they also commission and/or develop independent articles) and depend for their effectiveness on the thorough reading of many other periodicals and careful selection of the right items to abstract and report.

CHAPTER FOUR

Necessary Planning Details

DECISIONS ON SOME OF THE MOST BASIC DETAILS

There are many decisions to make in planning a newsletter, most of which have been discussed here in broad and general terms to provide an orientation and to gain a philosophical overview of newsletter publishing. But there are many things to consider in planning the actual details and making firm commitments. In this chapter we will consider those and weigh the pros and cons of the various options and choices available.

Primary Objective

Probably your first detail decision concerns your main purpose in publishing a newsletter of your own, for that affects other decisions about the content, the frequency of publication, and many other planning details, as you will soon see. Here it is necessary to analyze your purpose objectively.

There are two possible main objectives for publishing your own newsletter: To provide a good medium for promoting—marketing—your services and to establish a separate profit center within your practice. You are sorely tempted to decide that your main objective is to do both of these things. That is a compromise. And while compromise is the best solution in some situations, in this case that compromise is a mistake. It is a mistake because you must base other decisions on this one, and you cannot make the best decisions later when you have avoided facing the issue squarely here. It is important, if you wish to arrive at the best final design and plan, to commit yourself firmly here to one or the other as your primary objective. This does not mean that you may not pursue both objectives, but only that you must decide which is primary and subordinate the other to it as a secondary objective. That will enable you to make the right decisions about other matters. It does not mean that you may not change your objectives later. But then, again, having a clearly defined primary objective will help you in making the other changes necessary to implementing the new objective most effectively.

Decide, then, whether your newsletter is to be primarily a marketing tool and only incidentally a possible income producer, or primarily a separate source of income, incidentally useful for marketing.

Having decided that, you are ready to go on to deciding what the content is to be.

Main Content

In general, of course, the main content of your newsletter must relate to the field in which you practice—the field that is of interest to your intended readers—and include information and materials that are of use to them. Obviously, the interests of your various readers are not identical, so you must include a variety of items. Initially, you will make your best guesses, some of which will probably be right and some almost certainly off the mark. In the end, it will be your readers themselves who tell you what they want, if you are careful to solicit their reactions to what you publish and their ideas as to what they would like. Some publishers try to do this by a direct appeal to write and comment, others by printing up a questionnaire and sending it out. Neither of these direct approaches works as well as you would like, usually, so it is necessary to use indirect approaches, such as careful and continuing reading of letters from subscribers and other means, some of which will be suggested as we proceed later to discuss contents.

Frequency of Publication

The frequency of publication is a matter that should not be taken lightly, for it is a commitment with long-term implications and consequences. By far the majority of newsletters are published on a monthly basis (although some publish only 10 or 11 times each year, skipping December because it is the holiday season and/or June or July because it is the vacation season).

This is no small commitment. It means meeting the schedule each and every month over the long term. Unless you do your newsletter preparation on an overtime basis—evenings and weekends—you are reducing your available time for consulting by nearly 25 percent. (The alternative is to use outside help to get some of the chores done for you, which can be costly for a small newsletter struggling to become established.)

Don't underestimate the work that is required to produce each issue. There are many functions required: You must review the raw data—the source material and leads you have been gathering (and possibly following, as they develop)—choose the material you will use, decide which is to be the lead for the next issue and what other pieces you will use, write the stories, edit them, do the copy fitting, and do the production work. The latter includes composition or typesetting, layout preparation, and pasteup in preparation for printing. And, finally, there is the mailing each month, no small chore in itself.

Admittedly, it does become easier with practice and as your system becomes organized into a set routine. A computer and desktop publishing system are great assets, making the task easier still. Nevertheless, it is still time-consuming and you must still meet what may turn out to be a far more onerous and demanding schedule than you had ever dreamed it would be. A great many newsletter publishers wisely choose to start with a more leisurely publication schedule, which can always be advanced to monthly publication at a future time, far more easily than you can retreat from monthly to less frequent publication. (Aside from the question of committing your time to a monthly publishing schedule, there is also the question of whether a monthly schedule is even necessary or justified. If you publish a newsletter strictly for marketing purposes, for example, there are distinct advantages in and good arguments for a more leisurely schedule.)

The schedules for which others often opt include bimonthly, quarterly, semiannually, and "occasional." Probably the most sensible schedule to start with, if you are unsure whether you can or even need to cope with the demands of a monthly deadline, is quarterly, although more than a few who publish newsletters strictly for marketing purposes and make no pretense that the publication is anything but a free handout do resort to that occasional schedule.

The Disadvantages of the Occasional Publishing Schedule

Publishing an issue occasionally means publishing it whenever the publisher thinks it's time for a new issue, so that there may be many months between issues or even a year or more. There is nothing inherently wrong in this idea, but it does have several disadvantages, as well as advantages.

The obvious chief advantage is the freedom to publish a new issue whenever it is convenient or expedient to do so. The informal occasional schedule also allows you to experiment freely with formats, content, and size, since you cannot charge a subscription fee for a publication whose appearance is to be irregular and unpredictable, at best. (Of course, you may be able to put the results of your experiments to profitable use later.)

The necessity to give the occasional newsletter away free is a drawback. Presumably, you hope to eventually charge subscription fees for even the newsletter launched as a free publication for marketing your services, and would normally list a nominal annual subscription fee even though you don't actually charge anyone. Another disadvantage is that you cannot build up in readers a habit of reading your newsletter and an automatic anticipation of receiving it regularly. Consistency and regularity of publication are among the assets that help a newsletter venture become successful. But perhaps the greatest disadvantage is the almost irresistible temptation to make the free, occasional newsletter actually an advertising brochure disguised thinly—and usually not very successfully—as a newsletter. This corruption of the newsletter idea is self-defeating and will, if you succumb to it, seriously hamper any efforts you make later to launch a true newsletter. Hence, should you decide to start with an occasional publishing schedule, publish a true newsletter—one in which at least a goodly portion of the content is information of direct use to the readers, rather than pure huckstering of your wares. This will help you "get your feet wet" in newsletter publishing, and will also help you establish the seedbed of a future newsletter for profit.

In general, unless you firmly intend to use your newsletter strictly as a marketing aid and never charge subscription fees or try to use it for generating income directly, you will probably do best with either a quarterly or bimonthly schedule.

Regular Features

The decisions as to the features you wish to appear regularly in your newsletter are not totally arbitrary ones. Perhaps in some cases you know in advance that you will be able to produce service articles for each issue, for example, because you plan to write them yourself. But you may or may not be able to produce a Letters to the Editor column every month because you can't be sure that your readers will write frequently. (But you can solicit letters from individual readers, as some magazines do!) In short, your ability to commit yourself firmly to specific kinds of content is going to depend, in part at least, on the sources of your information. In deciding what features you wish to include regularly in your newsletter you must be sure that your decisions are practical ones—that you *can* provide those features regularly. Therefore, give some thought first to the sources you expect to have available to you. As a starter, here are a few possibilities, some of which may or may not be appropriate to your own field and situation:

Distribution lists of PR and "information" offices.
Relevant associations.
Published information in relevant periodicals.
Cooperative arrangements with other newsletter publishers.
Your own personal and professional contacts.
Government offices.
Legislators' offices.
Conventions and conferences.
Contributions from guest writers.
Contributions from professional free-lance writers.

These and other sources will be discussed and explored in greater depth in Chapter 10.

Method of Composition

Examples shown earlier (Figures 3–1 and 3–2) illustrated, respectively, composition via formal typesetting and composition via electric typewriter or computer printer, which are essentially the same thing; the results are almost indistinguishable from each other. The formal typesetting has the advantage of superior appearance and more efficient use of space: You probably get about 20 percent more copy into a given space when you use formal typesetting. You also get the automatic advantage of vending the composition job out so you do not have to do it yourself.

On the other hand, many newsletter people feel that formal type suggests stale, boilerplate copy, whereas the typewriter or printer composition imparts the sensation of greater immediacy. So the choice is not entirely an economic one, although formal type does cost real dollars, usually much more than typewriter composition (but even so, that cost is not a major part of the total cost of producing the newsletter).

There is another possible choice today. Desktop publishing programs offer an opportunity to produce text that is quite close to formal type in appearance and typographical quality, if you have a personal computer and a modern laser printer or even a good-quality dot matrix printer. (Desktop publishing will be discussed in Appendix A.)

My suggestion is to start with the less expensive "homemade" composition, using your typewriter or word processor and printer. You can always "graduate" to formal type later, if you wish to.

WHO WILL PRODUCE YOUR NEWSLETTER?

At a certain point you are ready to put your copy together and send it to the printer, if that is what you decided to do. You have finished your writing and editing and are ready for that composition we just discussed and for whatever else is needed to get ready to print the next issue. There are a great many details to these production processes that will be covered in later chapters. Briefly, the other chores, after composition, include laying out the issue—deciding how it all fits together and drawing up a plan for that, first with a rough layout, then with a "comprehensive layout"—and pasting all the final copy together into pages called "mechanicals." The latter are also referred to as "camera-ready copy" because it is ready for the photographic process that makes printing plates of it.

In many commercial publications the illustrators in the organization's art department are responsible for handling all these production chores. But in the typical newsletter publishing operation we are discussing here there is no art department; you must handle this yourself, and you have three options:

1. You can do it yourself. (You can learn to do it by the conventional means, but if you have that desktop publishing system we discussed, your computer can handle a great deal of the work for you.)
2. You can hire someone to come in every month and handle this for you.
3. You can use a printer who has the facilities for handling this work—some of the larger print shops do.

Actually, there is a fourth option, which is something of a variation of the second option listed here: You can retain a specialist— another independent consultant, that is—to handle the entire job for you every month.

The Consultant Newsletter Specialist

There are a number of consultants who can take over your entire newsletter-publishing responsibility for you, if you prefer to avoid doing it personally. You have a number of choices available to you if you choose to do this, for there are different kinds of publishing consultants and specialists. Some of them regard themselves as publishing consultants, some as free-lance writers, and others as editorial services vendors or letter shops. Some may prefer to work in your office—or you may prefer that arrangement—while others have their own facilities with suitable equipment and are far more comfortable—and probably far more efficient—working there. In fact, it is likely that some will insist on doing the work in their own offices, and that would probably be to your benefit, too. Some have their own illustrators and production specialists, while others will subcontract portions of the work, assuming that you contract out the entire job. Alternately, you can contract for portions of the job or simply retain a specialist to advise and assist you wherever and whenever you feel the need for some assistance.

No matter which option you elect, you won't relinquish control in agreeing to have a consultant handle the work for you, nor will you be totally relieved of all responsibility for and work on the newsletter. It will still be your responsibility to make all final decisions—the consultant will advise and recommend, but you must decide—and it will be up to you to establish the sources and get the raw material flowing in, to decide what to use, to review and approve or disapprove all copy, layouts, and other items. You will retain both the control of and the responsibility for the final product—or as much of each as you wish to retain.

PRICING YOUR NEWSLETTER

As in the case of many other products, especially in the information business, the price charged for a newsletter subscription has little relationship to the cost of producing and distributing the newsletter or even the cost of winning subscriptions. Those costs merely establish the rock bottom—what must be recovered before the venture is profitable. The true yardstick most newsletter publishers use to establish the subscription fee is a far more subtle measure that we can only identify as "the market" for the item—what the information is worth to the subscribers. (Cynics call this price "what the market will bear," implying exploitation, which may be a fact in some cases, but certainly not in all.) Only the market accounts for one newsletter commanding several hundred dollars a year from each eager and willing subscriber, while another, apparently comparable, newsletter has difficulty persuading subscribers to part with as little as $40 a year for the opportunity to read the newsletter every month.

Newsletters offering to guide investors through the shoals of the stock market are one excellent example of this. Most tend to be somewhat high-priced, when compared with the cost of producing them, but those prices reflect the confidence subscribers have in the advice of the publisher. If the newsletter furnishes truly valuable advice, the product is well worth whatever it costs (especially in those cases where the advice translates directly into profits!).

But the philosophy applies to newsletters in all fields. Here are a few examples of monthly newsletters and their annual subscription fees, selected at random from Howard Penn Hudson's *The Newsletter Yearbook Directory*, 3rd ed. (The Newsletter Clearinghouse, Rhinebeck, NY).

Health Funds Development Letter: $55
Hospital Peer Review: $79
Cereal Industry Newsletter: $25
Telecom Insider: $225
Referrals Limited: $18
The National Bar Bulletin: $12
Monthly Newsletter Reports on a Selected High Growth Technology: $975

There are several criteria you can use as aids in deciding what your own annual subscription fee should be. The first one is what other newsletters, similar to the one you plan, cost subscribers. You can use whichever is the latest edition of *The Newsletter Yearbook Directory* or any other such guide as one source of information, although that has obvious limitations, as the example of newsletter subscription fees has already demonstrated. You will get a better idea if you gather up a few samples of comparative newsletters to study. (Many newsletter publishers will send you a sample edition without charge, but you should enclose a stamped, self-addressed envelope when requesting a copy.)

Some publishers list a relatively high subscription price on their newsletter but rarely, if ever, try to collect that full price. Instead, they use that listed high price as a sales inducement by always running "special offers," in which the list price is heavily discounted.

Even if you are planning to give your newsletter away free or for a nominal fee you should publish a list price to suggest a value claimed for your newsletter.

However you price your newsletter, you should first set a floor on the price—the lowest price practicable—by simple cost analysis. First, estimate and calculate the following costs:

Your own time expended on each issue multiplied by your rate.
Hired labor, contract, and/or vendor services.
Advertising, sales promotion.
Mailing.
Other.

Now estimate the number of subscriptions you believe you can capture and divide the total estimated cost by that number to arrive at an estimated cost per copy. One way to arrive at an estimate is to use *Hudson's Newletter Directory* (see Appendix B) or another directory of newsletters to look up similar newsletters and their circulation figures, add them to get an estimated market total for such a newsletter, and assume that you can capture some reasonable percentage of that market—perhaps 10 to 20 percent. However, do take into account also the number of regular clients you have and/or other factors that you might count on as representative of almost a captive market. Now add a profit figure to that—say 25 percent—and that is the *minimum* fee you must collect.

For example, if you spend 16 hours each month on the newsletter and charge $75/hour for your time, you have $300 per issue in your own time alone. If you have other related costs of, let us say, $900 per month, you must recover $1200 per month plus $300 profit. That is $18,000 per year in costs plus markup, assuming 12 issues a year. And if you estimate that you can capture 1,000 subscriptions, you must charge at least $18 per subscription as your rock bottom minimum.

That is a very modest subscription fee, probably far too modest for these times, and it does not really take into consideration all costs. Even if you do manage to capture 1,000 subscriptions, it won't be immediate. You will almost surely lose money in the early months while you are building your circulation. (As in virtually all ventures, it takes time to become established and profitable, and reaching your break-even point at the end of the first year is an entirely reasonable goal, in most cases.)

But there are still other considerations in pricing and the figures postulated are purely hypothetical. To make a simple point: The newsletter represents a cost, and you must know what that cost is when you consider pricing. Even so, the cost is not constant. That is, there are both fixed costs and variable costs to be considered. The cost of your time is essentially fixed, for example. That is, you may spend somewhat more or somewhat less time on one issue than on another, but you will spend as much time getting an issue prepared that sells only 100 copies as you would on an issue that sells 10,000 copies. In that sense, typesetting and other editorial costs are fixed. But printing, mailing, and some other costs are variable, according to how large your circulation is—how many copies you need. And the per copy cost for printing declines rapidly with rising size of print order.

Your advertising and other sales promotion costs are also variable, in that what you spend to market your newsletter is entirely at your option, and will almost surely not be constant. In fact, it will probably be heaviest at first, when launching your newsletter, then it will probably decline as your circulation begins to grow (and as you learn what is effective and what is not).

It is fair to say, then, that the major cost of publishing a newsletter lies in producing the first copy—that first copy bears all the costs, if there are no more copies. But given even a rather modest run of 1,000 copies, the physical cost of *manufacturing* the product is relatively small—perhaps 25 cents, on a broad average, depending on several factors, but declining rather swiftly as the press run grows in size.

This makes it clear that direct economic success in newsletter publishing—as an independent profit center, that is—lies primarily in your success in building paid circulation. Price has something to do with this, of course; obviously you can usually sell more subscriptions at a low price than at a high one. On the other hand, 1,000 subscriptions at $48 per year is more profitable than 2,000 subscriptions at $18 per year. It is more profitable, even, than 2,000 subscriptions at $24 per year, although the gross income is the same in the two cases.

Pricing, therefore, is a quest for the *right* price. You may need to experiment a bit to find it. But if direct profit from your newsletter does not represent your primary objective—if you publish a newsletter primarily to help you win clients for your consulting services—the right price is the one that brings you maximum readership, not maximum net dollars.

Don't be misled by this into thinking that "free" is necessarily the right price to maximize readership, however. Even if you give subscriptions away, every subscriber should be required to pay a "price" in some form, even such a simple one as requesting a subscription on a business letterhead or accompanied by a business card, responding to a few simple questions—kind of a miniquestionnaire—or otherwise being required to do something to *ask* for a free subscription. Your advertising and/or sample copies should demand some specific action on the part of the prospect to win a free subscription.

This has a dual purpose. On the one hand, it adds perceived value to the newsletter. (But isn't all value something that results from perception?) On the other hand, it goes a long way toward ensuring that your readers are qualified, that they are at least potentially valid prospects for your services.

CHAPTER FIVE

The Newsletter as a Marketing Tool

WHY A NEWSLETTER FOR MARKETING?

Whether you do or do not ever make a dime of profit from your newsletter, or even try to run it as a profit-making venture, you should most certainly not neglect to make it work in your behalf as a most effective marketing tool. A good newsletter can be such a tool and that alone, as has been suggested many times already in these pages, is sufficient reason to justify owning and publishing your own newsletter. Even if you must underwrite or subsidize its costs 100 percent, it is almost certain to be worthy of that support as a marketing medium and to return your investment many times over.

The underlying reason for using a newsletter principally as a tool for marketing your professional services is simple: It is difficult to market professional services, as every professional in such fields as medicine, law, and consulting soon discovers. Even where the law and/or ethical codes do not proscribe conventional advertising for professionals, practical considerations do. A great many (if not most) desirable prospective clients almost instinctively mistrust a professional who uses the same conventional commercial advertising that manufacturers and traders do. Of course, there are exceptions: The lawyer who specializes in divorces or accident cases, for example, normally works with individuals who may respond well to such advertising, and so he or she may be able to turn to advantage the recently gained freedom of lawyers to advertise commercially. But the lawyer who wishes to be retained by large corporations or seeks clients with large and important cases such as major lawsuits is not likely to win many such clients through newspaper advertisements or radio and TV commercials. And that principle applies almost exactly to the case of the typical independent consultant who is busily seeking clients. In fact, it may apply even more to you as an independent consultant than it does to the legal practitioner, for you are far more likely, as a consultant, to find your practice centering on organizations rather than individuals as prospective clients.

This does not mean that you should not advertise. You must advertise to build your practice just as other professionals must. But it does mean that you must do your advertising by other, much more discreet and much more dignified methods than by conventional huckstering. You must advertise in a way that does not appear to be advertising at all. You must advertise in a way that builds your image as a competent, dignified, and prestigious expert in your field, one who is, moreover, in demand and accepting but not actively seeking new clients. It is that which inspires the confidence in you of prospective clients and inspires them to call you to discuss how you can help them with their needs and problems.

Building that image is primarily a matter of gaining enough visibility, or what is called, commercially, publicity. But it must be visibility or publicity that is in keeping with the image you want to create, that presents you as a dignified professional. There are a few basic ways to gain this kind of visibility:

- Get yourself cited and listed in the press and elsewhere as often as possible in connection with many professional activities. (This is not as difficult as you may think.)
- Create your own direct mail campaigns in which you send out those quiet and dignified cards that announce the launching of a professional practice, the opening of new offices, the creation of a clinic or a new service, or other such event.
- Make as many personal appearances as possible in appropriate conduits—speak at conferences, seminars, and symposia; appear on panels; be interviewed; and participate actively in other such events.
- Make as many appearances as possible via the printed word, in articles in journals and even in popular periodicals, in books published commercially, in brochures, and—especially—in your own newsletter.

That latter avenue, your own newsletter, is especially important because it frees you from dependence on anyone else for achieving publication; you own the medium, and you control what appears in it and to whom it is sent. It solves that difficult problem of achieving publication in at least two other ways, for aside from the obvious fact of being your own publisher, your own newsletter opens other avenues that we shall discuss. For one, you can arrange to have other publishers republish some of your material with attribution, thus enlarging the visibility achieved by your writing. For another, once you have established your newsletter and its readership you can use it as a launching pad for many other publications bearing your by-line and intensifying your professional image.

CONTENT OF THE NEWSLETTER

Inasmuch as we are considering here the newsletter used primarily as a marketing weapon, we must face the issue of what is to go into that newsletter. Your objective in undertaking this burden of cost and effort is to solicit and win clients; obviously the content of your newsletter must be such that it pursues that goal. And yet it is not to be pure Madison Avenue–type advertising. It must be far more subtle while still based on sound advertising and marketing principles. Therefore we must consider some relevant marketing considerations. Not the least of these are the peculiarities of the humans who constitute the market, for many of these humans exhibit certain characteristics that bear directly on the design of marketing campaigns generally and, in this case, on the content of your newsletter.

Some Relevant Advertising Considerations

Ultimately we will discuss many marketing considerations. But for now there are two characteristics of human behavior that are especially relevant here:

1. Many people will discard, without a second's hesitation, any solicitation made to them for the first time, but will respond positively (with an order, that is) to that same or similar solicitation on the second, third, fourth, or even later time. They evidently gain confidence in the solicitation and the solicitor as they become familiar through repetition. This often results in a solicitation pro-

ducing increasingly better results each time it is made until it reaches some peak, when it begins to decline. Oddly enough, however, in many cases it declines only slightly and then continues to produce good results for many months and even years after. There have been advertisements running successfully in print, once established, for as many as 40 years!

In connection with that there is another factor at work: My experience in marketing my own services demonstrated that many recipients of my appeals were not prospects when they first received my appeal because they had no need of what I was offering—they did not "identify" with the needs or wants I offered to satisfy. Subsequently they did experience such needs, and they may or may not have remembered my earlier solicitation or may or may not have saved a copy of it. But when a new solicitation of mine arrived fortuitously they seized upon it and responded immediately, for I was no stranger: My earlier appeals had made me an "old friend"! They recognized me and greeted me gratefully. I was, in fact, often astonished at hearing their profound regrets that they had not saved my literature or newsletter and their gratitude that my literature or newsletter arrived again so soon after. They were almost apologetic for not having called sooner!

2. Many people will respond to an offer months and even years after it is made, even when the offer is identified as "special" and for some limited time and valid for only that time. This very week I was rewarded with an order for a newsletter I haven't published since 1978! Evidently these people either procrastinate to an exaggerated degree or they tend to mislay things and act on them when they finally find them.

These facts mean that you must not expect a single appeal or presentation—a single speech, a single brochure, a single sales letter, or a single free issue of your newsletter—to bring in more than a few scattered responses. It is likely that only repeated appeals and presentations will produce substantial results. Persistence and patience count in this endeavor as much as they do in most things, so you must expect to mount an entire *campaign* and not a single all-out effort so that you can encourage and facilitate the occurrence of those "fortunate" accidents of needs coinciding with opportunities. But even that is not the whole story.

Those characteristics of so many individuals also means that you must incorporate in your newsletter items that induce the reader to keep the newsletter for future reference, rather than discarding it after a brief reading. The real payoff is often many months downstream, but that does not make it less rewarding or desirable. The most obvious of such methods is to suggest to the reader that he or she file the newsletter by furnishing it already punched for mounting in a 3-ring binder. Perhaps you might even offer an imprinted ring binder at a modest price, such as your cost, to suggest that it is easier to save and file each issue for future reference than to clip items from it. The binder would bear your name and advertising, of course!

Two other principles of marketing too important to save for later (although they will be discussed again) are these: (1) everyone, and especially everyone in their business or career matters, has problems. Problems and the solving of them are a fact of everyday life; and (2) people are concerned with what they want, not what you want. To make effective marketing appeals you must understand this and employ it. Consider these four items of human behavior and marketing principles as you study the rest of this chapter, for they are the key to both understanding the rest of this chapter and learning to put it to work effectively in your behalf.

I currently receive more than a dozen publications regularly (probably the figure is much closer to two dozen). Most are monthly publications, but several are weekly or biweekly, and probably nearly one half of them are free, to me at least. I simply do not have time to thoroughly read all of them, *but I always make time to at least skim through each one.* The reason? Because I occasionally mine a gem of information or an idea, something of value to me. I cannot afford to risk missing that gem.

Ideas for Items to Encourage Saving of Issues

To induce readers to save issues of your newsletter, especially if they are free or sample copies, you should include material in each issue that is definitely useful as reference and/or has immediate application. For example, after I purchased and learned to use my first personal computer and word processor (WordStar®), I was annoyed by the interminable sign-on greeting of MicroPro (WordStar's manufacturer), the necessity for laboriously turning off all those help menus that took up about one half of my available screen space, and several other time-consuming preliminary chores

I had to perform before I could begin work each day. And, new as I was to the use of a personal computer and word processor, I was not aware that I could do anything much about these things. But one day I happened to read somewhere that James Fallows, writing in *The Atlantic* magazine, had furnished a list of instructions for changing all these things and customizing WordStar to one's own taste so that WordStar appeared on the computer screen automatically formatted as the user wanted it. Revelation! I hastened to find and buy a copy of the relevant issue of the magazine and kept that magazine in my desk for many, many months after as an indispensable reference, should a need for WordStar "patching" arise anew. (I did subsequently subscribe to the magazine!)

Following are just a few general ideas as to what normally constitutes such material, to illustrate the principles and to suggest new and different ideas of your own. Most of the items are generalized enough to apply to any or to at least most fields, rather than to any single one, and so most of the items may be adapted easily to your own purposes. I sincerely hope that these examples will serve to inspire much better ideas from your own imagination:

- Calendar of significant annual events—conventions, conferences, trade shows, other such conclaves within or of an industry.
- Measurement standards, such as metric system, conversion tables, mathematical symbols (e.g., Greek letters), and units of measurement.
- Checklists of various kinds, such as basic rules of grammar and punctuation, proofreading symbols, and do and don't lists.
- Lists of useful tips, short cuts, checklists, bibliographies.
- How-to-do-it articles.
- Where-to-find-it articles.

Advertising Yourself in Your Free Newsletter

The most basic mistake some make in publishing a free newsletter as a marketing tool is to devote the entire newsletter to advertising their services. In fact, for some the newsletter is simply a special format for an advertising brochure, a lengthy advertisement most thinly disguised as a newsletter. That may produce an occasional client, but it is self-defeating in the end. The reader recognizes the sham for what it is, and that compromises any future effort you might make to establish a legitimate newsletter.

Of course, self-advertising *is* the purpose of the newsletter, so you must include a reasonable share of it. But remember that the classic huckstering of commercial advertising is not very effective for most consultants. Your newsletter is designed to advertise you and your services in far more subtle ways by developing your professional image suitably. And to do that you must limit the out-and-out "Come to Ajax Associates for the very best services" type of appeal. There are, in fact, two basic principles to observe vis-à-vis the need to limit the advertising:

1. Limit the percentage of total space you devote to your open and blatant self-advertising.
2. Present at least some of your self-advertising indirectly.

In line with the first injunction I would suggest that you devote not more than about 20–25 percent of your total space to out-and-out commercials—direct appeals for assignments or projects. And even then be careful to avoid the typical "hype" (extravagant hyperbole) that characterizes so much commercial advertising. This kind of treatment is damaging to your dignity and especially harmful to an image of integrity, since it is obviously inflated and stretches the truth.

Far more important and far more effective in the long term is more subtle material that builds your image generally and advertises what you do and what you are indirectly. With a little thought you can actually create powerful advertising that does not appear to be advertising, and so is not automatically suspect, as obvious advertising always is. You should, of course, include in your coverage some of the typical newsletter items—news items about the industry and the people in it—but it is essential that you also have as much as possible of the types of items that advertise you and what you offer clients. Following are a few examples of and ideas for that type of material, some of them from my own newsletters. Keep those marketing principles introduced earlier firmly in mind as you study these items, and remember that you must select items and handle the writing of them in such a manner that they reflect and suggest the kinds of services you offer and your skills in providing them.

- Abstract of a speech or some remarks you made from the platform at some recent event, especially if your remarks were of the "how-to" type.
- An editorial in which you clearly identify yourself as the writer.
- A first-hand report of people and other significant coverage of some recent major event in your professional field. (Again, be sure to identify yourself as the writer.)
- Your responses to readers writing Letters to the Editor or to letters seeking information—perhaps even a Questions and Answer (Q&A) column.
- Just about anything else you can think of that identifies you clearly, suggests the kinds of services you offer, and reflects your qualifications and credentials as an expert in your field and, especially, as an expert with creative imagination that can produce fresh and resourceful new ideas for your clients.

WINNING CIRCULATION—THE *RIGHT KIND* OF CIRCULATION

For most periodicals, the "name of the game" (the criterion of and key to success) is circulation—large numbers of readers. Big-city newspapers, such as the *Washington Post* or *New York Times*, count their circulation in the millions of readers, as do the largest and most successful magazines. In fact, the prices paid for most periodicals, including daily newspapers, do not cover the production costs; most periodicals (other than newsletters) depend entirely on advertising revenue to cover the remainder of their costs and produce a profit.

Even free periodicals, such as many trade journals are, must measure their success by their circulation—subscription—figures because their advertising rates are based on those figures. For such publications as these success depends on getting enough advertising and being able to charge high enough rates for the advertising to turn a profit—ergo the absolute necessity for some minimum number of qualified readers. And readers must be qualified in much the same sense that sales prospects must be qualified as individuals who are reasonably good prospects as potential customers for the advertisers. Thus, most so-called controlled circulation (free) trade journals require applicants for free subscriptions to furnish information, usually via a simple questionnaire, to prove to advertisers that the circulation is to legitimate sales prospects and so justifies the advertising rates.

The situation is identical, in principle at least, in the case of a newsletter turned out strictly as a marketing tool (and it is not only independent consultants who turn to this as a marketing tool, for many large organizations also turn out free publications for marketing purposes). Here, too, circulation is also the criterion of success. Here, you are the advertiser, the sole advertiser, and it is important that the newsletter get out to qualified prospects. If your newsletter is at all effective in helping you win clients, the degree of that effectiveness is linked directly to the newsletter's total circulation—the number of readers you have managed to win—readers of the right kind, of course.

Controlling the Circulation

Those who get involved in mail order in any direct way and to any significant extent soon learn that a carelessly worded or otherwise uncontrolled offer of something for nothing—free samples, gifts, or novelties of any kind—brings lots of responses from *un*qualified respondents—from children, for example. It is possible to waste a great deal of effort and money sending sample copies of your newsletter and advertising literature to such respondents, extremely few of whom are likely to ever be of value to you as legitimate prospects or catalysts for business. But the only way to avoid or at least minimize this kind of wasted circulation—we might call it *noncirculation*—is to control your circulation as trade publishers normally do.

Despite this need, asking applicants to fill out a questionnaire is a bit impractical. Trade publishers do so because they need to meet the standards of the Bureau of Public Audit who validate and certify controlled circulation figures for publishers. But since you are not going to seek other advertisers, your concern is somewhat different: You want merely to certify to yourself that you are reaching legitimate prospects and not wasting your time and money.

There are several ways to do this. Some of these ways require the prospect to go to some trouble and thus inhibit building your circulation slightly. However, other ways accomplish the same thing without in any way requiring special effort of the prospect (although they may require some special efforts of you) and so do not inhibit the building of your circulation. Four basic ways to minimize the waste of unsuitable circulation through qualifying prospects are suggested here, although there are many variants of these possible:

- Select, rent, or develop your mailing lists carefully.
- Require those asking for a subscription to do so on a formal business letterhead or by enclosing a business card.
- Advertise the availability of your newsletter in professional journals that would normally be read only by those who are suitable prospects.
- Distribute copies through suitable organizations such as professional societies and/or at seminars, conventions, and other such conclaves, where it is unlikely that other than legitimate prospects will be in attendance.

Newsletter as a Profit Center

THE BASIC INCOME SOURCE

It is clear that a properly managed newsletter pays for itself as a marketing tool, no matter what other benefits you derive from it, either directly or indirectly. At the same time, a newsletter can play a dual role as both a marketing tool and profit center, and many newsletters are used that way, starting life as marketing tools and later becoming profit centers. But now let's have a look at that side of newsletter publishing, your newsletter as a producer of income, without regard to its values and virtues as a means of building your practice.

The first and most obvious source of income from newsletter publishing is the subscription fee. Unlike most other kinds of periodicals, newsletter subscription fees normally produce a profit of themselves. For many newsletter publishers, subscription fees must produce that profit because these fees are the only source of income from the newsletter. And the profit from subscriptions is possible because the typical newsletter costs, for printing and mailing, are something on the order of 25 cents per copy. Admittedly, this is a rough average that can vary quite widely according to individual circumstances, but it does set the scale in general. When you double or even triple that figure to cover other costs—labor and overhead— it comes to something on the order of $9.00 per year maximum for the typical monthly newsletter. Even an inexpensive monthly newsletter today bears a subscription fee of at least $18 per year, and most are considerably higher than that. So even a modestly successful newsletter ought to produce a gross profit each year from subscription fees alone.

A FLY IN THE OINTMENT

The cost and markup figures supplied here are attractive. They make newsletter publishing appear to be a no risk, can't lose proposition. However, these figures do not take into account the high cost of newsletter promotion—selling subscriptions—which is not an easy nor an inexpensive task, for you must achieve two marketing goals: (1) you must win the original subscription; and (2) you must win renewal. And therein lies what many regard as the most critical element of newsletter success.

THE RENEWAL-RATE PROBLEM

It is generally conceded by those experienced in newsletter publishing that newsletter success lies in winning a certain minimum renewal rate, such as 65 percent, a figure I have often seen cited. The major expense in newsletter publishing is by far (for most newsletter publishers) marketing. (We will discuss this in some depth in Chapter 14, but it is necessary to touch on a few major points here.) It is neither easy nor inexpensive, in most cases, to get those subscriptions initially, and if (according to this logic) you must replace more than about 35 percent of those initial subscriptions to hold your ground, you are likely to be spending all your profits and perhaps a bit more than that.

Obviously, that figure cannot be equally valid for all situations. I could think up a dozen scenarios where it would not be. However, the principle is valid. It ought to be far less costly to keep the subscribers you already have than to find and convince new ones. So we will give a good bit of thought to this in discussing marketing later. And we will be looking at many exceptions to this and ways of being exceptions to this rule also!

Fortunately, the foregoing is not the entire story of successful newsletter publishing, for subscription fees are not the sole possible source of income from a newsletter, and many newsletter publishers take advantage of other newsletter profit potentials.

SECONDARY SOURCES OF INCOME FOR NEWSLETTER PUBLISHERS

There are several secondary sources of income from newsletters. A few—a very few—newsletters accept paid advertising, but this is marginal because it compromises the integrity of the newsletter and does so at too low a price. The limited amount of space in a newsletter does not permit enough advertising revenue to be worth either the trouble or the adverse psychological effect of such an untraditional action. Even if you add a page or two to your newsletter, the increase in space and income is not significant, especially given the limited circulation of most newsletters.

The simple fact is that the very concepts of print advertising and newsletters are adverse. Advertising is based and depends for its effectiveness on exposure to many, many readers, whereas the newsletter concept assumes a relatively small and highly specialized readership. Moreover, even if this were not a powerful argument against accepting advertising in your newsletter, if you are going to sacrifice some of your precious editorial space to create advertising space, it is much more profitable to use that space for your own advertising, which we will discuss in a moment. However, even that aside for the moment, there are much better ways to add to the earnings of a successful newsletter than selling a little advertising space.

Selling Other Information Products

One of the most popular and successful ways to enhance newsletter performance as an income producer is to sell other useful publications to your subscribers. For example, more than a few newsletter publishers operate mail-order bookstores. Kennedy and Kennedy, publishers of *Consultants News*, Jerry Buchanan of *Towers Club, USA Newsletter*, Dottie Walters of *Sharing Ideas*, and Howard Ruff of *The Ruff Times*, are newsletter publishers who do this. Some newsletter publishers actually stock books and ship directly, in fact—have literal bookstores—while others use "drop-shipping" to fill orders. That means that while they may accept a somewhat smaller profit per book, they do not have to carry an inventory. Instead, they send the orders on to the publishers to be filled, and the books are then shipped out under their own labels, which they supply to the publishers for the purpose.

Typically, you can profit—earn as your share, that is—from about 25 to 60 percent of the books' cover prices, when having books drop-shipped, depending primarily on the type of book and the size and importance of the publisher. However, you can almost double that when you stock the books and handle the shipping yourself.

There is also an arrangement referred to as "PI" or "PO," for *per inquiry* or *per order*, respectively. In this arrangement, which is somewhat similar to that just described, a book publisher furnishes advertising copy for you to run or to enclose with your newsletters, and you receive the orders that are drop-shipped by the book publisher. (This can also be done with merchandise other than books, and often is.)

Publishing Books of Your Own

There are newsletter publishers who publish their own books. Phillips Publishing, Inc., a Bethesda, Maryland publisher of a number of newsletters, is an example of this, as is Federal Publications of Washington, DC, who produce and present seminars as well as publish newsletters and books. On the other hand, some who are primarily book publishers, such as McGraw-Hill, Dartnell, and Prentice-Hall, also publish newsletters.

Obviously, there is a larger margin of profit in selling your own publications. But not everyone, and especially not the small, independent consultant, is able or willing to make the rather substantial investment required to become a book publisher. (But even that has exceptions, as you will soon discover.) And that does not refer to the financial investment alone, for the commitment to book publishing means also an investment of time and effort. The first step of making the cash investment may only make you "pregnant," as a former business associate of mine was fond of observing: Once you take the plunge you discover that you must spend a great deal of time—maybe much more than you had anticipated—to protect your original investment and make good your commitment to book publishing, so it is important to understand that in advance. Jeffrey Lant is one who has made that commitment, for example, and I suspect he would agree that he has become far more the author and publisher than the independent consultant. (Certainly he devotes a great deal of his time and energy to his work as author and publisher.) Gerre Jones, on the other hand, has produced other publications under his own Glyph Publishing Company imprint (*Newsletters, Hot Marketing Tool*, for example), but has entrusted the publishing of books he has written to a major book publisher,

McGraw-Hill. Barbara Brabec, who publishes the *National Home Business Report,* is at this time producing the second edition of her successful book, *Home Made Money,* which she sells to her subscribers, but she does not publish it herself. (Her publisher is Betterway Publications.)

Publishing on a More Modest Scale: Reports and Folios

On the other hand, there is a possible compromise here, one that offers you the best of both worlds: the profits in self-publishing additional items to sell your subscribers, while doing so with small financial risks and a limited commitment of your time. The Gerre Jones's Glyph publication is one example. It is a 40-page, 8½- × 11-inch booklet (as he himself refers to the series), formally typeset, saddle stitched (folded with staples in the center), with a paper cover, nicely done and professional in appearance, and yet not an expensive production.

Even so, it is possible to produce small ancillary publications on an even more modest scale costwise, composing them via electric typewriter or computer line printer, binding them with side stitches (staples) or corner staples, and using what is referred to as a "self-cover," which means simply that the cover is of the same paper as the pages and serves as both cover and title page or first page. In fact, if you need only a limited number of copies it is possible to do most of the production work yourself in your own office with ordinary office equipment. In fact, today's xerographic office copiers produce such excellent copies—even improving on originals, in many cases—that they have largely replaced offset printing presses as the method of choice for short runs (small number of copies, such as 50–100).

The significant thing you must understand is that when you publish such items, what you are selling is not paper and ink or the handsome bindings of formal library editions; what you are selling is information. The publications must be legible and presentable, of course, but they need not cost a great deal of money to print and bind.

Such little reports or "folios," as some call them, can be as small as three or four typed pages, since each is devoted to a single topic. In my own case I produced over 30 such reports (as well as several manuals and other special publications). They varied from a minimum of 2 pages to a maximum of 20 pages. Here are just a few examples of the topics with which they dealt:

- How to become authorized to accept credit card orders. (This convenience for clients can alone mean as much as 25 percent increase in sales volume, and a surprisingly large number of people do not have the vaguest notion of how to go about arranging for this.)
- How to write copy for small print advertisements. (There is an abundance of bad advice offered on this subject, and I have found good advice on the subject welcomed.)
- How to write direct mail copy, especially salesletters. (Same comment as previous item.)
- The OPM (other people's money) plan for financing operations. (See further discussion and explanation at the end of this chapter.)
- How to negotiate with hotels for meeting rooms and other tips on seminar planning and production.
- How/where to get government publications free.
- Lists and descriptions of newly authorized and funded public works projects as business opportunities.
- Where/how to get surplus and closeouts.
- How to start/operate singles clubs.
- Getting free advertising (publicity).
- Do's and don'ts of direct mail.
- Where and how to find any information you need.
- How to build your own mailing lists.

Of course, your own reports and folios will be far different, dealing with those things in which you are the expert. The idea is the same, however: Build each around a single topic, and focus sharply on some common problem and benefit. The degree of accuracy with which you identify a commonly recognized problem is probably the most important element in achieving sales success in this profitable business.

Selling Other Items

We have been dealing here with selling information to your newsletter readers, a most appropriate thing for a consultant to do. Yet, it is possible that in your own field you may be able to sell your newsletter subscribers some other kind of equally relevant prod-uct—vitamins, health foods, special diet calculators, training pro-grams, and/or a great many other things. The methods for selling these are not different than those described earlier here. You can stock the items and sell direct; you can have merchandise drop-shipped; and/or you can be a broker, with a PI or PO plan. All are legitimate methods, and all are a service to your clients and subscribers. You can also sell special services of some kind, such as a research service or acting as the client's representative. On one occasion, for example, I found quite a number of clients willing to pay me to simply scan the government's daily requirements and have appropriate solicitation packages sent out to them. (One small-business association in Washington does this on a regular basis and charges a rather substantial fee for it.)

The possibilities to turn a newsletter enterprise to a number of profitable ancillary ventures are virtually unlimited, hackneyed as that phrase may be. My experiment to discover how much people would pay for convenience surprised me: I found a profitably large number of prospects willing to pay me to order free government publications for them, although I had been absolutely clear in ad-vising them that these were free and, if they ordered them through me they were paying for my service only, and not for the publi-cations. It was a most gratifying experiment, as well as a profitable one, I confess.

My experience forces me to trite phrases, but they are true, never-theless. For example, I must agree that the possibilities of turning a newsletter to a direct profit advantage are limited only by your own imagination. Here is just one other idea, one in which I used the good offices of a friendly newsletter publisher because I had not yet started my own newsletter.

This gentleman publishes a highly successful newsletter, *Business Opportunities Digest*, which is several pages of telegraphically worded short items that are predominantly of the "opportunities to buy and/or sell" category. I was at the time just beginning the writing of a book I planned to self-publish, and we struck a deal: He would write and publish an announcement of the forthcoming book and invite advance orders for it, and I would pay him a commission of 20 percent of the cover price. The result was that he earned approximately $500 by running that brief item, and I financed the printing and binding of the first edition of that book with customers' dollars! Later, when I had my own newsletters and loyal reader following, I would do similar things for others, as well as for myself. Also, I used this and other experiences to write "The OPM (Other People's Money) Plan," a report that I sold to many of my readers, revealing several methods for financing business operations without applying for loans or otherwise borrowing in classical methods.

So, you can see, it is entirely possible to make money from your newsletter even if the profits from subscription fees are minimal, and perhaps even nonexistent. Many newsletter publishers, in fact, do not even attempt to use their newsletters as profit centers in themselves but, rather, as vehicles in which to launch and transport other profit-making ventures.

The key to doing this successfully is a loyal following of devoted readers, and it is sometimes necessary to deliberately forgo direct (subscription-fee) newsletter profits to develop that loyal following. They are often the *real profits* of newsletter publishing when you use the newsletter as a vehicle for other ventures.

CHAPTER SEVEN

Typical Costs and Income Projections

THE BASIC COSTS

We have looked at some rough figures to reflect the cost of producing a newsletter—and they are exceedingly rough, for there are many, many possible variants that affect your costs. And we are speaking here of only the cost for getting that first copy off the press. We'll explore the per copy cost a bit later. But consider these costs first and how they inevitably must vary from case to case.

Initial Investments

Note that the plural term *investments* is used here. We must consider both the out-of-pocket cash investment and the investment of your time—*sweat investment*—that goes into all the preliminary work before you even begin to write and produce Volume 1, Number 1—your first issue—or begin to solicit and collect the first subscription fee. (And in the newsletter business, as you will soon learn, you must extend credit, at least in the form of extending to subscribers the "bill me later" privilege.)

Depending on how much you can do yourself, versus how much you must pay out to have done by others, you can soon have a substantial out-of-pocket cash investment. Many have put this figure as high as $50,000, but if that were a universal truth there would not be 35,000 or more newsletters in the United States.

In any case, that $50,000 figure is small, compared with the $200,000 to $250,000 some have put into launching a newsletter. But it is high—extremely high—compared with the modest (but successful) newsletter launches of many independent consultants for whom newsletter publishing is only one of their activities, such as in the case of Steve Lanning, publisher of the popular *Consulting Opportunities Journal.*

The difference is principally in how rapidly you get the venture off the ground. With a large front-end cash investment you build circulation rapidly (if all goes well!), but you pay a large price for each subscription, of course. With limited capital you build much more slowly, although you may pay an equally large price for each subscription. But even then the pain is less severe, for you subsidize a large part of that cost with revenue produced by the newsletter, so that it becomes at least partially self-supporting even in the initial buildup stage.

Still, even that is not necessarily the case. There are many ways to minimize the front-end investment, if you are willing to forgo that initial big-splash promotion that is so typical of many newsletter launches, and willing to build carefully and slowly, bringing in subscriptions at a modest per subscription cost.

Bear in mind that if you have a large overhead to support—a suite of offices in a modern (and expensive) office building, several secretaries and clerks, editors and production specialists, and an administrative staff—you *must* win a large number of subscriptions rapidly before you can hope to operate in the black. But if you are operating on the modest scale that is typical of a great many independent consultants, avoiding the costly trappings others affect, a circulation of a few hundred subscribers will represent at least a modest success. And that has been the secret of success for many independent consultants and their fledgling newsletters.

Ongoing, per Issue Costs

You may have invested several thousand dollars out-of-pocket and an even greater number of dollars' worth of your time to simply design the newsletter, develop a marketing plan, and prepare for the marketing battle. That is a one-time cost, a front-end investment. And yet it is not something to simply write off—to forget—when all the front-end work is finished, for it automatically and immediately becomes an ongoing, operating cost that endures even after the newsletter is launched, has been through several editions, and is selling well. You do not shed that initial cost simply because you have gone beyond it and turned out the first issue. It is a debt the newsletter venture owes you and/or your practice, and it must be paid. That is, you must arrange things so that you eventually recover that cost through repayment by the newsletter.

THE IDEA OF AMORTIZATION

Everyone knows, painful as it is, that a new automobile loses much of its initial value as soon as it is titled to an original owner, for it is immediately a "used" or "formerly owned" car. And its value declines steadily over the years. It *depreciates* in value with age, even if it is kept in sparkling, like-new physical and mechanical condition.

Even the IRS recognizes depreciation of value as a fact of life and allows you to charge off capital investments—purchases of capital equipment, property, and fixtures with a useful life of one or more years, that is—through annual depreciation write-offs. So, over the course of a few years, you derive all the benefits of the item as a tax deduction by writing off a portion of it each year until the item has been entirely depreciated, reaching the end of its useful life. (That does not mean that you may not go on using that item for many more years, but only that you may no longer regard it as a deductible expense. "Useful life" and/or "end of useful life" is a hypothetical measure used strictly for tax purposes as the time allowed for depreciation, not to measure actual possible years of use.)

Amortization is somewhat analogous in principle, but is generally applied to items that have been developed at some cost, such as a book, a hardware design, or a newsletter. It is not a physical item that you can depreciate, nor is it something whose cost you can hope to recover immediately. Instead, its cost must be recovered—amortized—over some period of time, usually by considering it in pricing the item.

Let us suppose, as an example, that you have invested $10,000 in designing and developing the newsletter. (That figure should include the cost of your labor, even if you have not yet been able to pay yourself for it.) And let us suppose, further, that you decide to recover—amortize—that cost over five years. That means, of course, $2,000 per year.

Normally that $2,000 would come from subscription fees. You must estimate how many subscriptions you can reasonably hope to win and prorate that $2,000 accordingly. If you think you can win and sustain 500 subscriptions, for example, you must include in the subscription $4 for amortization. That is, you must include that $4 as one of the several costs that must be recovered in the subscription fee, along with all the other typical costs. The items to be calculated and added up to help you arrive at a suitable subscription fee would then include at least the following items:

- Amortization allowance.
- Labor.
- Vendor costs.
- Printing and binding.
- Postage.
- Overhead.
- Miscellaneous (fees to contributors, toll calls, other).
- Profit.

ESTIMATING COSTS

Only by taking all of these into account in fixing the subscription price can you be sure that you will indeed recover all costs and realize a profit. Of course, all the figures you start with will be based on estimates, and experience may force a different set of figures on you in time, but let us assume some reasonable figures. Those hypothesized here are based on an assumption that you do all the editorial and production work in-house, either by yourself or via employee staff. Included are the circulation and amortization figures based on the 500-subscriber paid circulation hypothesized in discussing amortization.

Amortization	$ 4.00
Labor, editorial	14.40
Labor, mailing	0.60
Overhead	9.75
Vendors	1.00
Printing and binding	0.25
Postage	0.22
TOTAL	$30.22

Translating Costs into Subscription Fees

This set of figures mandates a subscription fee of at least that total, although $36 per year would be the typical price. That is well within the range of reasonably priced newsletters, although there are certainly many newsletters priced more highly. The actual out-of-pocket costs are modest ones. The major costs are for labor and overhead. Note, for example, that the largest single cost item is editorial labor. This results also in the second-largest cost item, overhead, on the basis of an estimated 65 percent overhead rate, a not unusual rate for a small service business. But that, too, is a hypothetical figure based primarily on the editorial labor dollars.

One thing this means is that you do not require a great deal of cash to get your newsletter started. By far the bulk of these costs are for your own labor and the overhead to support your own labor. In fact, this will continue to be the pattern of costs—primarily labor and overhead—as long as you handle most of the editorial work in-house, doing it personally or by using hired help. (The alternative is to have vendors or free-lance writers handle most of the editorial work.) But the figures also illustrate that the normal profit markup for the average newsletter is quite a modest one.

Cost Centers

There are distinct types and groups of activities typically required to publish even the simplest newsletter. In fact, they fall into certain specific classes and subclasses, as listed here.

> Editorial activities
>> Research (information gathering)
>> Writing
>> Editing
>> Illustrating
>> Layout, makeup, and copy fitting
> Production
>> Printing, binding, and mailing
> Administrative
>> Marketing/advertising/sales promotion
>> Billing and accounting generally

Information gathering is a tedious chore initially and could be a time-consuming task, which would make it also an expensive one. However, if you establish avenues of regular input, it soon settles into a routine of sorting the information coming in every day so that it does not require a great deal of time until you begin to assemble materials for the next issue and begin actually writing. Then the major expenditure of time is for writing and assembly of materials into formats and creating the camera-ready master copy for the printer.

Fortunately, that is becoming an easier and easier task, with the aid of modern computers and desktop publishing programs. (See Appendix A.) But there is another way to reduce costs.

Editorial Contributions. It is possible to get many contributions of articles and news stories from your contemporaries and associates, from free-lance writers, and from other published materials. In Chapter 10 we will discuss in detail the methods for getting these at small costs and even without cost. Note that these are cost-avoidance measures because they save your time in both research and in writing and editing labor.

Formatting and Page Makeup. Completing the physical makeup of a newsletter can be a time-consuming chore, requiring you to make rough and final layouts, fit the copy, physically cut and paste up camera-ready materials, and produce the mechanicals for the printer. With modern desktop publishing programs and computers these chores can now be almost completely automated, with the resulting saving of time and money.

Production Chores

Printing and binding are chores normally left to and carried out by your printer. Costs vary rather widely, especially with quantity. The basis for these costs depends on certain specific tasks, some of which present options. "Makeready," the chore of adjusting a printing plate on the press and getting it ready to start printing pages, is a standard item of cost with most printers and is a fixed and unvarying cost for any given press and size or type of plate. Paper, on the other hand, varies widely in cost and you will have to choose a paper that suits you. The following are the various items for which the printer will normally charge you:

Platemaking—cost per printing plate (plates may be metal, foil, paper, or plastic).

Negatives (camera work)—required if metal plates are used, but not usually used today for short runs of a few hundred copies, unless photos are to be printed.

Makeready (explained in text).

Paper (as chosen by you).

Impressions (cost of actual printing).

Collating (if required).

Folding and/or binding (if required).

Cutting or trimming (if required).

Three-hole punching (actually *drilling* three holes, to be technically accurate).

Following are some typical costs for most of these chores. These are based on small-press and short-run requirements, with 11- × 17-inch plates, sheets of paper, and final product folded to 8½- × 11-inch size. Use these only as a rough guide, however, for costs vary in different parts of the country and with different shops.

Platemaking—paper or plastic: $1.50–$3.00 each; metal: $7.50–$10.00 each.

Negatives—$10.00–$15.00 each.

Makeready—$1.00–$2.00.

Impressions—$1.00–$1.50 per 100 .

Collating, cutting, drilling, folding—$0.50–$1.00 per hundred for each.

Manufacturing Considerations

Manufacturing costs of publications in general—printing and binding—are heavily dependent on quantities ordered. That is especially true for printing itself, since the front-end costs of such items as negatives, plates, and makeready are the same for one copy as they are for thousands of copies. But it is also largely true for the other processes such as collating and binding, which also involve makeready preparation.

There are, in fact, two basic types of printing plants, which we can characterize as short-run plants and long-run plants. Short-run plants—the type you would normally be calling on for your printing—are usually labor intensive, using manual methods, small presses, and relatively little automation. Long-run plants, turning out printed materials in the tens of thousands and even larger quantities, are necessarily equipment intensive, using large presses and much automation. Such a plant can no more print and bind newsletters and brochures for you efficiently than the neighborhood copy shop can turn out 100,000 copies of a brochure efficiently. The modus operandi of each type of plant is dictated by economics, not by preference. Or, to look at it from the user's viewpoint, your needs and the economics related to those needs dictate which type of plant you must use.

You will, therefore, find it necessary to seek out a small printing establishment rather than a large one to handle your work. In fact, today you can probably find a neighborhood copy shop with a small press to handle your newsletter printing. Such shops use inexpensive platemaking equipment, machines that work on the principle of the common office copier (the xerographic process), and these are perfectly satisfactory for printing runs to several thousand copies. (Manufacturers of these machines tend to suggest that these plates are not suitable for more than 5,000 copies, but my own experience demonstrates that 5,000 is an overly conservative estimate.) On the other hand, these types of plates are suitable for type and line drawings only, but not for photographs; the latter require negatives and metal plates for good reproduction, and so most small newsletter publishers minimize or even avoid using photographs in their copy. This is a wise idea if you wish to minimize costs.

Administration and Overhead

The principal administrative cost is usually that required for marketing the newsletter, and these costs are reflected in the overhead figures, as are all administrative costs—unless you choose to set up a special accounting system for your newsletter venture. (You may wish to so isolate your newsletter from your other consulting activities for any of several reasons, such as establishing a separate asset for possible sale.) Later, in discussing marketing per se, we'll examine the marketing activities and get a better idea of what they cost.

It should be apparent by now that the typical newsletter does not normally produce great riches from subscription fees, although it can provide substantial income and reasonable profit. There are exceptions, such as the newsletter that happens, for one reason or another, to command a very large circulation (of many thousands) or to command a very large subscription fee (several times that $36 hypothesized in the example used here).

On the other hand, it is not absolutely necessary for a newsletter to achieve an exceptionally large circulation or subscription fee to produce greater than average income and earnings. Many newsletters of only average circulation and subscription fees reward their publishers with gross income and net earnings that are well above average. They do so usually by utilizing the well-established newsletter and its readership as a base for other income-producing activity.

CHAPTER EIGHT

Maximizing Newsletter Income

OTHER, NEWSLETTER–BASED, PROFIT CENTERS

As already noted, many newsletter publishers do not rely for their profits on the subscription fees they charge their readers, or at least not on those fees alone. Instead, they rely on the sale of those ancillary reports, seminars, and other information products described in Chapter 6.

The marriage of newsletter publishing to these other activities, especially the publishing and selling of other information products, is an entirely logical one, offering more than one direct benefit. First of all, loyal newsletter subscribers are virtually captive customers. It is almost inevitable that a direct mail appeal to a customer list brings a far higher rate of response than one made to almost any other kind of list. But there is also the advantage that both the newsletter and the accompanying direct mail offer are mutually supportive: Both ventures benefit by sharing costs, thus adding to each others' profits—helping to *ensure* profits, in fact.

Types of Information Products

Most other information products are of the "how-to" type—how-to-do-it, how-to-find-it, and/or how-to-understand it—but they can assume any of several forms and formats, from that simple sheaf of typed papers with a corner staple, to a little saddle-stitched booklet, to a paperback manual, to a formal, cloth covered (hardback) book. There are pros and cons for each, however, as might be expected.

The formal, cloth edition book is prestigious and (presumably) helps build a highly professional image for you. But in practical— profit and loss—terms, the story is a different one. In fact, the information products you offer need not be massive tomes—thick, scholarly books. Instead, there are certain advantages in offering a number of small publications, rather than a few large ones. Consider the economics alone, for example.

Both cost and selling price are relatively small. It's usually much easier to persuade readers to part with $3–$5 for a booklet or report than to remit $30 to $50 for a formal book. Too, your total investment in a report or small booklet can be held to a few dollars, whereas it is difficult to produce even the simplest book for less than $2,000 or more, which conjures up other problems.

One reason for this is the front-end cost of manufacturing a book. It is so high that it simply does not pay to manufacture less than 1,000 bound copies. In fact, the economics of printing and binding are such that it is the practice of many publishers to print 3,500–5,000 books, although binding only 1,000 initially and holding the unbound remainder as "flats" until it becomes apparent that more books should be bound or the flats should be "remaindered"—sold off to liquidators of surplus stocks.

The problems you face when publishing a book include not only the initial investment, but also the need to store the copies somewhere until all are sold, as well as the pressure to sell them before the content is obsolete, an additional and not insignificant hazard.

With reports of a few thousand words the economics are far different. If you produce them in their simplest form—8½- × 11- inch sheets, corner stapled—you can afford to produce as few as 50–100 at a time without suffering unduly. And even if you produce a report as a little saddle-stitched booklet or manual you can order as few as 250 copies at a reasonable per copy price.

Building a List

One major advantage of developing a series of small, specialized reports is that you can build a list of titles—subjects—quickly. This becomes a great asset for more than one reason. The reader who might hesitate to spend $20, $30, or even more dollars on a book is not so hesitant to venture $5 on a report. If he or she likes the report, orders for other reports soon follow, and they usually add up to far more net profit than you could have realized from a single book. (Here, the "economies of scale" work in your favor.)

In the end, you find the series of reports far more profitable than most books. Moreover, it is relatively simple and inexpensive to build and "maintain" a series of reports, since they usually can be updated quickly and easily so that few need to ever go out of print.

Publishing a Compendium

One frequently overlooked benefit of publishing a lengthy series of short (and specialized) reports is their ready conversion into a book that is a compendium of the reports. Suppose, for example, that you have produced 20 how-to reports about your field and they have been well received and sold well. It may be time to consider assembling them into a single volume, perhaps your first *book.* This is a virtually painless way to create a book. Even better, you can create a book whose success is assured, since the reports have sold so well. In fact, even those who have bought many or most of your reports will buy the book because it represents a permanent, bound record.

It is a good idea to consider this possibility before writing your first report and plan for it—plan your reports, that is, so that they will fit together logically into a single, useful volume.

Typical Costs of Ancillary Publications

As in the case of most publications, the major cost lies in the labor to create the product, rather than in its manufacturing cost. This is especially true in the case of most of the products under consideration here, for they are usually of extremely simple design—a sheaf of typed pages bound with a corner staple, a saddle-stitched booklet, or a paperback manual, publications that are manufactured by the most basic and simple publication manufacturing processes. Too, they are usually ordered in short runs, so that what was said in the previous chapter about newsletter manufacturing costs is equally true here: We are talking, for the most part, about short-run printing and binding.

Even in relatively small quantities of a few hundred copies, therefore, a simple report of a dozen pages may cost as little as 25 to 50 cents to manufacture, a saddle-stitched booklet about a dollar, and a bound manual two to three dollars. And these manufacturing costs would decline sharply with greater quantities. But because you are selling information, not paper and bindings, you generally encounter no difficulty in getting $5 for a small report and as much as $30 to $50 for a complete bound volume.

Of course, that does not mean that you are making overwhelming profits, for there is the original investment to consider—your own time, if you write all these products yourself, and/or fees to others for editorial work to create the products. (In fact, many freelance writers are hired to create such products for others to sell.)

Amortizing the Cost

The method for recovering the cost of development is the same as it is in the case of your newsletter, but with this significant difference: As far as you know or can judge, your newsletter, once created, will go on indefinitely. If it must evolve and change, it will do so spontaneously, over time, since it has a kind of life of its own. But a report or manual is a different proposition because once published it is locked into its form and format, as well as its content, and thus tends to have a shelf life all its own. It will almost surely become obsolete in time and then have to be abandoned or revitalized through revision and a new edition—if, in fact, a revised edition is a worthwhile proposition. (It sometimes is not, even when the original edition sold well.)

The length of that shelf life is indeterminate; you can only estimate it, and that is likely to be little more than a guess. In fact, the shelf life may be far longer than you expect it to be, but it may also be far shorter. Amortization is thus a problem: If you plan to amortize the original investment, that R&D-type cost, over several years and the shelf life of the product proves to be far shorter than expected, you may never recover all your costs. In consideration of that I recommend the following procedure and guidelines:

1. Estimate the shelf life of the product—how long before it must be scrapped or revised.
2. Plan to amortize the R&D cost over the first one half of that estimated shelf life.
3. If you cannot see your way clear to do this, either because the estimated shelf life is extremely short or you believe that

you would have trouble getting a large enough price for the product to enable you to amortize it on this basis, then you must consider the viability of the product: Perhaps you ought not to undertake creating that product at all.

In short, this method for amortization provides a go/no-go gauge for you also, helping you judge the practicality of a proposed venture into an ancillary product.

GETTING IDEAS FOR ANCILLARY PUBLICATIONS

You have a wide universe of choices in conceiving and creating ancillary and supplemental publications. There are at least three general approaches to creating these: (1) they may be completely original manuscripts; (2) they may be wholly or partially based on material that appeared previously in your newsletter; or (3) they may be collections and reprints of material published earlier. Perhaps the easiest or most direct way to get started in producing such lucrative supplements to your regular newsletter is the third idea, so let us look at that first.

Reprints

Reprinting published materials as separate publications is a common practice, especially in trade and professional journals, but it takes more than one form. When the publisher of a periodical carrying commercial advertising has reason to believe that many readers would have use for multiple copies of a published article—perhaps to distribute to a staff or to associates—he or she often announces that reprints are available. Usually, in such cases as this, the expectation is that reprints will be wanted in quantity, and they are offered at a nominal price as a service to readers. (The trade journal publisher is interested primarily in advertising as a principal source of income and profits, and the professional journal is usually published by a nonprofit organization as a service to members.) But that is of little or no value to you as a newsletter publisher. What is referred to here is the idea of assembling and publishing sizable collections of previously published articles. Each edition of the newsletter *Boardroom Reports,*® for example, is made up principally of brief excerpts from various published sources, with a few slightly longer pieces commissioned to special correspondents. It is relatively easy to create a book by assembling collections of these items. Boardroom Reports, Inc., creates and uses such publications as a bonus for subscribing to their newsletters. For example, they sent me a 62-page book titled *Personal Business* for subscribing to one of their newsletters. Items in the book were organized into such categories as Real Estate, Insurance, Investment, and other classifications of obvious personal interest to a great many people. (But the firm also creates and publishes books in much larger volumes and commands good prices for them. One that they managed to sell me, for example, is titled *The Book of Business Knowledge* and is a large format ($8\frac{1}{2} \times 11$ inches), hardcover book of over 500 pages. It is not exactly a reprint, however, although it reflects coverage of the newsletter *Boardroom Reports*.)

Gerre Jones makes the reprint approach clear enough in a statement appearing under the title of his 40-page book, *Newsletters, Hot Marketing Tool.* His notice on the title page of this book makes the following statement:

> The text of this book consists of articles from *Professional Marketing Report,* Volumes I through VI. The guide originally was compiled for the Marketing Management Workshop series, *Newsletter Design and Production.*

(You will note that the astute Gerre Jones first utilized his newsletter articles as the basis for a series of workshops and a workshop manual and then offered that manual as an independent publication.)

Since most publishers begin a new volume each year, this book represents a six-year collection of articles and columns from the monthly newsletter, but the actual number of articles constituting the content of the book appears to be about 15. They do not appear in the book in the chronological order of their publication, either, but were reorganized to fit a five-part format and pattern, in which the author treated the subject progressively, from general introduction to printing.

For Gerre Jones this was an almost inevitable idea, since he is a skilled writer and long ago recognized the merits of newsletter publishing as a valuable marketing tool for the professionals his newsletter addresses. Your own case will be different, of course, depending on your field, your chosen specialties, and what you publish in your own newsletter. In my own case, logic dictated collecting my articles on proposal writing, and since I made those a two-page monthly feature in *Government Marketing News*, they accumulated at the rate of 24 pages a year. But there are many possibilities, and the following ideas may suggest choices of your own:

- Most often asked questions and your answers (from a regular Question and Answer column or from letters received and published).
- A collection of how-to-do-it articles.
- A collection of how-to-find-it articles or lists.
- A collection of how-it-works explanations.
- References of various kinds.
- Insider tips, hints, ideas.

Publications Based on Previously Published Material

Boardroom Reports' *The Book of Business Knowledge* is an example of a book based on previously published material. Although it was largely a new and original work by the editors of *Boardroom Reports,* they were inevitably heavily influenced by the materials they had published previously.

A common avenue to creating such new works as outgrowths of the newsletter coverage lies in expanding coverage treated briefly in the newsletter. The space limitation of a newsletter compels economy in writing, and only rarely can a subject be treated in depth in a newsletter. Even when a subject is made into a series of articles or a regular feature of every issue, as in the case of my own two pages on proposal writing in each issue, the result is only 24 pages a year, hardly matter for a book of any size. At that rate, even a modest-sized book made up of reprints would require 5–10 years' worth of articles!

Obviously, if you are to produce a book of any substantial size based on previously published newsletter articles it must include a substantial amount of new material. But that in itself is the key to producing an ancillary book: Because the space limitation of your newsletter compels you to treat all subjects only cursorily, it is relatively easy to find ideas for ancillary publications. Make notes, in writing your newsletter articles, of which subjects are important enough and of great enough interests to your readers to merit more extensive coverage than you can give them in a newsletter. Be especially conscious of subjects and situations where the limitations of space compel you to reluctantly trim far more out of your articles than you wish to. These are probably targets of opportunity.

This should result in deciding whether each topic merits a complete book of its own or a chapter in a book. *The Book of Business Knowledge,* for example, is quite a substantial tome with chapters on many subjects—22 chapters, to be exact—including the following:

Advertising	Computers	Insurance
Financial management	Investments	Marketing
Office management	Purchasing	Security
Credit management	Compensation	Unions

Of course, any of these chapters could be the subject of an entire book, and books have been written about all these subjects. However, you must decide what is appropriate for your own readers. (I originally wrote and sold a single manual on selling to the government generally, but later wrote and published another, devoted to proposal writing, and finally wrote still a third one, this one a directory of government purchasing offices in the U.S. These were in addition to the many small reports I published and sold later.)

New and Original Publications

New and original publications are not as difficult to conceive and create as many people think. If you are writing a newsletter, you can hardly help but get frequent ideas for new publications, often for material that you find you cannot fit into your newsletter, either because of the space limitations or because the material is simply inappropriate for a newsletter. My directory of federal contracting and purchasing offices is one example: It is almost impossible to fit such material into a newsletter, but there proved to be a demand for the information, making a viable idea of a separate publication for it. (Magazines and tabloids will often publish such directories in a special annual edition or as a separate publication accompanying a special annual edition.)

MAIL-ORDER BOOKSTORES

Many newsletter publishers run mail-order bookstores as part of the service they offer. If they publish books of their own, they sell them via their own bookstores, of course, but many sell books published by others as well, including the major book publishers. But not all actually stock books, since many publishers will drop-ship for dealers, as explained in Chapter 6. And since it costs little extra to include a catalog sheet in the newsletter you mail every month, because the newsletter budget bears the bulk of the postage cost, you can afford the limited markup possible in this arrangement, for you are usually working at from 25 to 40 percent of gross or selling price. (This would normally be considered unacceptably risky were the bookstore mailing required to bear the entire cost.)

OTHER SERVICES

There are other services you may be able to offer your newsletter subscribers. Matthew Lesko founded Washington Researchers, a firm that taught the art of mining the rich Washington, DC mother lode of information on just about every subject conceivable. He published a newsletter and instruction manuals, conducted training workshops, and provided research services in kind. This is not unprecedented; other newsletter publishers have provided research services and conducted training seminars and workshops.

Associates and Associations

Before I had published a newsletter for very long I noticed, as I mentioned in Chapter 2, what appeared to me to be an odd phenomenon: In writing to me as editor and publisher, readers often referred to themselves as "members" of "BSE," which was our familiar abbreviation for *Buyer's and Seller's Exchange*, the newsletter I was then publishing. I soon learned, in talking to other newsletter publishers, that I was not alone in this. Many others had experienced this also.

A little research turned up the information that this was not a phenomenon peculiar to newsletter subscribers: Psychologists were well aware of the human need to "belong," to be part of something; *everybody* (or nearly everybody, in any case) has that need.

At the same time I noted in mail I received from readers that many sought a bit of advice, such as how they could find a source of supply for some gadget they wished to sell, where to learn hypnosis, how to become a "finder" or financial broker, what to charge in certain special situations, and many other such things. That is, they turned to me as their "answer man," making me their special consultant. This is also a common experience of periodical publishers. Readers think of the publishers as natural sources of advice and information, and many magazines encourage such questions by running regular columns devoted to them.

Applying simple marketing logic to this, I decided that it added up to my having recognized two needs, and the satisfying of needs is the most basic and probably most widely recognized basis for a business venture. In short, it seemed to me that I should be able to turn this to advantage by finding some way to satisfy these needs. After a little thought I devised the following plan.

Subscribers to BSE ($36/year) were invited to become "BSE Associates" for an additional $12/year. As BSE Associates they would get three reports—their choice—free, a 10 percent discount on anything BSE sold, and the privilege of several free consultations (by mail or telephone) and/or research assistance.

More than one half the subscribers opted to become BSE Associates, and virtually all new subscribers opted for the $48 package, rather than for a mere subscription. But I was in for one more surprise: Although my BSE Associates were glad to get the free reports and take advantage of the discount, few ever took advantage of the free consultation and research, which were probably by far the more important benefits and, as far as I could determine, by far the most attractive part of the offer! Evidently the availability of and opportunity to use the latter services was important to those who chose to become BSE Associates (as a source of comfort?), regardless of whether they ever had need to use the special services.

Seminars and Workshops

Many newsletter publishers run training seminars and workshops, which are often the natural outgrowth of a newsletter. The marriage of newsletter publishing and seminar production is a natural one for several reasons:

● The major cost in most seminar ventures is advertising. Advertising space in newspapers is quite costly, and direct mail campaigns—by far the more popular and more widely used method for promoting seminars—can involve a major expense also. Ergo, the natural advantage of using your newsletter, which is already in place and readily available at only a slight additional cost, as your chief advertising medium.

● Your subscribers represent the best possible mailing list: current customers. Whereas typical "cold" mailing lists are not likely to produce responses of more than 1 to 4 percent at best, customer lists often produce 12, 15, and even higher percentages of response. Moreover, if you provide notice of a seminar program far enough in advance of the event, you can often persuade your readers to help you publicize the event to their friends and acquaintances.

● If you have maintained contacts with many other newsletter publishers via exchanges of complimentary subscriptions and permission to reprint information from each other's newsletters (with attribution, of course), you can enlist the aid of other newsletter publishers in publicizing your seminars, adding many more prospects.

Promoted widely and effectively in this manner—at low cost for advertising—seminars and workshops can become highly profitable ventures, since the costs for printing (advertising brochures and handout literature) and meeting rooms are relatively minor: Perhaps $100–$150 for printing, $50–$100 for a meeting room, and another $100 for such amenities as coffee and cold drinks. (Some seminar producers include a luncheon in the program, but most avoid this expense.) Typical fees charged seminar attendees are on the order of $200 per day, but the range is usually from lows of about $100–$125 to highs of $300–$400 per day. And while one-day seminars are probably the most popular, many run for as much as five days. (My experience, based on experiments with different schedules and formats, has been that busy people are often reluctant to be away from their offices or jobs for more than one day, so I usually favor one-day programs, even for in-house programs for client organizations.)

Here is a rather typical seminar, as described in a solicitation I received recently (on the all too typical four-page, 8½- × 11-inch glossy brochure mailed under a nonprofit organization bulk mail permit). The program is titled "Training & Computers Seminar: How to Teach People to Use Computers." It is a three-day program, includes lunches and a 200-page manual, costs $795 per attendee ($725 for attendees from government and nonprofit organizations), and is presented by an individual represented to be a trainer and consultant in computer applications. A note in the brochure advises the reader that if there are five or more people to be trained, arrangements can be made to present programs—several are named—in-house as custom programs. (This, too, is almost a staple offer of seminar entrepreneurs.)

There are at least two basic ways you can approach seminar and workshop ventures, and even there, one of the two ways offers alternatives, so that there are actually three possible approaches:

1. You can pursue the conventional approach of developing a program and offering it to the public on what I term an *open registration* basis—anyone can attend. This means that you will rent a meeting room, advertise the event, sign up attendees, and make the presentation.

2. You can develop a basic program but offer it to organizations as an in-house, custom program and charge a fee for the use and presentation of your program.

3. You can develop a program and offer it to one of the many producers of open-registration seminar programs, who will do all the selling and administrative work, take all the risks, and pay you a fee for making the presentation and using your program.

Only the first method involves investment and risk on your part, although you may be able to keep the investment and subsequent financial risk small, as explained. But it does require a great deal of your time to handle all the details, so there is that risk of wasting your time, which is an asset worth money, too. Of course, there is also the prospect of earning much more income and profit when you present a seminar as an independent entrepreneur, rather than as a fee-paid consultant.

Setting Fees. In presenting seminar programs to an in-house group for a client, there are at least two separate options for pricing:

1. A flat fee, as a consultant.

2. A fee based on number of attendees. (Some presenters also make a charge for seminar manuals and/or other handout materials.)

It has been my practice to charge clients a flat fee for in-house seminar presentations. However, the fee I charge has no relationship to my normal consulting fee (it's considerably higher) for several reasons: (1) It is my copyright program, a proprietary product, that I present, and I am entitled to a usage fee for the program, as well as a fee for my time in presenting it; (2) I charge no extras (except for travel and related expenses), I customize the program as much as it is possible to do so without actually revising it, and I supply a copyright seminar manual without charge (that is, I supply a master copy and permission to make as many copies as the client needs to distribute to the attendees); (3) there is a distinct tendency on the part of clients to judge the worth or value of the seminar by the price, and $1,000 per day appears to be the minimum price that makes a seminar appear to be a worthwhile program; (4) I offer specific guidance in solving specific problems—virtually a free consulting service—during frequent Question and Answer periods. And, finally, (5) I prefer to keep things as simple as possible, which I can do by setting a large enough flat fee to cover everything and still not be out of line.

My experience over the years in marketing this has been that clients tend to prefer a flat fee. Setting out a menu of items and their costs tends to lead to nit-picking disputes and endless negotiations, which often result in an aborted effort to reach agreement. It is necessary to explain to the client in some detail—detailed explanation of what the client gets, that is—what your fee covers, but avoid scrupulously pricing individual items other than your fee and your expenses—travel and subsistence. And a note on that also:

As anyone else does these days, I try to maximize my cash flow, while I also make it a practice to charge clients only my actual expenses, rather than a fixed or standard per diem allowance. I therefore usually suggest to clients that they can benefit by providing my airline tickets and arranging my hotel accommodations to be billed directly to them so that I can charge them only my actual costs while giving them the opportunity to take advantage of any discount privileges they enjoy. Otherwise, I explain, if it is necessary to furnish a more detailed explanation, I must add a G&A

(general and administrative) cost to my expense account. I have found many clients entirely amenable to this—it is in their interest as well as in mine—and I am thus able to minimize invoicing and cash flow problems. (I have found many large, private corporations even slower than government agencies in paying their bills.)

You may be able to make the same arrangements when you are presenting seminars for a seminar-production organization. I do, in fact, and far prefer it because it is simple and risk-free. (If money were my sole motivation, I would deliver only seminars I produced myself.) But these organizations are in the middle, as brokers of a kind, taking risks and trying to earn a profit on what I do. They are also a source of income for me on a continuing basis, which may stretch over years. I therefore find it necessary to give them a kind of "wholesale" price, and so I set my fee a little lower for them than I do for a client ordering an in-house program. However, you may find, as I did, that some seminar-production organizations tend to offer you compensation on a percentage basis, possibly with a small guarantee. This is not necessarily a bad deal, but you need to be alert for built-in traps. One client, a division of a very large and prestigious corporation, made me just such an offer but set the commissions on only attendances in excess of the first 65 attendees, with a small guarantee of $250. It was unlikely, under those circumstances, that I would be paid more than the minimum guarantee, so I regretfully declined. While some seminars attract as many as 150–200 attendees, they are very much in the minority. It is far more likely that any given seminar will draw from 20 to 50 attendees.

Probably, in most cases where you make a custom, in-house presentation of a seminar to a client's staff, it will be a one-time sale. However, that is not always true. I have often had the pleasure of making more than one presentation of the same program to a client's staff. In some cases, the client has numerous offices or facilities and has me visit each with the program. In others, the client wishes a large number of staff trained, but since the client recognizes that it is unwieldy to deal with large numbers of trainees, I am asked to make repeated presentations at the same location but to a different group each time.

But there is still another way to do repeat seminar business with clients: You need not confine yourself to a single seminar program. You can develop several programs and probably keep yourself quite busy with such presentations. In fact, some consultants have found seminars more to their taste than any other activity and devote most of their time and efforts to such undertakings.

Special Approaches.   There are other ways, special ways, to begin marketing seminars or small lecture courses. Probably the easiest way is via local colleges and universities, especially community colleges, who offer extension or adult education courses. These organizations offer a wide variety of programs on dozens of subjects and are always ready to consider new ideas or better programs. For example, I have presented brief courses and seminars on getting ideas for small businesses, marketing, proposal writing, consulting, and other topics at such colleges. Government agencies—federal, state, and local—often fund such seminars. I have, for example, presented seminars to a number of federal and state agencies—the Department of Commerce, the Office of Personnel Management, and the Michigan Employment Training Institute, among others. Associations hire speakers to present seminars at annual conventions, and I have spoken at conclaves of the Automobile Accessories and Parts Association and the Land Improvement Contractors Association, among others. Finally, there are such organizations as Open University in Washington, DC and Learning Annex in New York City, private sector organizations that function very much like those extension courses of the community colleges, offering mini-programs in a wide variety of subjects, from wine tasting to computer programming.

You can, of course, pursue any or all of these methods and approaches. (I pursue only methods in which I am paid a flat fee for my program and time, since I became involved in so many activities that I simply cannot find the time to attend to all the details of organizing and producing my own open-registration programs.)

There is one final and pleasant surprise: There are special rewards for the consultant in all these activities. The appearances before groups of people almost inevitably leads to consulting assignments. My experience has been that approximately three quarters of my speaking engagements have produced either another paid speaking engagement or a consulting job.

CHAPTER NINE

Designing the Newsletter

PRELIMINARY CONSIDERATIONS

There are both artistic/editorial judgments and standard practices involved in newsletter design. There is much to be said for originality and novelty, of course, but you must also remember that readers anticipate and expect to find certain features by which they can immediately recognize the newsletter for what it is—a newsletter. So you must strike a reasonable balance between what is novel or striking design and what is simply bizarre. But first it is necessary to be familiar with certain standard features and practices in newsletter design.

THE CLASSIC PHYSICAL ELEMENTS

As in all things, certain de facto standards have developed in newsletter publishing. The physical elements we expect to find in most newsletters include the following items—but don't be dismayed if the names are strange; they will be explained as we go. Perhaps they are not terribly important, but unless you become familiar with the names and know what they refer to, our communication will be handicapped.

The Nameplate

First of all there is the matter of the nameplate. That is (usually) the area at the top of the first page where the name and a few vital statistics of the newsletter are identified. If you refer to Figure 3–1, *Professional Marketing Report,* you will find a rather simple nameplate, which includes only the title, the volume and issue numbers, and the issue date.

Figure 3–2 has a somewhat more ambitious nameplate, which includes information about the publisher and several other data items.

If these are extremes, Figure 9–1 is a compromise between them. *Desktop Graphics;*™ is a newsletter intended to serve newsletter publishers, among others. And Howard Penn Hudson's *The Newsletter on Newsletters* (Figure 9–2) is equally middle-of-the-road in its nameplate.

Audrey Wyatt, founder and Executive Director of the American Consultants League, gets the League's credentials up front in the nameplate of its newsletter, *Consulting Intelligence* (see Figure 9–3).

The Masthead

Traditionally, the masthead is a column on the editorial page of a newspaper in which are identified the principal functionaries and other vital data of the newspaper. It tends to assume the general form of Figure 9–4, the masthead of the popular *Sharing Ideas*, published by Dottie Walters for speakers and consultants, which is probably more a small magazine than a newsletter, owing to its size alone. But mastheads can assume many other physical formats, and in some cases the masthead becomes part of the nameplate and/or copyright notice (see Figure 9–3) or appears elsewhere in the publication.

Copyright Notice

The matter of a copyright notice is an entirely different matter because this involves the law on copyright. This is a law that changed considerably a few years ago, not necessarily for the better, depending on your viewpoint. Certain basics are little changed. However, one thing that has changed is that you do not necessarily lose your right to the copy simply because you have failed to proclaim that right. Still, you are well advised to pursue older conventions; they are the safer course to pursue in safeguarding your rights, and we shall recommend those here.

The proper notice is "Copyright (date) by (name)." You can add such notations as "all rights reserved," but they really add nothing

FIGURE 9–1:   Front Page Typeset, Ragged Right, with Ilustrations

DeskTop Graphics™

The How-To Newsletter for Desktop Graphic Designers

| Volume 1, No. 3 | Published by Dynamic Graphics, Inc. | September, 1986 |

The basics of stationery design and production

Quick! If you are setting up your own shop or have taken on a client that is a start-up, what is the first design project you tackle? More than likely, it is letterhead, envelope and business card—business stationery.

As a desktop graphic designer selling laser printer output, the design/production of your own stationery might be a problem. You want to put your best foot forward, but yet you may need to demonstrate that you practice what you preach. A strong effective design can go a long way to overcome the limitations of the microcomputer and 300 dpi resolution. Too, there are ways to optimize the output of your laser printer. Read on as this article covers all these points and more.

The basics

No matter what additional design elements you may have on your stationery, no design is complete without the person or organization's name, mailing address and phone number. That's all that is needed. You or your client may be tempted to list his entire product line or board of directors, but try to steer clear. This type of information often becomes obsolete before the stationery does. A good sensible design can define the company without verbalizing it. If required, a short label that describes the nature of business will do nicely.

CONTINUED ON PAGE 2

How to produce a business card at 300 dpi and have it printed at 600 dpi.

Recently, when I suggested to a desktop designer that she could easily produce a business card with 300 dpi laser printer output and have it printed in quantity at 600 dpi visual resolution, she expressed disbelief. Here is the simple solution that makes that possible, thanks to an old trick of illustrators and production artists—working oversize. •RLK

The standard business card in the United States is the 3 1/2" X 2" horizontal format that will be used in this article. To achieve your objective, you will work at a size that is 200% of the finished size, or 7" X 4" and print out camera-ready art at that size.. Note that both width and height are doubled.

Any draw program (i.e., Windows Draw/IBM PC, MacDraw/Macintosh) or layout/pasteup program (i.e., ReadySetGo, PageMaker, etc.) can be used. Always remember that you are working oversize; that the width and height of everything in the design will be half of the original when printed in quantity. If your program has a 50% view option, it is a good idea to use it as you work as it will give you a WYSIWYG perspective of your final printed card.

The example design used here is for a design studio named Orchard Studio. Basic name and address information appears on the card. If the name of the firm does not communicate the nature of its business, add a brief description of its product or service. In this case, it will read "Advertising Design and Production."

Define your card design by first drawing an outline rectangle that is 7" X 4" at actual size. Before you begin placing graphics and type, however, go to a 50% view of the area.

Type is the most important element in a business card design. The type carries the information that

CONTINUED ON PAGE 3

to your legal protection. It is best to use the word *copyright*, rather than *copr.* or the symbol (C), because some nations do not recognize the latter symbols as authentic notices. For safety's sake, most publishers use both the full word and the symbol.

FIGURE 9–2:   Front Page of a Special Promotional Issue

ISSN 0028-9507

THE NEWSLETTER ON NEWSLETTERS

FOR THE NEWSLETTER PROFESSIONAL: Reporting on the newsletter world—editing, graphics, management, promotion, newsletter reviews, and surveys.

Vol. 23, No. 10A   (SPECIAL ISSUE)   May 21, 1986

Dear Subscriber:

You'll recall that last summer our Aug. 15 lead story was "How Personal Computers Will Revolutionize Your Newsletter Production." We quoted James Cavuoto and his initial issue of MicroPublishing Report NL:

"The personal computer will soon supplant much of the dedicated and expensive equipment used in many publishing operations, including typesetter page make-up terminals, and outside mailing services."

In the fall we visited Cavuoto in California. And more and more we have been reporting on this phenomenon, generally termed laser writing or desktop publishing. Now Jim Cavuoto has written the book-- LaserWrite It!, "A Desktop Publishing Guide to Reports, Resumes, Newsletters, Directories, Business Forms and More."

It's a timely achievement. No, it's not perfect because laser writing isn't either, as our review will mention. But, in one fell swoop, Cavuoto brings us all up to date. Stop collecting those weekly articles and ads on desktop publishing. For the moment, you need only one resource on your desk: LaserWrite It!

We state unequivocally that if you are in newsletters or publishing of any sort you need this book--now. You may obtain it through The Newsletter Clearinghouse. Order form enclosed.--H.P.H.

YOUR GUIDE THROUGH THE LASER MAZE

What laser technology offers the publisher is complete control of the typesetting and graphic design of any publication. Newsletters, of course, with their emphasis on typewriter composition, have long been in control since the development of the Selectric typewriter. Word processing has offered greater flexibility and typographic capability. However, when publishers wish to handle

You can register your copyright with the Copyright Office of the Library of Congress for a small fee. However, it is not absolutely necessary to do so; your publication of the copyright notice furnishes what lawyers call "common law" protection in that it es-

FIGURE 9–3: Newsletter of a Consultant's Association

Advisory Board

Eugene Hameroff, Director Ementus
The Consultants Institute

J. Stephen Lanning, Publisher
The Consulting Opportunities Journal

Hubert Bermont, President
The Consultant's Library

Herman Holtz, Author, Consultant

Audrey S. Wyatt
Executive Director

Consulting Intelligence

$8

Published by and for the

American Consultants League

ISSN: 0887-0314   July 15, 1986

The Consulting Boom

Over the years, we have continually received phone calls and letters asking when would be a good time to enter the consulting profession. Our reply has always been the same: NOW! And never has that advice been more accurate than at the present time. Indeed, all portents show that it will continue to be accurate for at least the next five years. Ours is the fastest growing profession of all.

Never before have we had such enormous publicity. When we appear as the cover story of U.S. News & World Report, we know that we are in the professional forefront of the American public.

First, a few pertinent statistics:

Income from consulting rose as much as 28% in 1985 according to ACME and "The Consultant's U.S. Statistical Guide & Source Finder."

The percentage of GNP contributed by the consulting profession has never been higher.

Concomitantly, taxes paid to the IRS as a result of consulting income is at an all-time high.

Educated estimates put income from consulting at over 15 billion dollars in 1986, with far greater increases for the remainder of this decade.

Personal finance consultants alone number over 100,000. So it is safe to assume that that there are at least 200,000 consultants selling their advice and expertise in any one year.

Large consulting firms are hiring MBA's fresh out of Harvard for starting salaries of $55,000 a year.

Now let us examine the causes of this most extraordinary professional growth phenomenon. Consider if you will that:

In This Issue:

Your Advice For Free?...............1
The Consulting Boom................1
The Other Side of the Coin.........2
Book Reviews......................5
Why Consultants Fail..............6
Sound Advice......................6
Savings on International Travel....7

Your Advice for Free?

Virtually every advertisement you come across for a book or seminar on consulting touts the fact that it will teach you how never to give your advice away for free. Although it is true that many clients will attempt to get your expertise free of charge at one time or another, and although it is also true that in most cases you would do well to side-step this ruse, the impression that consultants should never, ever give free advice is false.

There are many times when it is actually in your best interests to give away a certain amount of free advice. We list these propitious times here:

When and if you publish a newsletter for the purpose of marketing your consultancy, you must give away a certain amount of concrete expertise. This is good advertising and shows you off to your best advantage.

Oftentimes in an exploratory interview, the client will ask meaningful, pertinent questions concerning his project. This is not always done with the object of getting free advice

tablishes your claim. Should you get involved in litigation over your copyright or claim to copyright, you must have registered the copyright with the Copyright Office. But you need not have done so at the time of publication; you can do so when and if litigation ensues and enjoy the same legal protection you would have had you registered it earlier.

FIGURE 9–4: Masthead of Speakers' Newsletter

Editor - In - Chief & Publisher
Dottie Walters, C.S.P.

Editorial Assistant
Patti Blair

Advertising - Credit Manager
Judy Johnson

Editorial Assistant
Audrey Lohr

Mailing Department
Dianne Severin

Printing Production
" Cowboy" Bob Walters

Speakers Bureau
Lillet Walters

Office Manager
Lorine Lasch

Reproduced with permission of Sharing Ideas

Most periodical publishers print their copyright notices as part of the masthead, but that is not a universal practice, especially in the case of newsletters, where the notice may be found in the nameplate or at the bottom of the first page, as in Figures 3–1 and 3–2. This is a common practice in publications of only a few pages.

The laws governing copyright are not as clear as we might wish for, even after being updated a few years ago. The basic intent of copyright law is to protect the author's and publisher's rights to the combination of words—and it is only the rights to that specific combination of words that is protected—but the publisher is obligated to let everyone know by publishing a copyright notice that the combination of words—the expression—is his or her property.

Volume and Number

It is a common practice of periodical publishers to print identifying numbers on each issue of the publication. Some publishers number the issues serially, from the first issue forward indefinitely, but most publishers use the volume concept, starting a new volume each year so that Volume 2, Number 3 identifies the third issue of the second year of publication. The numbers are usually part of the masthead, generally on the dateline.

Address Box

Although many publishers mail their newsletters in envelopes, it is also a common practice to make self-mailers of newsletters, usually by using the bottom half of the last page, attaching an address label. Figure 9–5 illustrates this.

TYPE STYLES

There is an almost endless array of possible type styles in both typewriter/computer-printer composition and in formal type. (From here on I will use the term *typewriter composition* to refer to both, since there is little practical difference between the two.) The first decision you must make about type is whether you will use typewriter composition or formal type. Figures 3–1 and 3–2 were good examples of each: Figure 3–1 is in formal type—"typeset," to use the jargon—while Figure 3–2 has a frame page that is typeset, but each month's issue is in typewriter composition.

Probably typewriter composition is by far the more widely used, but with modern computer systems—desktop publishing—distinc-

FIGURE 9–5: Typical Address Box of Self-Mailer Newsletter

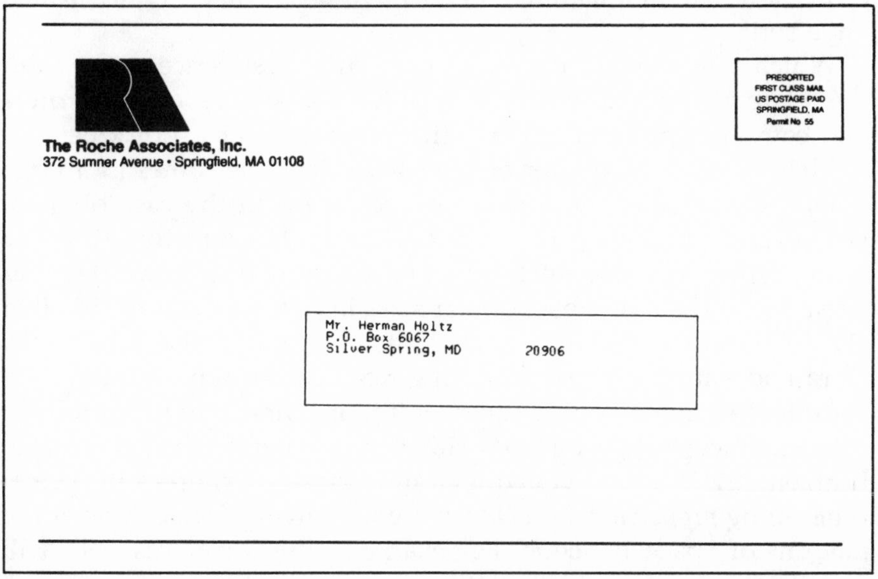
The Roche Associates, Inc.
372 Sumner Avenue • Springfield, MA 01108
PRESORTED
FIRST CLASS MAIL
US POSTAGE PAID
SPRINGFIELD, MA
Permit No 55
Mr. Herman Holtz
P.O. Box 6067
Silver Spring, MD 20906

Reproduced with permission of The Roche Associates, Inc

tions are becoming blurred, and the economics of the choice, once heavily weighted in favor of typewriter composition, are less and less a factor. However, that may or may not be true for any given case, for it may depend to quite a large extent on your working habits. If you actually write—and that includes rewriting and editing—at the computer (word processor) keyboard, printing out the copy is a mechanical chore and not a costly one. And this is especially so if you are working with a modern desktop publishing program because then you use the computer to do the formatting, layouts, and makeup, with camera-ready copy emerging from the printer. But if you are still scrawling out copy longhand and paying someone to keyboard it and print it out, it may pay you to consider formal typesetting.

The companion question of right-justified copy versus ragged-right copy is especially insignificant today. With almost everyone using a word processor, you can right-justify your copy quite easily, if you prefer that appearance. (However, many favor ragged-right copy, even when it is typeset.)

There is an almost endless variety of type styles, but at the root is first a basic division between typefaces with *serifs* and those without serifs, known generally as *sans serif* typefaces. Figure 3–1 is an example of a sans serif typeface, a letter gothic type, while other newsletters illustrated so far have used roman types, which have serifs.

Which you use is a matter of your own preference, since even the relatively limited variety of type fonts available for typewriters and computer printers offers both roman and sans serif types.

There is also the matter of type sizes, for type comes in a large assortment of sizes, designated by *points* or, in the case of typewriters and computer printers, *pitch*. Point refers directly to the size of the typeface, while pitch refers to the number of characters per linear inch. The two most popular sizes in common use are 10 pitch (12 point), also called *pica*, and 12 pitch (10 point), also called *elite*. (Pica and elite are terms stemming from earlier typewriters.)

Letters are not all of the same width, of course, but for simplicity of mechanical design of typewriters each occupies the same space horizontally in most typewriters and printers, whereas in formal typesetting *proportional spacing* is used, allowing each character the amount of space it needs. For example, the lower case "l" will usually occupy about one fourth the space allotted an "m" or "w."

It is largely for this reason that you can get a great deal more copy on a formally typeset page than on one you have composed via typewriter, even if you have used the proportional spacing available on some typewriters and printers. (There are also "condensed" typefaces that compress the type even more.)

But these are primarily mechanical and physical factors in the design of a newsletter. There are many editorial considerations that enter into the basic design, some of them fairly technical, perhaps, but many easily understandable as purely of the "horse sense" category, requiring no special publishing knowledge or experience to understand and appreciate.

COMMONSENSE COMPOSITION

In *Newsletters: Hot Marketing Tool,* Gerre Jones begins a chapter headed "Publication Design Principles" with the logical observation that since we read from left to right and top to bottom, prudence dictates bearing this in mind in designing a publication. Among many other sensible remarks he also notes that text set in capitals and lowercase letters is far easier to read than text that is all capitals. This is also due to our being conditioned, through basic education and ingrained habit, to read in capitals and lowercase letters. All deviations from this are strange and require us to break our comfortable old habits to readjust. Hence, we do not find it easy to read text that is all capitals or set in an unusual type style such as italic, script, or Old English. Even sans serif types, such as letter gothic, are less comfortable for many than are roman types.

Variety for Eye Relief

Readers find large, solid blocks of unbroken text formidable. The eye tends to go first to illustrations and short items, items distinguished by such devices as bullets, sideheads, and color, and other items that represent relief from and alternatives to that forbidding solid text. Figures 3–1 and 3–2 are both examples of such design, although not in color, as are Figures 9–1 and 9–2.

This is not to say that a newsletter must look typographically like a child's primer. But lengthier text, even in solid blocks, becomes far less dismaying when the reader's interest has been aroused and when there are islands of relief in the sea of text. Certainly, the overall appearance of the front page ought to be one that is not forbiddingly dense.

Single-Column versus Double-Column Format

Most typeset newsletters use two- or three-column format (as in Figures 3–1, 9–1, and 9–3), while typewriter-composed newsletters tend to single-column format (as in Figure 9–2), although Figure 9–3 is an exception. The idea behind two-column format is that the human eye has a little trouble scanning a six- or seven-inch line, and is more comfortable with one of about one half that length. Experience provides little evidence, since by far the majority of newsletters are composed in single-column format; but they are also usually typewriter composed, which makes it rather difficult to make a valid comparison of relative or apparent readability between the two.

COLOR CONTRASTS

By far the majority of newsletters are printed in black ink on white paper. Some publishers use off-white paper, and others use colored paper. Studies suggest that black and yellow offer the best contrast—probably the reason so many traffic signs are in black lettering on yellow backgrounds. However, some publishers make the mistake of printing on dark papers, and even of printing in ink colors that offer a low contrast to the color of the paper, such as red ink on dark brown paper, one particularly ill-advised combination I have observed.

This is not a proper use of color, of course. Paper should be of light colors—pastels, if not white or off white. Inks should be of contrasting dark colors, preferably black with colored inks used sparingly, if at all, for headlines, captions, special notices, and other such applications.

THE PROPER ROLE OF NEWSLETTER DESIGN

Note, in general, that while it helps to make your newsletter as attractive physically as possible, cosmetic considerations have little lasting effect on the success of a newsletter. Many highly successful newsletters are pure "plain Janes," typewriter composed, printed on simple white offset (sulphite) paper in black ink, without photos or illustrations, and without any frills at all. They are successful because of their content, because they deliver the news, information, ideas, and whatever else their readers want. Never lose sight of the fact that it is that—information—that your newsletter is supposed to deliver. The design should be attractive. It should please the eye. But most of all, it should make it as easy as possible for the reader to glean what he or she wants from it. And there are still a few other ways to help your reader use your newsletter most effectively.

Guiding the Reader

One particularly useful thing you can do for your readers is to furnish them with a road map to the contents of each issue—a table of contents—on the first page for maximum convenience. In Figure 3–1 you find such a contents listing in the lower right corner.

The *Mail Order Connection* (Figure 3–2) does this a bit differently, posting a boxed notice as part of the nameplate and listing therein a summary of the issue's contents, without listing page numbers. The coverage is different in a subtle way, too: Where the publisher of *Professional Marketing Report* is simply guiding readers objectively to columns and features, the other is providing teasers, written as benefits—inducements to read the newsletter. (Perhaps this is inevitable, considering the nature of this latter newsletter!)

The publisher of *Consulting Intelligence* (Figure 9–3) also lists the issue's contents on the first page, immediately under the nameplate. This is more an objective listing for convenience, however, in the style of Figure 3–1, than of motivation to read the newsletter thoroughly, as in the case of Figure 3–2.

Routing Box

Despite copyright laws that forbid it, many subscribers will make copies of your newsletter for distribution to others in their organizations. In an effort to discourage this, while at the same time adding income, some publishers offer additional subscriptions at a fraction of the charge for the original or first subscription, hoping to make it uneconomical for subscribers to make copies. Steve Lanning, publisher of *Consulting Opportunities Journal* (Figure 9–6),

FIGURE 9-6:   Example of Newsletter with Routing Box

CONSULTING
OPPORTUNITIES JOURNAL®

America's Continuing Education Source For The Marketing of Professional Services
Published By The Consultants National Resource Center

Vol. 6, No. 1	September-October 1986	ISSN: 0273-4613

ROUTE TO:

Some Ideas We Have Been Gathering

MARKETING PROFESSIONAL SERVICES— THE ADVANCED COURSE

By J. Stephen Lanning

SELLING HAS TAKEN ON A NEW DIMENSION

By Don Reid

The pressure from competitors and the greater awareness by consumers are probably the two primary factors that are influencing the new style and dimension that sales representatives need to adopt: the role of an extremely important resource person to one's clients.

One of the greatest assets of high achiever salespeople is the ability to have knowledge of their client's business, and the ability to suggest ways of improving it. High achiever salespeople make it their business to know as much about their client's company as they possibly can. And not only in their company but also in their client's industry—they know the trends and the vital changes that the trends are bringing about in their clients' field. How this important information is used can truly "make or break" a sale.

Successful salespeople have a great deal of skill in the questioning technique area. What is vitally important is that when they ask their client a question, they also have the ability to listen. They tend to be up-front and understand the client's business, getting a handle on what is happening so they wind up being more of a "consultant."

More and more, sales management is recognizing that the sales call has risen dramatically from $75.00 in 1975 to

(See SELLING . . . pg. 7)

I really wish every subscriber could listen in on the conversations of marketing ideas from their fellow professionals. Some are new but many are as old as the hills—but with a new twist.

It's been said (by whom, I've forgotten) that an idea only has to be 10 percent new to make a million dollars. And that we should tread very lightly on ideas that are over 50 percent new.

However, management consultant, entrepreneur and all-around businessman Brian Tracy brings out the fact that research shows that 80 percent of the things we have today either didn't exist or existed in a very limited format just five years ago. And five years from today 80 percent of the things (gadgets to processes) we'll be using then don't exist today. SOMEONE is going to bring them into the various markets. And it might as well be you—since you are on the leading edge of your industry anyway, yes?

We want to share some of the things we've been hearing and learning about ourselves with you. Now please bear in mind, some of the things we simply cannot share in print. This is not because they are illegal, but because some of the ideas are being used by our C.A.R.E. clients. And they have simply asked us to wait a few months as they implement them into *their* marketplace.

New Networking Ideas We Like

Several twists on this one. Anytime you get a group of people together, what do you have? (Keep the jokes to a minimum, please!) Well, you could call it a network. But you also could call it an association, a consortium, a league, a roundtable and so on.

Do you think you have a certain niche, a unique selling point, a purpose for getting together that you could share with others in your discipline? It's being done every day—forming associations (for-profit and non-profit) and other business clubs under the above names and others.

The Business Breakfast

One consultant couldn't seem to get appointments with the right *people* in her industry. Yes, she got business, but it was a trickle compared to what she felt she COULD get. After sitting down with (who else?) another consultant and taking a hard look at her industry, her city and the people she was trying to reach, she decided on an end-around play.

The people she was trying to see were C.E.O.s and marketing V.P.s. They had a common field. And common problems and needs. And, through doing a little research found that most all of them got to the office early several days during the week. She found Thursday was the morning most of them had in common.

She started a "Grant County Marketing Opportunity Breakfast Club." (The real name was MUCH better, but you get the idea.) It was promoted through the local Chamber of Commerce. And got press releases picked up regularly. (Didn't seem to matter to the press that it was a for-profit arrangement on the part of the consultant.)

She charged companies $100/month membership. And for that the company could send up to three of the management brass. (One had to be the

(See MARKETING . . . pg. 2)

takes the opposite view: He encourages subscribers to circulate their issue by printing a routing box on his front page. He believes that maximum readership is in his interest, even if much of it is by nonsubscribers, because his newsletter is a vehicle to reach prospects for other goods and services and because many who read a pass-along copy of his newsletter will decide that they want their own, personal subscription.

CHAPTER TEN

Gathering the Information—Sources

THE MOST BASIC SOURCES: OTHER PUBLICATIONS

Consciously or unconsciously, all newsletter publishers are greatly influenced by and depend to at least some extent on other periodicals, probably as their most basic source of information and ideas. Your newsletter would begin to perish from lack of nourishment quite rapidly if you failed to keep up your own reading, especially of periodicals, which fall into specific classes:

- General-interest newspapers and newsmagazines.
- General-interest (newsstand) magazines on specialized subjects.
- Special-interest (by mail only) magazines and other periodicals.

The kinds of news and other information you pursue depends on your own professional or technical interests and what you cover in your newsletter, of course. Unless you are deeply involved with computers and with specialized considerations about computers, for example, you probably are not even aware of *MIS Week* or *Network World,* much less a subscriber reading their weekly issues. But there are undoubtedly some other specialized periodicals, perhaps general-interest but almost surely trade or professional publications, that you do read because they relate to what you do and would therefore relate to the coverage of your own periodical.

Your motives and objectives in reading whatever periodicals you do read also vary according to your field. There are many newsletters—*Boardroom Reports,* for one—that are almost entirely quotations and abstracts from other publications, probably from as many as 50 or more other publications. In fact, the concept underlying such newsletters is that of acting in behalf of readers who would not have the time to do all that reading for themselves, and of abstracting for the readers the best information and ideas. Such a newsletter represents a virtual reading service, and its success depends on how accurately the publisher gauges what will interest and be appreciated by the readers. But even those other newsletters, based on far different concepts, require the publisher to be conscious of what is happening that has some relevance to his or her field and newsletter. The need to read rather voraciously is, with only rare exceptions, a basic requirement for publishing a newsletter.

That need to read extends to books also, for more than one half of the 40,000–50,000 books published annually are nonfiction works, many of them on rather specialized subjects, as is this book. It is a rare field that is so highly specialized that it is not covered in some manner by at least a book or two every year or so. (In fact, you may wish to review books that would be of interest to your readers and publish those reviews as one of your regular features.)

Improving the Process

Information gathering through reading is routine, and while it may seem a forbidding task, you soon learn to do it efficiently. For one thing, you begin with a wide range of periodicals, but you soon learn which are worth the time spent in reading them and which are not, so you winnow the list considerably in a rather short time and are soon concentrating on a much smaller range of periodicals and perhaps an occasional book.

You also soon begin to discover other sources, some of which duplicate and are better sources than some of the periodicals you read, so you winnow that latter even further. In fact, although you can never afford to stop reading rather widely if you wish to truly remain on top of your subject, you ultimately come to depend rather heavily on other sources (unless, of course, yours is a newsletter based on quoting other periodicals).

The Traditional Legwork

Most of this chapter is going to be devoted to those other sources and, you may be pleased to know, how to do the bulk of your editorial research and information gathering at your own desk. The sources and methods include, generally, the morning mail, your personal computer, contributions from others, and a few miscellaneous ones.

It has become almost traditional and certainly conventional wisdom that a reporter must depend on legwork—deep, persistent, detailed probing in pursuit of information—to do a good job. Of course, as a newsletter publisher you are not going to be in pursuit of hard news, with perhaps only an occasional exception. Nevertheless, the legwork is a must: You will do lots of it if you want a top-notch newsletter. But legwork is not now literally hiking around, probing, pushing, cajoling, urging, and pressing many people, as it once was. Today's legwork, at least for your purposes, is carried out largely in the comfort of your own office, although you will have to make at least occasional forays, following up leads and ferreting out details.

What makes this possible—necessary and inevitable, in fact—is the modern information/communications age. Today, the problem is not one of discovering information as much as it is one of sifting through a surfeit of information in quest of truth and relevant data. We are, in fact, drowning in information, bombarded with it from innumerable sources, harassed by radio, TV, mail, newspapers, magazines, and computers. There is as much "junk" on the air and in print as there is in the morning mail. But once you become a newsletter publisher you can no longer afford to turn a deaf ear to junk radio and junk TV and an unseeing eye to junk mail and junk print media. Some of the junk becomes valuable now, for leads to ideas and stories, if not the ideas and stories in themselves.

Library Research

Editors who buy articles regularly from free-lance writers are generally opposed to what some have called "the library job"—an article based entirely on library research without going into the field to talk to people and do personal investigation. Still, library research is a necessary part of preparing your newsletter, and you should be building a personal library in your own office, although you will still have to resort to the public library from time to time. For example, I keep a number of directories in my own office, but there are some important ones that I don't have because they are costly and I don't use them often enough to justify the investment. Too, I sometimes need the help of an experienced librarian, which I can get in the public library, of course.

Contributions

Writers whose work is published in periodicals are often referred to as "contributors." This does not mean that they have donated money (although that is another way in which the word is often used), nor even that they have donated articles. Even professional free-lance writers who are paid for the articles they submit to editors are contributors. However, a commercial, general-interest periodical, such as most of those you find on newsstands, has usually paid for all material (other than Letters to the Editor) contributed by free-lance writers, whereas you may very well be able to get much material contributed without paying for it. But you can also buy material from free-lance writers, which may prove to be a bargain after all.

How do all these sources fit together? Which takes priority? Where do you start? What is a "lead?" Where/how do you get them, and what comes next?

The answers to these are the heart of newslettering, and we will explore them in greater depth as we go on.

THE RELEVANT PERIODICALS

Local drugstores, convenience stores, and supermarkets all carry newspapers and magazines, some of them on a fairly elaborate scale. Of course, you are familiar with or at least generally aware of most of those popular general-interest magazines that appear on those racks and stands, are you not? Or are you? If you think you are, try an experiment: Look in the Yellow Pages directory under "magazine dealers" for newsstands, and visit a few. If yours is a fairly populous city or county, you are likely to get a sharp surprise. Those who specialize in selling magazines and newspapers, as opposed to those who handle them as a sideline or as a convenience for their customers, will usually display dozens of magazines, newspapers, tabloids, and sometimes miscellaneous other publications, all completely strange and new to you. The average neighborhood drugstore or supermarket carries a relative handful of periodicals by comparison.

Simply browsing in such an emporium of periodicals will probably spark a dozen new ideas in your head. You will probably go home with an armload of new and interesting publications. And still you will have encountered only a fraction of the periodicals published regularly—probably 150–250 titles at most.

The current (1987) edition of *Writer's Market* (Writer's Digest Books, Cincinnati, Ohio) lists periodicals in numerous classifications under two general headings: Consumer Publications; and Trade, Technical, and Professional Journals. There are then listed 51 subclassifications of Consumer Publications and 72 types of Trade, Technical, and Professional Journals. That adds up to 123 *types* of periodicals, with such descriptive classifications as these few:

Animal	Art	Association
Business and finance	Child care	Ethnic/minority
Health and fitness	Hobby and craft	Humor
In-flight	Military	Retirement
Accounting	Aviation and	Clothing
International affairs	space	Law
Medical	Jewelry	Real estate
Selling and	Photography	Travel
merchandising	Transportation	

The listings run from page 203 to page 876 inclusive, describing well over 2,000 periodical publications in those nearly 700 pages of closely packed type. Nor is this a complete list by any means, but a list of only those periodical publishers who choose to be listed—primarily because they are interested in buying material from contributors—and/or whom the editors believe to be of value to free-lance writers (for whom the volume is intended). There are other directories that list an even greater number of periodicals.

Controlled Circulation Periodicals

You may recall mention made earlier (see Chapter 5) of free periodicals, periodicals often referred to as "controlled circulation" publications. These are trade publications for whom maximum possible circulation among the types of readers their advertisers most prize is far more important than the dollars resulting from subscription fees. To achieve that ideal, which then maximizes their advertising rates and income, they grant subscriptions free to those who qualify as the most-desired types of readers.

To control the circulation to "qualified" readers, each reader is required to fill out a simple questionnaire to gain a free subscription and another each year to renew the subscription. A computer periodical, for example, might ask whether you buy computers, as well as your position in your organization, in qualifying you for a free subscription.

How to Learn of Free Journals

Many of these free trade journals accept paid subscriptions from those who do not qualify for free subscriptions, so you will sometimes find copies of such publications offered for sale at exceptionally well-stocked newsstands. That is one way to learn of their existence. However, many of these publications run advertisements in other periodicals, inviting readers to apply for free subscriptions. And, finally, you will often find advertisements in your morning mail, especially in "card decks," those packages of advertising post cards. After a while your name will have been added to dozens of mailing lists, and the quantity of mail you receive will increase by several orders of magnitude. (And you will eventually develop the habit of reading all your mail, even that which is obviously advertising matter, instead of throwing it away without a glance.)

There are also all those reference directories, such as *Ulrich's International Periodicals Directory* (R. R. Bowker, New York, NY), and *Ayer Directory of Publications* (Ayer Press, Bala Cynwyd, PA), to name only two of many. One of the numerous directories I keep at hand is an annual, *The National Directory of Addresses and Telephone Numbers* (Concord Reference Books, Inc., New York, NY). Each year it gets considerably thicker than the year before, and while it lists little more than names and addresses of many things, I find it most useful throughout the year as a quick and accurate source that is right at hand. For example, I put it to use a few minutes ago to verify the names and publishers of the other two directories I named here.

THE MORNING MAIL

For many newsletter publishers, the morning mail is the richest source of information, ideas, and leads. In my own morning mail, for example, I am likely to find the following:

Press releases.
Complete publicity packages—press kits.
Brochures galore.
Memoranda and bulletins.
Reports of various kinds.
Salesletters and direct mail packages.
Periodicals that I may or may not have subscribed to.
Decks of advertising cards.
Business correspondence.
Chatty letters from friends.

Any of these may include information useful for newsletter publishing (although in my own case I gave up my newsletters some years ago in favor of writing books, consulting, and lecturing). Probably, however, the press releases are most consistently useful for the average newsletter publisher if they are from sources that are truly relevant. (Somehow—mysteriously—once you get on a few distribution lists for press releases, you find yourself getting releases from people, organizations, and places you never heard of!) But you also soon find yourself getting many other kinds of reports, special bulletins, brochures, booklets, and advertising matter. Let's look a bit more closely now at some of the goodies that arrive many mornings.

Press Releases

The press release is probably one of the more important items in your mailbox, when you learn how to use it well. Typically, a press release looks about like the one illustrated as Figure 10–1. This one actually says "Press Release." Others may say simply "Release" or "News." And some people refer to such a document as a "Publicity Release," for it is that, too.

Note the words "For Immediate Release." This means that it may be used immediately. In some cases a release is "embargoed" until some specified date. This might be the case when the release

FIGURE 10–1:   Typical Press Release

Practice Management Associates, Ltd.

Ten Midland Avenue
Newton, Massachusetts 02158
617-965-0055

FOR IMMEDIATE RELEASE

PRESS RELEASE

For more information
Contact: Stephen Kliment
(617) 965-0055

PUBLISH 1987 EDITION OF
DESIGN AND BUILDING INDUSTRY PUBLICITY DIRECTORY

The 1987 (Fourth) edition of the Design and Building
Industry Publicity Directory is scheduled for publication in
October.

The Directory has nearly twice the number of entries (400)
as the previous edition, and comes in a revised, more
spacious format to allow for annotation by the user.

Designed as a handy reference for architects, engineers,
interior designers, landscape architects and other design
professionals, as well as contractors and product and
materials vendors, the new edition of the Publicity
Directory lists some 400 professional trade and business
publications which design and construction firms can select
as targets for their publicity efforts.

Each entry provides the following data:
   -- Name, address, telephone number and owner of the
      publication   (more)

contains the text of a speech yet to be given. The issuer of the release does not want it to appear in the press until the speech has been given and so advises the reader with a suitable notice.

Most important, however, is the note near the head of the release on the right side that says, "For more information . . ." and gives a name and telephone number as a contact for follow-up. This is the means for following up a release if you have questions concerning it or sense a more important story behind it. It is this action, a follow-up, that may convert an unimportant and routine release into an important article for you.

The bottom of the page says "(more)," which tells you that there is at least another page. When you reach the end of the release you will normally be so advised with the word *End*, the symbol -30-, the symbol ###, or some other device to signify the end. This is a carryover from the old wire services, with their teletype machines that clacked on spasmodically, so that it was difficult to know whether more was yet to come unless each transmission signified that there was, or that the message was now complete.

Releases are properly double-spaced to facilitate editing. Although you may run them exactly as received, few editors do. Most edit them, revising them to fit available space or otherwise editing and/or adapting them for use.

You may wish to call the contact given to ask questions, seek more background data, ask about the availability of photos, or otherwise follow up the item. That is, the release may be treated as a lead for a larger and more important story. Or you may find that the item fits into something else that you have ready to run or have been working on, and you may wish to incorporate the release into that other piece. Or you may wish to drop it into a file or folder of material you have been gathering on a subject for later use. (I keep numerous open files on subjects of interest for books or articles.) These may be literally file folders in a drawer or they may be cardboard boxes on my shelves, depending principally on how bulky and voluminous is the collection of clippings, brochures, releases, bound reports, photos, drawings, and other materials. As the authors of *The Newsletter Editor's Desk Book* observe, "Organized editors keep good files. . . . Good files are indispensable. They save time. They fill out stories that would otherwise be too sketchy or too obviously one-sided. They promote accuracy."

Press Kits and Other Advertising and Publicity Packages

My morning mail often brings me complete press kits and publicity packages, especially when I have made inquiries and asked for more information, as I often do. Such a kit usually includes a heavy paper folder with two pockets, into which are stuffed press releases, brochures, photos, circulars, reprints of published articles, copies of other newsletters, and/or whatever else the mailer thinks is an appropriate element of the total package.

But many of these kinds of items also arrive individually in separate envelopes almost every morning. My practice is to sort through them and decide which to add to my files and which to discard. A seminar brochure on a subject of interest, with an outline of content, for example, may be useful and therefore saved. The result is that I save a great deal of what others call junk mail, which draws frequent criticism from my spouse as she surveys the several cardboard cartons overflowing with my gleanings.

You soon realize in all this that the easy part is drawing in this flood of material; the hard part is knowing what to keep and what to dump. But there is more to it than that. Just collecting material interminably does you no good if you allow it to become unmanageable. To make it manageable and useful you must organize that material somehow. In my case, except for the occasional article I write for periodicals, I collect materials for books, for projects of many months' duration. I therefore sort out and organize a growing file by chapters or, if that is not practical, by subject matter, or the collection would be nearly useless by the time I am ready to begin serious writing. But you must prepare a newsletter every month and use, probably, not more than 20 percent of your time in doing it. You therefore need to maintain at least two kinds of files.

One, you need a "morgue" or library of general materials organized into files on and about individuals and subjects and containing clippings (including those from your own newsletter), photos, letters, and whatever else is available, as described here. This is a general resource for the future. These are files that you should be adding to regularly. In fact, I keep files on floppy disks, too, of materials I have generated. All my book manuscripts written on my word processor are archived on disks, of course, as well as in print, but I also have created special floppy disk files of drawings I have created on the computer, special statements such as acknowledgment of various registrations and trademarks, forms, and other material that can be reused, either directly or via adaptation. Of course, you should do likewise, keeping floppy disk copies of your newsletters (assuming, of course, that you are using a word processor) and such source materials as you happen to have on disks or in machinable form.

Two, you need to keep a current file on a subject about which you are currently developing or planning a future article; or, as a variant, a file in which you are collecting materials hoping that eventually they will provide a useful article. These, too, may be partially in computer disk form. (Actually, once you have become thoroughly comfortable with computers and word processing, you will probably find disk files far more efficient to work with, as I have.)

ON-LINE DATABASE SOURCES

There are, today, a large number of information banks available on-line—that is, via your computer and telephone line, implemented by a modem, an inexpensive electronic device that enables your computer to communicate over telephone lines directly with other computers at other locations. (These on-line databases are installed in other computers, which respond to dial-up applications for connection and access to their files constituting the databases.)

Perhaps the most widely publicized and hence best known of these are The Source, in McLean, Virginia, and CompuServe®, in Columbus, Ohio. But there are literally dozens of others, most of them rather specialized, whereas the two named here are of general interest. NewsNet, for example, is primarily an on-line bank of newsletters, but there are extensive databases of heavily detailed information intended for engineers, doctors, lawyers, and many other specialized professions, industries, and businesses. There are also some services that provide "gateways"—connections—to many of the specialized services, in sort of a brokering arrangement. (Representative lists of these and sources for more information on the subject are supplied in Appendix D.)

Most of these are subscription services. Typically, subscription requires a "connect-time" charge (cost per minute of connection), with a minimum monthly charge, and sometimes an initiation fee. Each is a rich source of information available almost instantaneously and at your own desk, where you can record it on your own disks at 1,000–2,000 words per minute (depending on your modem and some technical factors) and print it out at your leisure at the far lower speed of your printer. Typically, printer speed is on the order of 200 words per minute in final copy (letter quality or near letter quality), or several times that in draft quality; but still so much slower than recording on disk that it would be uneconomical to print the information as you receive it. Moreover, you may not want all the information in "hard copy" (printed form), but may want to study the material on-screen to decide what you want to print and how, if at all, you wish to edit it first.

GLEANINGS FROM OTHER PUBLICATIONS

Even if you do not set out deliberately to exchange complimentary subscriptions with other newsletters, you will soon find yourself in contact with other newsletter publishers who offer to swap free subscriptions. Moreover, you will find it possible to reach agreement with most of these to reprint each others' materials with attribution—with acknowledgment of the original source, that is. But even aside from this, many publications—magazines and tabloids, as well as newsletters—carry notices that any material may be reprinted as long as attribution is included. And, finally, you can usually get permission from other publishers to quote or reprint their material. But this idea needs some clarification.

First of all, permission is not always granted, and when it is, the grantor sometimes demands payment for using the material if it is of any great length, as distinct from a paragraph or two. Copyright law allows brief quotations without payment or permission, under the "fair usage" provision of the law, but it is so difficult to determine what that is and when or where it applies that it is wise to get written permission in any case where you want to use more than a few words or a sentence fragment. A letter of permission from the copyright owner is perfectly satisfactory, but that requires the other to take the time to compose a letter. You are far more likely to get a response or, at least, a prompt response, if you supply a release form that requires little but a date and a signature. (Remember always that when you want someone to do something you must make it as easy as possible to do it.) The release form can be a simple one such as that of Figure 10–2, one that I have used successfully for some years. However, I have used that form in connection with a general request for information and quotable or reproducible material. When you wish to quote or reprint some specific material that has already been published, you generally

FIGURE 10–2: Sample Release Form

RELEASE

Permission is hereby granted to Herman Holtz and his publishers to reproduce, cite, comment on, and/or quote briefly from material supplied herewith, with the understanding that full attribution will be made.

_____   _____
(Typed/printed name/title)   (Signature)

_____   _____
(Company/division)   (Date)

HERMAN HOLTZ   * POB 6067   *Silver Spring, MD 20906   * (301) 649-2499

must identify exactly what you wish to quote or reprint, for the copyright owner will almost surely want the release limited to the specific item or items. You will therefore want to modify the form so as to adapt it properly to your own purposes.

CONTRIBUTIONS BY OTHERS

Most newsletter publishers depend to at least some extent on specific contributions by others—material written especially to be used in the newsletter—as well as on the general contributions already covered. And although you often have to pay free-lance contributors for their materials, you can often get them free. Each case merits separate discussion.

Buying Free-Lance Contributions

Professional free-lance writers, whether they are full time in that profession or practicing it on a part-time basis (as a great many free-lance writers do) usually work for money, not only because they pursue writing as a career work but because payment is a symbol of recognized worth of the writing. (Presumably, it is no mark of success as a writer to have your work published without payment, although even that is not entirely true.) Payment for contributions to a newsletter, however, is generally rather modest.

Payment and even the basis of payment for such contributions varies widely, according to several factors. In the case of newsletters, it may be a scale of flat fees—for example, $5 for an item of less than 50 words, $10 for a personnel notice, $7.50 for a news item, and so on—or it can be (and most often is) payment by the word, likely on the scale of from three to five cents per word, although some publishers go to as much 10 cents per word. That applies to the number of words you *use*, however, regardless of the number of words in the original manuscript. That is, an author may contribute a 750-word article, but you judge that you would edit it down about one third, and so you offer the writer $15 or perhaps $25 for the piece. (Most writers will accept.)

You may very well find, as many other publishers have, that free-lance contributors are among your best—and most reliable—sources of informative articles. They tend to be well worth the modest fees they cost.

Attracting free-lance contributors is not difficult. You can have notices published in *Writer, Writer's Digest, Writer's Market, Writer's Yearbook,* and other media (listed in Appendix B), explaining generally what kinds of material you want, where and how to submit or query, and what the payment schedule is. You can also offer prospective contributors sample issues and/or writer's guidelines. (Some publishers make a charge for sample issues.) Published in the sources noted, these notices are almost certain to bring you many contributions for your consideration.

If you pursue this route, you will ultimately find certain contributors who are especially reliable in understanding your needs and producing appropriate material, and you may begin to assign them articles to do for you. If you reach this stage, you will have relieved yourself of much work and anxiety.

Free Contributions

There are many opportunities for and ways of getting contributions without cost to you. Even professional free-lance writers may be willing to contribute occasional pieces free of charge (I do, for several publications), but there are also many executives, consultants, and others who are quite willing to contribute articles and guest editorials free of charge. And some of them write quite well.

Their motives in doing so vary. Many are well established in their careers and have no need of supplementary income, but feel a kind of *noblesse oblige*, with regard to speaking and writing to others in their professions. Some are simply flattered to see their names in print. And an amazing number of people are frustrated would-be writers and will gladly agree to write for publication without payment.

There are, in fact, some successful journals published nationally that are supported entirely by free contributions, many from professional writers, who wish to see the publications succeed and remain in existence. One of these is a journal for writers, and another is a journal for ham radio operators and computer hobbyists. Both examples referred to here are growing steadily and presumably will one day reach the stage where they can afford to pay their contributors. (I have contributed to both on more than one occasion.)

There are several kinds of pieces most commonly used for "guest" writers who write without demanding any kind of fee or honorarium. If you indulge in editorials—and many publishers demand that as their prerogative—it is a popular spot to turn over to guests (and usually easy to find willing guests for), because almost everyone likes to vent his or her opinions. But there are many other kinds of pieces, even regular columns, for which you can find eager hands and minds. Later (in the next chapter) when we discuss some specific kinds of coverage in detail, you can consider which of these are among the best subjects to solicit guest writers' ideas and words, as well as interviews and profiles.

Entirely aside from the fact that you will get good material at no cost to yourself, there is often the distinct benefit of having well-known names appear as by-lines in your newsletter. It can do you nothing but good to publish editorials and articles by respected leaders and authorities in your field.

This is also an attractive avenue for exchange with other newsletter publishers whose journals are not incompatible with your own. You will find many quite willing, even eager, to exchange guest pieces with you.

All in all, if you use this idea effectively, you will make your newsletter a prestigious one shortly, with your obvious lines of connection to many other journals and the individuals prominent in your field and related fields.

Paid Contributions

Despite the attractive features of getting free contributions by guest writers, and despite the fact that many of these guests will be individuals of great professional distinction with thoughtful observations to make, the universe of opportunity represented by free-lance writers is far greater. There is no reliable way of estimating accurately the number of professional free-lance writers in the United States because only a small percentage of our professional writers are engaged full time in the profession, but it certainly numbers in the millions. An invitation to that community of struggling professional free-lance writers to submit manuscripts for consideration will bring a flood of responses. (I once made the mistake of advertising for a part-time writer, and it was weeks before I struggled to the surface of the resulting tidal wave.)

The journals in which to place your notices so that they reach free-lance writers include all those read regularly by writers (see listings in Appendix B), such as *Writer's Digest* and *Writer*. Typically, such notices are along the following lines:

> **Horse Sense** (ABC Publishers, Inc., 354 Newsprint Lane, Information, OH 43353). Editor: Horace Cameraready. 75 percent free-lance written. Monthly newsletter covering innovative management techniques, methods, problems, and results. Pays on acceptance, gives by-line, pays 3 to 10 cents per word, more on special assignments for writers with established records of success with us. Pays $40 kill fee. Buys all rights, but returns secondary rights after publication. Publication usually within 90 days after acceptance. Simultaneous, photocopied, and previously published submissions okay. Query first. Free sample copy and writer's guidelines.
>
> **Nonfiction** How-to, interviews with known executives, profiles, new techniques. We seek clear, jargon-free exposés, with how-to-transfer-the-techniques explanations.

You can add to this any other information you think appropriate, such as a more detailed description of your newsletter—for example, its features and coverage, what you seek in more detail, the writing style you prefer or insist on, and whatever else you think appropriate. You can also make a charge for sample copies of your newsletter, if you wish; many publishers do so. The writer's guidelines or style sheet is not a must, but helps you, as well as the writer, and so is a good idea.

There are certain items that differentiate publishers running such notices and determine how the average free-lance writer reacts to the notices. The first is between those publishers who promise to pay on acceptance, and those who pay only upon publication. Predictably, given that in many cases publication follows acceptance by many months, and occasionally an accepted piece is never published (I have had that joyless experience), writers are not overly eager to sell their pieces to "pay on publication" publishers, so "pay on acceptance" publishers get the pick of the crop.

Every field has its own jargon, and there is a bit of jargon in that sample notice that needs some explanation. The "query" idea is one.

Many editors today do not wish to spend time struggling through a mountain of unsolicited manuscripts every day, so they refuse to read unsolicited manuscripts and insist that would-be contributors submit queries. A query is simply a brief description of the article proposed and the proposer's qualifications. The editor then decides which proposed article appears to be worth reading and gives the proposer a go-ahead—"on spec." That means that the editor does not promise to buy the piece, but promises only to read it.

The "kill fee" applies in a case when the editor has assigned a job to a reliable regular contributor or has accepted a query with a guarantee. (The reliability of a contributor is almost always based entirely on the editor's personal experience with the writer, not on the writer's general credentials, no matter how impressive those credentials are.) The kill fee is the guarantee—what the editor will pay if he or she has a change of mind, or something arises that results in killing the article, no matter what the stage of its preparation. Usually it is approximately one third of the agreed-upon price for the article, although that can vary. (Most editors, finding a query attractive and deciding that it is worthwhile seeing the proposed piece, will negotiate a price with the writer before giving a go-ahead, even on spec.)

Unless you truly prefer to write the entire issue yourself—some publishers do—buying part of your material for each issue is a sound idea. Overall, the cost is not great—probably between $75 and $150 per issue at most—and the saving of your personal time is quite large. And remember that it is not only actual writing time, but also research time that you are saving. Moreover, you are researching a much wider range of areas and materials than you could cover all by yourself.

THE EDITOR'S "SAFE"

It is far from unusual for a small publisher (who is also the editor) to discover as deadline time looms that there is not enough copy for the upcoming issue. Sometimes a contributor you depend on fails to come through and leaves a hole in the schedule. Sometimes you discover that some facts in a piece are not facts at all, and you must kill the piece at the last minute. And sometimes information you counted on simply does not materialize.

It's panic time. But you can take out insurance against it by establishing and using your own editor's "safe," a supply of reserve materials—stories—that you can run at the last minute.

Some stories are time-sensitive. News stories, for example, are of no worth when they are no longer news. No one is interested in learning that Joe Getthejobdone was made general manager of Buckrogers Products eight months ago or that SuperSave, Inc. brought out a radical new kind of burglar alarm last year. But there are many other stories that can be run any time. It is never too late to run a piece on how to cut training costs by 33 percent or how Eager Maven chooses low-risk stocks successfully. These are stories you can save, keeping them in your safe—that can be a desk drawer, actually; "safe" is a euphemism—to fill a hole in an emergency.

Keep that in mind when contemplating queries or even your own story ideas. Try to build a stock of usable-anytime stories equal to at least one complete issue, and find replacements for them when you use them. In fact, don't sit on them forever—even they go stale eventually—but as you get new usable-anytime pieces, run some of your older ones and store the new ones.

Ideas and Guidelines for Content

POLICIES AND STANDARDS IN GENERAL

A publication requires standards and policies. Editorial standards of usage are easy: You need simply adopt any of the accepted style manuals, such as that of the U.S. Government Printing Office, and a dictionary, such as Webster's Collegiate. But not all editorial matters are that easy to standardize or to create a policy for.

First, decide what kinds of stories and/or other editorial content you will use and what kinds you will not use, choosing from at least the following possibilities:

News of the industry or profession.
Interviews of people in the field of interest.
Profiles of noteworthy people in the field of interest.
Personnel changes and related notices.
Feature stories.
Editorials.
Letters to the Editor.
Question and Answer column.
Humor.
Cartoons.
Photographs.
Line drawings.
Charts and graphs.
Service articles.

You may not be able to reach a decision easily on all of this in the beginning, and you may want to try all or most of these at first. Eventually, however, as you get experience with these various kinds of content, you will decide which fit best into your plans, which give you headaches, and which are easiest or hardest to come by. Gradually, you will be able to shape a policy or, more precisely, a set of policies and operating standards as to what you will publish and how you will handle problems—or what measures you will take to avoid problems as much as possible.

Still, there will be problems. They are inevitable. If you conduct an interview and paraphrase, abridge, or edit some of the resulting copy, the interviewee may become quite unhappy at what he or she thinks is unfairly slanted reporting. On the other hand, if you print the interviewee's remarks verbatim, some of those direct and spontaneous remarks made without careful thought may embarrass the interviewed party and still bring his or her wrath down on you. The same consideration will apply to any profiles or other stories you write about people, their deeds, and their organizations. There are potential booby traps and land mines everywhere, and you may soon come to believe that you can't win. But there are methods that minimize such problems and make life much easier for you as a publisher. Instead of waiting to learn the hard way, you can benefit from the hard experience of others.

In this chapter we'll take a close look at some of these kinds of items—close enough to see them, warts and all—and suggest some protective policies and standards for maximizing the benefits while minimizing any destructive fallout from them.

COVERING THE NEWS

News in a monthly periodical is not the same as news in a daily newspaper or on TV. Newsletters do not normally report breaking stories on murder, burglary, corporate mergers, or the deaths of prominent citizens. Yet, there is news in newsletters, news not covered by the daily press. There is news of personnel changes, speeches and public statements made by leading figures in the fields of interest, product news, legislative news, scientific developments, and other such items that the general public would not care about but have importance to those who read your newsletter. News may or may not be the most important feature of your newsletter—that very name is a misnomer in some cases, where the publication carries everything but news—but most newsletters do contain at least some material that can be fairly characterized as news.

Sources of News Items

The basic sources of news are direct (first-hand) observation, what others say (public statements, interviews, witness accounts, etc.), and what others have written. But these materialize practically in a great many ways.

Obviously, one source of news is the morning mail—those press releases, for one. But another is the daily newspaper, for there is some overlap in news coverage. For example, you might read a brief item in the newspaper that arouses your interest, and you might pursue it in quest of more information, just as you might follow up a press release. Still another source is the advertising brochure that arrives in the morning mail. An announcement of a seminar or a new product might spark your interest and inspire you to pursue additional information on the subject. There are also other ways news items and leads reach you: Pickups of items from other publications, calls from acquaintances, attendance at trade shows and conventions, and other spontaneous occurrences may be news items, sources of news items, or seedbeds of—leads for—news items. In less time than you might imagine you will be unconsciously and almost instinctively alert for leads.

Hazards

In today's litigious society you must be extra careful in handling news items. Daily newspapers use such escape hatches as *alleged, it was reported, according to unofficial sources*, and similar terms when they cannot verify the information or the source declines to be identified. Fortunately, the problem of possible libel does not normally arise with a newsletter as it does with a newspaper. Still, consider carefully whether what you are reporting can damage someone and, if so, how to avoid statements that could be considered libelous.

But even aside from the question of possible libel, there is the question of utility. It is not the business of a newsletter to entertain readers, but to supply useful information. Consider all news items— all items, for that matter—from that viewpoint: Is the information offered here of practical, utilitarian value to your readers? That is itself a first test of an item. But the item cannot be helpful if it is not true; it may, in fact, be harmful if not true—a false report about some stock issue or the fortunes of some company, for example. Your readers will not soon forgive you if you publish something that damages them in some way, such as costing them money.

But there is also the matter of avoiding the giving of offense. Don't lose sight of the fact that you are in the consulting business, and giving offense can cost you clients. Probably you can not avoid making someone unhappy with you from time to time, no matter what you do, but you can minimize the frequency of this by thinking carefully about items before you publish them.

Writing Style and Treatment of News

Unlike editorials and many other kinds of material, news items should be treated objectively, despite the fact that as a newsletter editor you are an advocate of sorts. It is not easy to be objective, and complete objectivity is a goal, not a reality. Still, you must strive for it in what are or purport to be straight news stories, even if you must consciously and deliberately stifle your own emotions and biases and manage to achieve a kind of detachment. (It is possible to do so, even when you feel strongly about the subject.)

Bias is the result of seeing only one side of an issue, whether deliberately or otherwise. Objectivity requires seeing all sides, and that means gathering all the available information possible, or at least as much as time allows. And objective reporting means reporting all sides, trying to be as even-handed as possible in doing so. (That latter is perhaps the most difficult thing to do.)

Journalistic style helps in doing that. It calls for telling the whole story, quite briefly, in the opening sentence—who, what, why, when, where (and maybe how, also). Each succeeding sentence then elaborates, adding detail. The beauty of the method is that as an editor you can cut the story anywhere (to fit the available space) and still have a complete story, even though lacking some of the available known details.

It's quite easy to lend bias to a story, even then, however. Consider the following two sentences:

1. Police reported that Smith had his car under control, although he was legally intoxicated.
2. Police reported that Smith was legally intoxicated, although he had his car under control.

The words are the same, and they do appear to offer a balanced view. But each arrangement lends a different emphasis to the report and suggests a definite bias. The difference here is between one of *denotation*—absolute definitive meaning of the words—and *connotation*—implied or suggested meanings and shades of meanings.

It's a common problem. *Stubborn, persistent, determined, mulish,* and *obstinate* are synonyms, but they don't have identical meanings to most people because each has an *emotional* content known as *connotation* or *nuance*—shade of meaning. *Determined* is an admirable trait, and sometimes—but not always—*persistent* is also. The others are negative, generally undesirable traits, as the words are interpreted by most people. You must therefore consider the effects of your words as you choose them. That is, an individual may welcome being referred to as *determined*, and may not object to being called *persistent*, but may or may not dislike being called *obstinate* or *stubborn*, and almost certainly will bristle a bit at being termed *mulish*.

INTERVIEWS

Interviews of people prominent in your field are usually of great interest to readers; they want to hear the opinions of individuals who represent marked success in the field. But interviewing is itself an art, and a few tips on interviewing techniques, with "do's and don'ts," ought to be helpful.

People who are successful enough and prominent enough to merit interviews are usually busy. Even if you succeed in getting their agreement to being interviewed for publication they are not likely to grant you an entire morning or afternoon. Usually, your best chances for success are when you ask for not more than an hour or, at most, two hours of their time.

That means preparation so that you get right down to business in the interview and do not waste time. But even aside from the elements of efficiency and time available, there is the psychological effect of arriving prepared versus arriving unprepared. Prepared for an interview normally means at least this:

1. You have "done your homework" and researched your subject. You know what is already available publicly about the interviewee. (You won't waste time with questions to which you should already know the answers if you had prepared properly.)

2. You have some specific theme and objective for the interview—a main question identifying that theme or objective—such as "What, in your opinion, is the trend of today's information industry?" or, "What advice would you offer for today's college student in choosing a career field?"

3. You have a prepared list of questions and starter observations, so that you can guide the interview suitably.

Tape or Shorthand?

Taking good notes in an interview is an art, and even the best of interviewers sometimes misquote their subjects. Tape recording appears to offer a solution, but it is not without its own pitfalls.

It is a good idea to ask in advance whether the interviewee objects to tape recording the interview. The response to that inquiry can be informative. It is possible that the interviewee has true "mike fright"—a psychological barrier. But it is more likely, when an interviewee objects to your recording of an interview on tape, that the subject has some fear of being tied down or of making unwise spontaneous statements, a not unusual fear.

Transcribing from tape is not easy. Recorders do not always pick up everything. Asides may be muffled and unintelligible, as may anything said, for that matter. Unless you have an excellent memory, it helps to also make notes of key items.

Writing the Interview Account

Conversation, even in a planned interview, is rarely totally organized, directed, and efficient. It usually rambles about a bit, is redundant, includes irrelevant and often banal asides, and is full of "uuhhhhs," "y'knows," and other such verbal doodles. Obviously, a printed transliteration of such a tape would be a highly impractical undertaking. A great deal of judicious editing is necessary to make a sensible written account of the interview.

One way to avoid problems is to permit the subject to review your draft manuscript. In fact, some individuals will grant interviews only on condition that they be allowed that review privilege, and some will even insist that they will grant an interview only if they have the right of approval or disapproval of the final manuscript.

How you react to that kind of demand is up to you, of course. Probably most professional newspeople would reject such a demand immediately, although they might agree to permit the interviewee to review and comment on the draft of the story. However, you have the right to do as you wish, and agreement with such demands may win you interviews you could not otherwise get.

FEATURE STORIES

A feature story is somewhat like a magazine article. It is not a news story, although it usually has a "news peg"—is related somehow to (or even inspired by) current or recent news. If a scandalous stock swindle is currently in the headlines, a feature story reviewing one or more of the most famous stock swindles of the past—the Ponzi swindle, for example—may be in order.

Unlike news items, features need not start with the essential facts and usually do not. Instead, they usually have a *delayed lead:* They start with some interesting and attention-getting detail and get around to sketching in the relevant essentials of the story later, after the reader's interest has been captured by the opening gambit, very much in the style of short stories and TV plays.

Ideas for Feature Stories

A feature story may be about almost any relevant subject. If your newsletter is on plant security, you might run feature stories on locks and alarms, reviewing the history of such devices, earliest models, especially novel or interesting ones, or the latest ideas, among many other possibilities. This approach can be applied successfully to virtually any field. A newsletter in the social services field might use the same idea to review some earliest types of such services, the kinds of programs that are found in other countries, the latest ideas put forth for possible future application, and some novel programs in place and operating today.

Of course, these are not the only ideas for feature stories. The possibilities are completely open-ended. Although they usually tend to be pegged to the news—insights into some angle or aspect of whatever is in the news—especially in the daily press, feature story ideas can be whatever your imagination suggests to you.

FEATURES VERSUS FEATURE STORIES

Every periodical has features, not to be confused with feature stories. Newspapers, magazines, and many other periodicals have various columns, crossword puzzles, cartoon strips, recipes, interviews, profiles, book reviews, movie reviews, contests, and many other such items. Each of these—just about everything that is not a news story—is a feature. But newsletters have features too, and most of the items listed earlier are typical of such features. You may wish to consider some or all of them for possible inclusion in your own newsletter. In fact, some of the items you will find discussed here themselves suggest other ideas for features, and these will be mentioned and discussed too, as we go on.

SERVICE ARTICLES

Service articles could be regarded as a special kind of feature story, but they are usually distinctly of the how-to-do-it, how-it-works, or how/where-to-find-it variety. That is, they have direct and immediate useful applications for the readers.

For example, *Government Marketing News* carried a two-page how-to-do-it service article on proposal writing in each issue, covering such topics as developing strategies, gathering information about competitors, building a proposal reference library, creating and using graphics, typical problems and suggested solutions, case histories, and other such topics. The nature of the subject provided a bottomless barrel of ideas and a wide variety of possible topics. But that should be true for just about any field. As in the case of features, the chief inspiration should be your own creative imagination, backed by your experience and specialized knowledge. However, this is a rich area for soliciting contributions from readers, from professional free-lance writers, and from anyone else to whom you can issue an appeal, possibly with a "best idea of the month" feature. You might even stimulate reader interest with a prize for the best idea submitted by a reader (paid contributors would not qualify), such as a book, a free subscription renewal or extension, or some other relevant item.

In fact, some newsletters offer how-to and where-to information as their primary functions. The *Business Opportunities Digest*, published by Straw Enterprises in Dalton, Georgia, is such a newsletter.

It is a business exchange medium, devoted nearly 100 percent to notices of merchandise, services, and business deals offered and wanted. And Barbara Brabec's *National Home Business Report* is entirely service oriented. Hers is a sizable publication, larger than most newsletters although not quite a magazine (6- × 9-inch format, saddle-stitched, current issue 30 pages of small—approximately 8-point—type). She manages to pack quite a lot of information, most of it service-oriented, into each issue. The issue currently on my desk (see Figure 11–1 for a reproduction of its cover) lists on its cover 7 feature articles and 12 "departments."

EDITORIALS

Editorials can be hazardous to the health of your newsletter, and should be handled—if you choose to use editorials at all—with great care.

The hazard is a simple one: Unlike news, editorials are pure opinion, and almost inevitably based largely on emotional biases. No matter how hard you and others who editorialize in print try to be totally objective, you can not avoid having your assessment of facts and conclusions drawn from them colored by your own desires and prejudices, even to the nature of the premises upon which you structure your logical arguments. However, your readers have the same human weakness, and an editorial can arouse a great deal of anger in readers, as the editors of any newspaper can verify!

This does not mean that you should not use editorials. It does mean that you should exercise great caution in judging what to run as editorial commentary. (One of my readers became quite angered and wrote me a scathing letter because I referred to competitive bidding for government contracts as part of the free-enterprise system, a characterization to which he objected violently.)

If you use guest editorials—invite others to write and contribute editorials to your newsletter—you should recognize and accept a responsibility for them. No matter who writes them, they are your responsibility if you publish them. Everything that appears in your newsletter is your responsibility, both legally and morally. So you must edit guest editorials to be sure that they neither libel nor offend others unduly. But first of all you must anticipate and minimize the problem by exercising some care and good judgment in

Figure 11–1: Cover of *National Home Business Report*

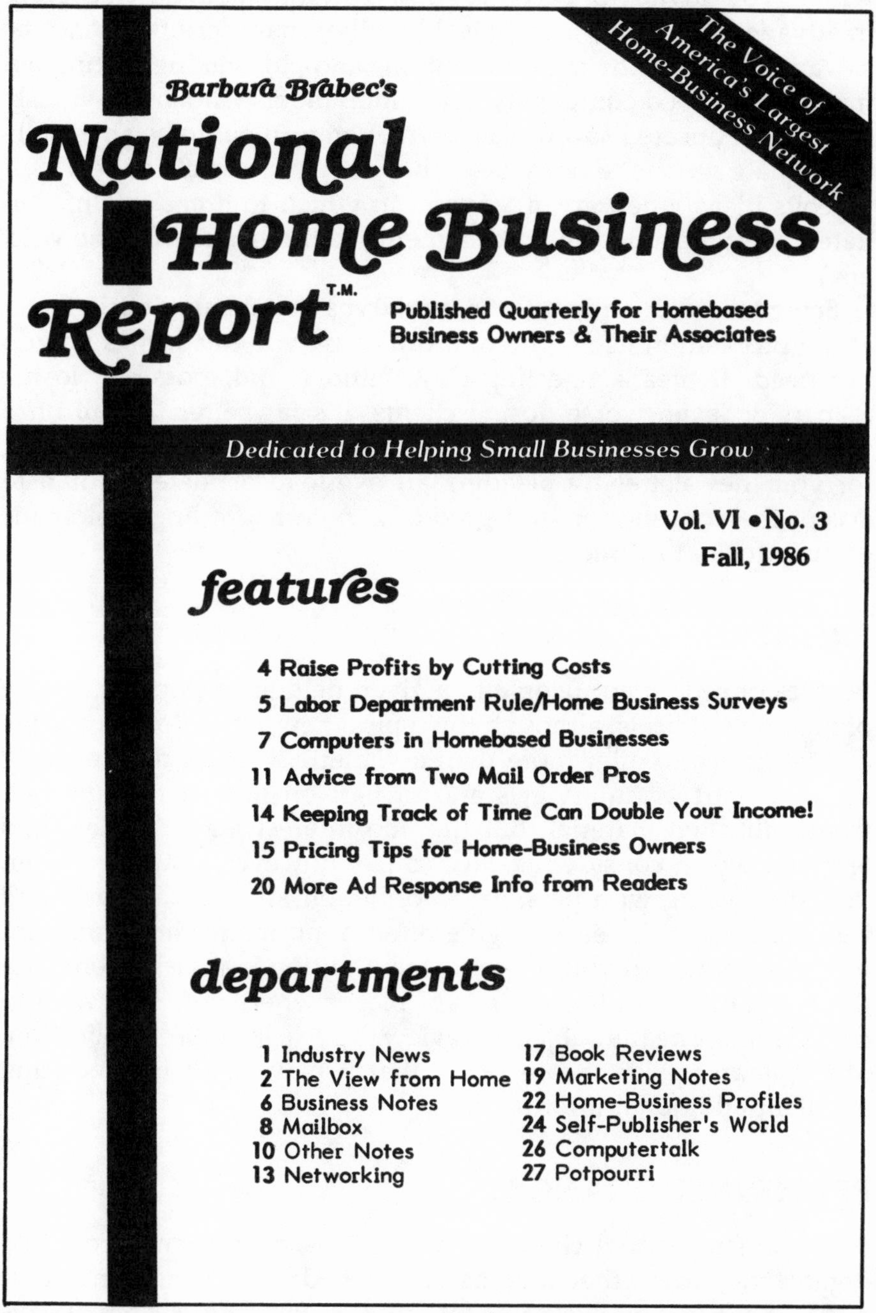

The Voice of America's Largest Home-Business Network

Barbara Brabec's

National Home Business Report T.M.

Published Quarterly for Homebased Business Owners & Their Associates

Dedicated to Helping Small Businesses Grow

Vol. VI • No. 3
Fall, 1986

features

4 Raise Profits by Cutting Costs
5 Labor Department Rule/Home Business Surveys
7 Computers in Homebased Businesses
11 Advice from Two Mail Order Pros
14 Keeping Track of Time Can Double Your Income!
15 Pricing Tips for Home-Business Owners
20 More Ad Response Info from Readers

departments

1 Industry News
2 The View from Home
6 Business Notes
8 Mailbox
10 Other Notes
13 Networking
17 Book Reviews
19 Marketing Notes
22 Home-Business Profiles
24 Self-Publisher's World
26 Computertalk
27 Potpourri

whom you invite to become guest editorial writers. Recognize in advance that some editorials, like other manuscripts, cannot be salvaged by even the most meticulous and painstaking editing but must be scrapped completely. Even individuals who are obviously quite well educated and well spoken often turn out to be abysmally inadequate writers. Even worse, they may express absolutely outrageous ideas when given a forum in which to preach. (Unfortunately, editorials become preachments in the hands of some writers.)

Being forced to scrap guest editorials as hopelessly deficient creates a problem in itself, one that can cause you headaches you do not need. It means rejecting contributions and, possibly, losing readers or, even worse, losing clients. It's far better to stall off a would-be contributor who holds views you know to be all wrong for your newsletter by pleading an overload of material than to accept the contribution and go on for months finding diplomatic excuses for not running it.

PROFILES

Profiles of prominent people in a given field are a popular feature of many periodicals, although the typical newsletter does not allow enough space to offer more than a vignette. Profiles are normally based in part on interviews and in part on information gleaned from published material. But they do interest many readers and are well worth considering. Recognize, however, that here again you are dealing with personal information about individuals and it is therefore quite easy to give offense, no matter how innocent or well intentioned your remarks are. Caution is advised here, and this is again one of those kinds of pieces where you may wish to consider inviting the subject to review the article before publication. This has an upside, however, in that it may result in producing excellent additional information.

PERSONNEL CHANGES

Notices of personnel changes—promotions, movements from one organization to another, awards, and related notices—are innocuous bits that can be quite valuable information for readers. I am always interested in new information about individuals with whom I do business—their movements, their promotions, their changing assignments, their awards, and anything else. I *use* that information, writing congratulatory notes or notes of concern to the individuals involved, as appropriate, and I have found that to be most valuable in marketing: It is essential to maintain your "contacts" and refresh the prospects' recollection of you. One person with whom I first did business when he was a rather junior person in his organization, for example, is today an officer of the corporation, and we do business together today on the basis of casual conversations as a result of the relationship I worked meticulously to establish and nourish over the years. Those newsletter notices of his progress in his company were valuable to me—I still make it a practice to send individuals I know a note of congratulation and good wishes or whatever is appropriate when their names show up in those columns of personnel notices—and they are in themselves reason enough to renew every year what is a rather expensive subscription to a periodical I skim rather quickly and casually otherwise.

LETTERS TO THE EDITOR

It is a drawback of the typical newsletter that space limitations bar a full-scale Letters to the Editor feature, for the lively exchanges that take place in such a feature generate a great deal of interest in many periodicals. The average newsletter must condense letters to their barest essence to find enough room to publish them, and even then be highly selective in choosing letters to use. You should know, however, that not all those letters are legitimate spontaneous actions. Many editors who are well aware of the attraction letters columns have for readers often solicit letters from readers (I have been the subject of such solicitations), sometimes by sending a selected reader advance copy of an upcoming article and asking for reactions to it.

The letters column is particularly valuable in two situations: one is when controversies arise in the forum among various letter writers; the other is when letter writers use the column as a Question and Answer forum, wherein either the editor or other readers answer questions. Both kinds of situations should be encouraged, unless you happen to have a separate Q&A department or column.

Such a column is a valuable asset, and I would encourage its development.

HUMOR

Humor or, more specifically, failed attempts at humor can be quite as deadly in print as on the lecture platform. Humor is far more difficult than it appears to many to be, and you are far better off to shun it unless you are absolutely certain that it is truly humorous, is in good taste, and is appropriate. To be an asset to you the humor must meet all three of those criteria, but especially that of being in good taste. And that does not refer to what *you* think is in good taste but what your readers think is in good taste.

At one time, in illustrating some literature with clip art—drawings that you can buy and paste up for use in any publication—I used, among other pieces, a sketchy and simple line drawing of a cocktail waitress wearing a typically brief outfit. It seemed to me to be mild and lighthearted, if not humor per se. But at least one of my readers— a man—did not see it that way. He wrote me a letter protesting my use of the illustration rather heatedly. He thought it in bad taste and an exploitation of womanhood. Unreasonable? Perhaps. But it illustrates one of many hazards in trying to be humorous: You cannot predict how readers will react.

But there is another side to this, perhaps an even more serious hazard. Giving offense to a reader or two is not usually fatal, although it may cost you subscribers or clients. But aside from the question of whether you might give offense to someone, there is the matter of how your use of humor reflects on you. Humor that readers consider to be coarse or in bad taste, even if it does not generate specific protests, does great harm to your dignity and to your own image as a serious professional. That can be a mortal wound to your professional practice.

Dangerous subjects in general include sex, ethnic and/or religious groups, women generally, and public figures. This is not to say that you may not mention any of these, but that it is easy to run aground with readers by jokes based on or at the expense of someone identified as belonging to some specific category. Any reader who identifies himself or herself as belonging to that category is likely to feel badly used by the humor. Therefore, do study carefully what you plan to write to see if any individual or class of individuals is being made the butt of the humor. If so, and if there is no way to retain the humor without making someone the victim, don't use the material.

There are no "safe" subjects, but only safe ways to handle subjects. For example, the one exception to that prohibition against making any individual the butt of your humor is the case when the laugh is on you, yourself. If you can make yourself the victim, it is unlikely that you will give offense. No one is likely to be offended by a joke on you if you are willing to laugh at yourself. (And if you can't laugh at yourself, you do not have a true sense of humor and should abandon the idea of using humor entirely.)

Here is an example: In explaining to seminar audiences that while government contracts can be "wired"—arranged to give someone a competitive edge over others—such things furnish only some advantage, not a guarantee that the favored someone will win the contract. "Indeed," I say, "let me tell you how I very cleverly managed to lose a contract that was wired for me!" That always brings a stunned silence for a moment and then a hearty laugh as the listeners suddenly realize what it is that I just said. But the point is that I am willing to invite them to laugh at my own misplay and I am obviously enjoying the joke on myself, too.

Of course, this can be overdone, to a point where it damages your image. But that only stresses the fact that humor is double-edged: It can backfire on you so easily that it is best left unused unless you are absolutely sure of what you are doing.

CARTOONS

Cartoons are generally intended to be humorous, although many are also pointed social or political commentary. They fall into very much the same category as does humor: They can be dangerous. And they are at least as dangerous when used to comment on social and political matters. But newsletters usually have little or no space to spare, and so most do not use cartoons simply because they are an inefficient use of space that is at a premium.

PHOTOGRAPHS

The chief problem with using photographs is the space they require, space that a newsletter can usually ill afford, despite the advantages of photographic illustration. Hence the advice: Use sparingly if at all.

LINE DRAWINGS

In certain cases, line drawings are well worth the space they require because they carry more information per column inch than would text, if they are well conceived and used effectively. Or, if they do not, they should not be used at all. There are many types of drawings you may use for various purposes, but the types you are most likely to have use for are plots, bar charts, scatter diagrams, and others of that type. (At least one sample has been shown already in Figure 3–1. Other samples will be shown in reference materials appearing later.)

In weighing the use of such material, always consider (1) whether the drawing is indispensable (many ideas and concepts simply cannot be conveyed effectively in words alone) and simply demands graphic presentation, and (2) if it is not a mandate, whether it is more efficient (in terms of space required) than text to convey the idea. In short, it is necessary to *justify* the use of a drawing in a newsletter where space is most limited.

THE COMPUTER AND DESKTOP PUBLISHING

There are several ways in which the computer can help you, especially if you have some of the new desktop publishing programs. Figures 11–2 and 11–3 present relatively basic and simple samples from two programs, Formworx™ and Fontasy®.

FIGURE 11–2:   A Computer-Generated Milestone Chart

PROJECT   SCHEDULE

Time in months	0	1	2	3	4	5	6	7	8	9	10
Task analysis...											
Preliminary plan......											
Review....................											
Revision....................											
Field research....................											
Interviews..........................											
Draft lesson plans....................											
Tryouts....................................											
Analysis of tryout results....................................											
Final revisions and turnover....................................											

Courtesy Analytix, Inc

FiGURE 11–3: A Computer-Generated Pie Chart

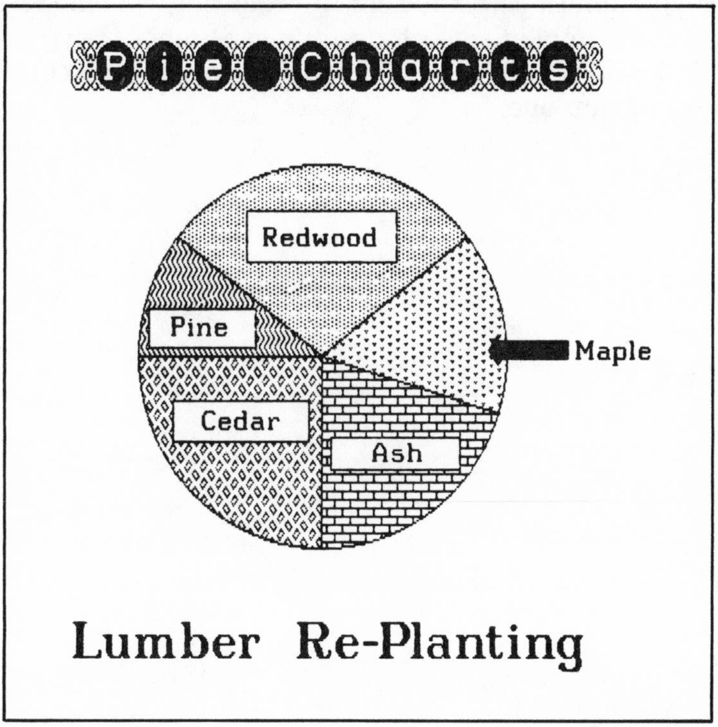

Courtesy Fontasy

Formworx is a program designed primarily for forms (hence the name). Many of the forms it can produce would require a trained draftsperson or illustrator and hours of labor to duplicate by manual means. Fontasy is a graphics program, and offers a modern version of clip art. Instead of line drawings and headlines printed on glossy paper to cut out and paste up, the art is recorded on computer disks in programs that will print them out on your printer at your command. This offers distinct advantages, including the ability it confers on you to manipulate the drawings—change their size, invert them (to their mirror images), emphasize them, and rotate them, among other things.

These and other modern programs produce much more complex and sophisticated graphics, type fonts, and other contributions that we will examine in greater detail in Appendix A.

In all, then, a good desktop computer, equipped with any of the several excellent desktop publishing programs available today, makes you almost self-sufficient in producing your newsletter. A good system, implemented by a little experience on your part, is your in-house graphic arts/illustrating/layout/makeup department rolled into one.

CHAPTER TWELVE

Notes on Editorial Work

JOURNALISTIC STYLE

The typical and traditional journalistic style of newswriting stresses the "inverted pyramid," in which the lead or opening of the story covers everything in a sweeping and generalized statement, and the rest of the story adds detail increasingly. However, the most important details appear in the lead, with information of decreasing importance following; hence, the inverted pyramid, reflecting the decreasing importance of the detail. Thus the ease with which an overlong story may be cut.

This has some relevance to newsletter writing, at least insofar as a newsletter reports news, but there is at least one other journalistic practice that is probably of far greater importance and utility to a newsletter editor. That is the practice of "jumping" stories—starting a story on the first page and continuing it elsewhere, on some later page.

The motivation behind this practice is pure marketing. It's a way of packaging the product to make it attractive to readers. The most important stories—and that means the stories judged to have the greatest appeal to and interest for readers—always begin on the first page, with headlines to mark and introduce them. But to get a maximum number of such stories introduced on the first page, together with their headlines, only the lead and a small part of the story appears there, with the rest of each story relegated to the hinterland of the newspaper.

In periodicals bearing paid advertising this has also the secondary purpose of inducing readers to read the interior pages, on which appear those advertisements. In fact, at least one study revealed that full-page advertising is generally less effective than is advertising that shares pages with editorial content for this very reason—that readers tend to see and note advertising when they turn to these pages to follow stories that have been jumped, while many readers simply ignore pages that have nothing but advertising matter on them.

Of course, this is not a consideration in most newsletters, because most newsletters do not carry advertising. But jumping stories is a good practice, for the reasons given. It does help the reader note quickly whatever you believe to be the most important stories and it does help you induce readers to leaf through all the pages of your newsletter.

HEADLINE WRITING

Headline writing is as important an element in jumping stories successfully as it is in general. In newspapers, headlines characterize, identify, and draw attention to various stories considered to be the most important ones, and newspapers tend to set headlines in type of a size proportionate to that importance. Few newsletters, however, follow that practice of using oversize—extralarge—type for headlines. Partly that is because newsletters cannot afford the extra space required for oversize headlines, partly because newsletters do not usually deal in sensational news, and partly because such headlines are simply inappropriate for newsletters—especially newsletters composed entirely by typewriter, which cannot create headlines in anything larger than the capital letters of the font used.

Of course, that latter situation is changing rapidly now, with word processors in common use in even the smallest offices, and the new desktop publishing programs furnishing even small offices with in-house capabilities for setting captions, headlines, and even body copy (main text) in a wide variety of sizes and styles. (See Figure 12–1 for examples.)

The few samples shown in the figure are from the same Fontasy program that produced the pie chart of Figure 11–3, and these are only a fraction of all the type fonts available in this one program alone. (Those shown here were produced on a 9-pin dot matrix printer.) There are many other programs that do this kind of work, some of them stressing the newsletter application especially.

The quality of the type produced in such programs varies widely, according to the quality of both the software—programs—and the

Figure 12–1: Computer-Set Type (via Desktop Publishing Programs)

DESKTOP PUBLISHING

DESKTOP PUBLISHING

Desktop Publishing

DESKTOP PUBLISHING

DESKTOP PUBLISHING

Desktop Publishing

Desktop Publishing

DESKTOP PUBLISHING

Desktop Publishing

Desktop Publishing

Desktop Publishing

These are just a few of the available
fonts. Moreover, they were printed by
a quite ordinary 9-pin dot matrix printer,
not one of the new high-quality laser
printers. True typeset quality is possible
with such a printer, and even a 24-pin
dot matrix printer produces good quality.

hardware—printers. The best printers available today are the laser printers, which operate on the principle of the familiar xerographic copiers. But whereas the copier photographs an original printed copy and transfers that image to a selenium-coated drum or master, the laser printer translates the digital information supplied by the computer into the characters, which are painted onto the drum or master by a laser beam. Unfortunately, these printers are today priced in the range of $2,000 and more, up to several times that amount. However, the industry is now producing 24-pin dot matrix printers that rival the laser printer for quality, and even the more modest 9-pin dot matrix printers produce quite good results when the software programs are of adequate quality.

However, that is part of production work, which we will discuss later in this chapter. Here, let us first discuss the editorial side, including such topics as the editorial considerations in writing headlines and captions.

THE ROLE OF THE HEADLINE

Newsletters carry headlines even if they are not the 72-point banners of big-city newspapers. Each story, column, feature, and illustration needs to be identified with some kind of headline or caption. Every figure showing a page of a newsletter reveals that clearly. When the newsletter is formally typeset, the headlines and captions are usually in a little larger and much bolder type than the body copy is, but that is a superficial difference in an editorial sense, for all headlines and captions do essentially the same job. However, when you study the samples used here so far, you find a rather wide variance in the philosophy of their usage.

In Figure 3–1, for example, each headline offers a clue to the nature of the text to follow. The one headline we are able to see in Figure 3–2 also does that, but adds an editorial comment. Figure 9–1 shows two headlines: The first one is clearly expository, but the second one piques the reader's interest by promising to reveal a way to do something highly desirable but apparently impossible.

Subordination of Headlines

It is standard practice to use different kinds of type to indicate different orders of "heads" (colloquial for headlines). If set in formal type, the first-order head, introducing the subject, is generally in the largest and boldest type, the second-order head is in somewhat smaller or lesser weight type, and the third-order head is in even smaller or more subdued type. When this diversity of typefaces is not available, such as when you are composing your copy via typewriter or ordinary printer, you can use even a fixed font in several configurations, such as this:

FIRST–ORDER HEAD (ALL CAPITAL LETTERS UNDER-
SCORED).
SECOND–ORDER HEAD (ALL CAPITALS WITHOUT UN-
DERSCORE).
Third-Order Head (Initial Capitals and Lowercase Un-
derscored)
Fourth-Order Head (Initial Capitals and Lowercase Let-
ters).

There is still another expedient available when using a single type font to identify subordination of topics. A head may be a stand-alone head or a run-in head. That is, the head may be followed by copy that begins a line or two below it or the head may be used as the first words of the paragraph, to wit:

This Is a Stand-Alone Head

The text paragraph begins one or two lines below the head in this usage. This is generally a higher-order head than the run-in head.

This Is a Run-In Head. The text begins immediately after the head. This is used more often for lower order heads than the stand-alone types.

By using these various options in all possible forms and combinations, you can create enough distinctive heads to accommodate all conceivable needs for heads at more than one level, if you are tied to a typewriter type of composition or a typewriterlike computer printer. (So-called letter-quality printers use elements similar to those of typewriters and have the same limitations of fonts, except for the decidedly tedious option of frequent changes of the printing element, a laborious manual process.)

The Controlling Logic of Headline Subordination

One problem in using heads at more than one level is sticking to the logic of the subordination. Any head identifies and introduces a subject. A subordinate head divides the subject, introducing a topic that is part of the subject. But you can't divide the subject into one topic; if the subject is to be divided at all it must be into two or more topics. So you must always have two or more subordinate heads if you are to have any.

It's easy to forget this logic. Even the most experienced writers sometimes find themselves committing this sin of having a single subordinate head. However, properly used, the heads present a virtual outline of the story. In that respect they are valuable to both you and your readers.

Sideheads or Centerheads?

Headlines may be centered or they may begin at the left-hand margin. From this they get their understandable designations as "centerheads" or "sideheads." There is no particular virtue in making your headlines of either type, but centering a head has always required a special effort, whereas no special effort is required at all to position headlines as sideheads; hence the preference for sideheads in so many newsletters and related publications. Of course, with today's word processing, centering of heads is done by the machine, so it involves no special effort (except when exercising the double-width option on dot matrix printers. (At least in the case of WordStar, I find, some calculations or cut-and-try experiments are necessary to center those extrawide headlines.)

Captions

Captions are a special form of headline. They are used to identify tables and illustrations, most commonly. The may appear above or below tables and figures; the choice is yours. (Probably they are used most commonly below the item they identify, although that has no special significance.) This does not mean, however, that every illustration or table must be assigned a figure or table number and/or caption. The use of such identifications is normally for those cases where the table or figure does not appear at the immediate point of reference—is not "run in" with the text directly at that point—and where there are other figures or tables so that confusion is possible. This is probably more often the case with manuals and other, lengthier publications you might produce. Still, many newsletter publishers prefer to assign numbers to and write captions for figures and tables even when they are run in with text and confusion is not likely, so it becomes a matter of choice.

WRITING EFFECTIVE HEADLINES AND CAPTIONS

Aside from the mechanics of *using* headlines and captions effectively, there is the question of how to *write* good headlines and captions. Partly because headlines stand out from the body copy but mainly because the reader deliberately scans the headlines to determine which stories are of most immediate interest, the headlines convey the first messages and establish the impact of the newsletter upon the reader. In a nutshell, your headlines ought to have a great deal of "punch"—use short, simple words, action verbs and nouns, be in active voice. The headline ought to accomplish these three things at least:

- Get attention—*demand* attention.
- Tell the story—in a nutshell, but *tell* it.
- Hook the reader—make him or her want to know more.

Following are several before and after examples, mostly from actual headlines found in newsletters. A few comments are included in the first few examples, but you are left on your own with the others to study and analyze yourself.

- PAY SCALES WILL BE SUBJECTED TO OPM REVIEW: Passive voice, excess verbiage. Better: GOVERNMENT TO REVIEW PAY SCALES. Not everyone knows that OPM is the former Civil Service Commission. Abbreviations generally are to be avoided, especially in headlines. ("FDR" and other abbreviations that are better known than what they stand for are exceptions.) Infinitives and the present tense are better than simple past tense, as in BANDIT FLEES versus BANDIT FLED.
- THE FATE OF 100,000 PAPER CLIPS versus 80 PERCENT OF PAPER CLIPS WASTED, which is what that story was about. (Any comments required?)
- 23,000 MILES OF FIBER OPTIC NETWORK versus $2 BILLION COMMITMENT FOR ALL FIBER NETWORK, which is what the story was about. Which version is likely to have greater impact, mean most to lay readers?

- OFFICIAL TO RETIRE versus SPEAKER TIP O'NEILL RETIR-ING: Always identify the individual as closely as possible when the headline is about someone.
- NOTE ON COMMISSIONS versus EARN $25 COMMISSION EACH REFERRAL.
- SKILLS ARE HARD TO FIND versus SKILLS THAT MAKE YOU MORE VALUABLE.
- SOUND ADVICE versus KEEP JUMPING: A SECRET OF SUCCESS.

Study these few examples and see how they meet the three goals of headline writing (mentioned a few paragraphs ago). Consider how you could improve them even further.

The writing of captions is not greatly different in principle. Captions should also be descriptive and dynamic—in active voice, using action verbs and simple words generally. Most important, however, tell the reader what the table reveals and what the figure illustrates. Instead of "Monitor Costs" under a table, try "Monitor Costs versus Resolution," "Costs versus Dots Per Inch," or "Costs versus Resolution for Three Models."

STYLES IN BODY COPY

What is most easily readable is sometimes at odds with what is most efficient when it comes to the matter of body copy, the main text passages of your newsletter. This is the result of the limited space you enjoy in a typical newsletter. You are more or less compelled to pack your copy as densely as possible and to minimize the "wasted" white space that makes copy appear less formidable to readers, thus maximizing the amount of information in each issue. There are several ways to accomplish this:

- Do not leave a blank line between paragraphs. But do remember to indent the beginning of each paragraph so that the reader knows where a new paragraph begins.
- If you are using formal type, choose a condensed type font. If you are using a typical typewriter or computer printer, use a 12-pitch (10 point) type and, if possible, proportional spacing. (This is an available option in many systems today, and is far more efficient in its use of space than systems with fixed units of space for all characters.)

● You can make up your original copy slightly oversize—between 10 and 20 percent larger than your newsletter page size—and have the printer reduce the copy photographically by that percentage. This reduces your 10-point type to 8- or 9-point type, which is still quite legible. (Eight-point type is generally considered to be minimum for normal reading, although some readers find anything smaller than 9-point type a bit difficult to read.) Of course, you can also begin with 12-point type on copy oversized by 20 to 40 percent and reduce it, but you would have to use type of a fairly heavy body—at least that which is designated "medium." (You will find both 11- × 14-inch and 11- × 17-inch paper, both sizes used for preparing oversized camera-ready originals, readily available at most suppliers of art and publications materials.)

A FEW BASICS OF WRITING

This is not a course in writing, needless to say, and yet we cannot totally ignore the subject because for you, as an independent consultant, to publish a newsletter is to undertake what is largely a one-person venture. Even if you get all your stories from contributors, you still need at least a broad appreciation of writing to manage the enterprise well. In any case, I will cover just a few basics here—especially some cogent do's and don'ts—as a general guideline, and in Appendix B I will recommend some excellent reference texts that you can keep by your side and consult as necessary.

The Most Basic Problem

I have some firm convictions, resulting from diverse experience as writer, editor, and manager of publications and of staffs of writers and editors. The first and, I believe, the most important is this one:

I believe that by far the bulk of really bad writing is much more a reflection of bad thinking than the result of an inability to express oneself in writing. Results of experiments I made over the years have supported and reinforced this belief.

Consider this: The only things you can say or write are those things you formulate in your mind. What comes out of your mouth or from your pen comes from your mind, reflects what is in it. You cannot write well if you do not think well, and you cannot think well without knowing your subject.

Unfortunately, many people who attempt to write make the mistake of trying to write without adequate planning or preparation. Those same people would not go off on a long trip, take a vacation, buy a car, or build a porch without preparation and planning, but they often fail to perceive writing as requiring that same advance work. Research and outlines are to the writer what drawings and plans are to an architect or engineer.

You must gather and assemble all the information you need, and you must study it until you understand it. I have constantly been amazed at the capacity of people to convince themselves that they understand something when they really do not. They manage to truly deceive themselves, and they set about writing a plethora of vague and rambling statements, dodging the truth, keeping it even from themselves! So often I have faced their outraged indignation when I questioned their understanding of their subject, and later watched their sheepish grins after they had humored me by going back to their research and study, after which they succeeded in turning out quite acceptable copy.

Outlining is a key. Some experienced professional writers use something called a "lead," but that is just a special kind of outline. (I use a lead for short pieces, but I always outline longer ones.) For others, the formal outline is by far the better way to plan and prepare. But there is this difference between preparing plans for a house or machine and preparing plans to write something: Developing the plans for a house or machine is *the* creative act; executing the plans is more or less mechanical. Preparing plans to write is only part of the creative act; actually writing is the rest of it. Therefore, developing an outline is more than drawing up a plan for what you are going to write; it is also an exercise to force your thinking and study. It compels you to think out the subject, to identify gaps in your knowledge or the resource materials from which you are going to work, and to decide exactly where you are going to go in your writing and how you are going to get there.

To work properly, therefore, the outline must be highly specific, not vague or general, not as depicted in the following sample:

A. Introduction
   1. Operation
   2. Maintenance
      a. Preventive
      b. Corrective

Rather, your outline should be along the following lines:

A. General description
   1. Operation
      a. Standard start-up procedures
         (1) Power-on sequencer
         (2) Indicators
         (3) Controls
         (4) Alarms
      b. Malfunction signals
         (1) Audible alarms
         (2) Visual alarms
         (3) Emergency controls
         (4) Emergency power-down procedure

The difference is obvious, of course. Although this example may be totally inappropriate for your newsletter, it illustrates the principle: It lists precisely what is to be in whatever it is you are planning to write. Unless you can list these specifics and provide the information they call for, you are not ready to write yet. You haven't gathered enough information, you don't know enough about the subject yet, and/or you haven't yet thought the subject out adequately.

That's what requiring yourself to prepare a proper outline does for you: It *compels* you to do your homework.

Simple Sentences

It is not because I think that you are a novice writer nor because I think that your readers are not completely literate that I (and just about everyone who is an authority of any kind in the field of writing and communication) urge you to use simple, straightforward sentences and simple, commonly known words. School-children read and understand the *Reader's Digest* without difficulty, but college professors and many other highly educated people also read it and are not insulted by the simple, straightforward language that has characterized it for so many years. It's an excellent model of how to write: You can never go wrong emulating *Reader's Digest* style.

A Few Do's and Don'ts

The do's and don'ts of writing are not complex, and we are not going to waste time here on such topics as infinitives and whether they may or may not be split. But there are just a few injunctions you would do well to heed and which, if heeded, will probably keep you out of difficulties insofar as usage of our language is concerned:

● Never show off your large vocabulary. A large vocabulary is quite valuable, but its chief use is to help you think well, not to confuse others with rare words. Stick with the simple words. It's far more important to be understood clearly than to be thought a great intellectual.

● Your actual sentences do not have to be short to be easily understandable, but if they are long they should have frequent stops such as semicolons, dashes, parentheses, and other devices that allow the reader to pause and digest what he or she has read so far.

● Use headlines freely to help readers orient themselves and also allow them an advance look at where they are going.

● Stop and summarize occasionally to help readers reflect on where they have been.

● Go back and edit what you have written.

THE EDITING FUNCTION

Unless you happen by chance to have ready access to some experienced editor who will assist you, you will have to learn to handle the editing function yourself. Actually, it is not a difficult task, and a knowledge of the basics of English language usage—grammar, punctuation, and spelling—is probably less important than some other matters. You should have a good dictionary, a style guide (mentioned earlier), and a grammar text near at hand. If you are using a word processor you should have a spelling checker. You may also find it beneficial to have thesaurus and grammar programs.

● First, review all the stories you have, deciding which are the most important and which will "keep" (will not age, so that you can save them for future use). Select what you will use for the issue and save the others.

● Review the facts reported in each—dates, names, places, and spelling of names and places. Check them for accuracy.

● Check your stories against the rules of your chosen style manual.

● Check for grammatical correctness, general spelling, and punctuation. (Many modern newspapers, even the biggest and most influential, have become quite careless about these matters, but you cannot afford to be.)

● Decide which is (are) your lead story (stories), and draft your headline(s).

● Tighten up the copy, editing and rewriting as necessary.

● Fit the copy.

Editing for Tight Copy

There are exceedingly few writers who write tight copy, copy that is all business and wastes no words and no time in getting straight to the point with perfect logic and in a perfectly straight line. Without exception, or with only the rarest of exceptions, writers *edit* their drafts into tight copy. They—and others, in organizations that have specialists designated for and assigned to the editing tasks— go back over the copy to make it tight.

The first measure in tightening up copy is editing to boil out all excess verbiage and extraneous information. Almost everyone overwrites, especially in a first draft, so it is usually not at all difficult to cut the size of the copy in a normal first editing. Probably about one third of most first-draft copy can be excised without losing anything of real substance. The editing surgery, properly done, trims out two kinds of fat: (1) extraneous information that contributes little or nothing to the subject; and (2) extraneous language that only slows down the flow of ideas and information. Under deadline pressures many writers and editors do this in a single editing and/or rewrite, but when time permits most careful writers prefer to edit and rewrite several times. Most true writers are never entirely satisfied with what they have done and only regretfully release the copy and turn to the next job. However, with a bit of practice you can probably learn to do the job with a high degree of efficiency in a single self-edit and rewrite.

But even then, copy can be reduced further, and by significant additional percentages, through the use of telegraphic style. That means a kind of superediting, including chopping out the articles and many other unneeded words, very much in the same style as in writing headlines, achieving a clipped, staccato effect. Witness a brief example:

Before (draft copy):

> Direct product benefits are those that are realized specifically from use of the product. Peripheral benefits are those that the customer gets, not from the product itself but because he or she does business with you, a cagey mail marketer.

After (edited down):

> Direct product benefits are those resulting specifically from use of the product, whereas peripheral benefits are those resulting from doing business with you, a cagey mail marketer.

After (telegraphic style):

> Direct product benefits result from product use, peripheral ones from dealing with you: cagey mail marketer.

Perhaps some fine nuances were shaved from the original text by the time we reached the final version, but the essence of the original meaning is still there. The first editing cut the copy approximately 30 percent, and the final cut to telegraphic style reduced the bulk by another one third. Actually, the copy benefits from the cutting: It becomes much more vigorous and efficient, acquiring a kind of dynamic quality it did not have before. Newsletter copy ought to appear clearly to be condensed, communication that is all meat and no fat.

FITTING COPY

One of the arts in publishing a periodical, even a newsletter, is something called copy fitting. In the case of a daily newspaper, the task is complicated by the necessity to allow space for advertising matter, but the size of a daily newspaper is generally flexible, while that of a newsletter is generally fixed. If you apply the pyramid idea as much as possible in writing your copy, you will help simplify the task by making it possible to chop off and discard parts of stories that run overlong. However, that particular surgery is only one of the several possible ways to deal with the problem of too much copy to fit available space. There are other expedients, some of which are basic and should be applied as a standard practice even before you attempt to fit copy.

Another Kind of Literary Operation

There is still at least one other way to make copy fit. One periodical to which I contribute occasional articles almost invariably finds them too long. However, the publisher/editor has a swift solution: She also performs surgery, but instead of discarding the remnant left after the cutting, she runs it in a subsequent issue as the second of two parts. And if it needs to be cut into more than two sections, she runs it as a series!

Again, there is a side benefit: Multipart articles and series contribute to the establishment of a sense of continuity, as do regular columns, and they help to sustain reader interest while they also build reader loyalty.

COLUMNS

There are many kinds of columns possible, some of which have been mentioned earlier without serious discussions of how to create and employ them effectively. In general, a major benefit of regular columns is that many of your readers will become especially attached to one or another column and will look forward to it each month. There is, therefore, definite benefit in running certain columns that appear regularly in each issue, and we will have a closer look at a few of these here.

Book Reviews

It is so easy to get books to review that it soon threatens to become a burden, rather than a blessing. You need merely address a letter to the marketing department of all suitable publishers advising them that you are interested in reviewing books in your periodical regularly. Of course, you must explain what kinds of books you wish to review—some 40,000–50,000 books are published each year, and you are interested in only a tiny fraction. But you must also determine which publishers publish the type of books you would review. For that you must turn to such reference guides as *Writer's Market* listed later in this book among recommended references. Before long, if you are too energetic in sending out your letters, you will begin to accumulate an overload of books to review. Moreover, you will almost surely be dismayed to find that a great many of the books you receive do not match the description you have— are not at all the types of books that are appropriate for you. You would do well to be discriminating and conservative in where you send those letters and in the number you send, at least initially. That will help to minimize the twin problems of too many books to review and too many of the wrong kinds of books arriving at your office.

Who Will Do the Reviewing?   Reviewing books that are not of direct interest, especially when you are already overbusy with other things, is far too burdensome a chore to do yourself. You need to find others to do the job, and fortunately, that is usually not too difficult to do. Moreover, you can usually find people to do it gratis, their reward the books and the by-lines as reviewers. However, you do need to maintain control over the process, and so you should provide a set of guidelines to those who review books for you.

Tentative Guidelines.   If you read the book review sections of the newspapers and magazines, you will probably note that most reviewers do more than merely report and comment on the books; they expand the review into what amounts to virtually an independent essay on the subject of the book being reviewed, on writing, on the author's credentials, and/or on whatever subject the reviewer thinks relevant and of interest. (In fact, I have often found the review far more interesting than the book!)

Although that kind of review makes for good reading, newsletter space limitations do not permit such wide-ranging excursions in book reviews. You must set size limits, probably 150–200 words maximum, if you wish to get at least two books reviewed in each issue. (Of course, you can always make exceptions for the exceptional book.)

Aside from specifying the obligatory reporting of the "head data"—title, author, publisher, number of pages, and price—and staying within the size limitations, in developing your guidelines for book reviewers you ought to consider the following points for inclusion. Of course, most of these points bear on matters that are not absolutes but are understood to be prefixed with the qualifier *in the opinion of the reviewer*. But that is inescapable in book reviews; they must inevitably reflect the judgment and even the biases of the reviewer. However, these are some things you might consider in developing a set of guidelines and specifying benchmarks or objectives for your book reviewers:

> Explain/identify the main point and theme of the book. (What was the author trying to demonstrate, prove, report on, etc.?)
> What are the author's credentials?
> How well did the author succeed in achieving his or her objectives?
> How worthy/useful is the objective of the book?How helpful is the book?
> Comment on clarity of writing, illustrations, other features (or lack of them) in the book.
> Any feature, style peculiarity, information, other item worthy of special mention (whether approving or disapproving)?

Question and Answer Column

The problem with most Q&A columns is that it takes as long as two or three months before the inquirer gets an answer to a question if the answer is delivered only via the printed page. That tends to discourage readers from asking questions. To solve this problem I devised another method of handling questions, although it did require special demands on my time.

I accepted questions or requests for information from those who were my "BSE Associates" by mail or telephone, as explained earlier, and responded directly to them. However, those questions which appeared repeatedly or which I thought to be of interest to many other readers I also answered in print—in a subsequent issue of the newsletter. (I also subsequently published any worthy suggestions of answers from other readers of the column.)

Letters to the Editor

Letters to the Editor is a topic discussed briefly in Chapter 11, but there is this additional notation that I believe to be worthy of mention here: You must be fair in running such a column and publish letters of criticism, as well as letters expressing approval, if you expect your readers to have faith in your honesty as a publisher. Read the letters column of any publication and you will find that this is the practice everywhere. But as far as reader interest generally, the best use of a letters column is to encourage controversy between and among readers, as well as between readers and authors of the copy in the newsletter. Let readers use that column to sound off, to let off steam, to argue their cases with each other and with or against items that appear in your newsletter. Controversy arouses reader interest, even among those not directly involved in it.

A Rogue's Gallery of Assaults on the Language

WHY A SPECIAL GALLERY?

We learn so much from mistakes—others' and our own—that no discussion of writing is truly complete without a few examples, injunctions, and tips. This was to be no exception. But what appears in this chapter was originally to be a portion of the chapter just concluded. However, as I gathered materials for this collection my problem became one of containing the flood, rather than of finding some representative items. It became apparent to me that our joint interests—yours and mine—would be better served by awarding this collection of English language do's, don'ts, clichés, platitudes, malapropisms, plain misuses, and other humorous and not so humorous uses, misuses, and abuses of our noble language its own easily identifiable place of honor and special prominence so you can return to it when you feel the need to refresh yourself.

Frankly, there are few do's here, except by inferring them from the don'ts; almost all the items presented here are horrible examples: What not to do. They are grouped in classes, each one introduced separately.

CLICHÉS

Few writing offenses make a reader's eyelids heavy faster than the dreary repetition of the most widely used clichés. Expressions that may have been fresh and even witty once, many years ago, are deadly, unimaginative bores today. Even single words and long-accepted colloquialisms included here have become virtual clichés because of overuse, misuse, and abuse. And some clichés are even double offenders—anomalies, oxymorons, or redundancies, as well as being trite and stale—and so may appear on more than one of the lists offered here. But here, in alphabetical order (for no good reason) are some of the most commonly encountered trite words, tired phrases, and worn out expressions commonly found today in the speech and writing of some.

acid test	irregardless
all in all	it goes without saying
along the lines of	it's a fact of life
a new dimension	its safe to say
a step in the right direction	know-how
(not to) belabor the point	last but not least
bottom line	leaves much to be desired
cutting edge	let me make this perfectly clear
each and every one	life goes on
easier said than done	matter of course
expertise	more often than not
fallout	plays an important role
few and far between	(this) point in time
for all intents and purposes	(to) put a fine point on it
hard data	reiterate
I submit	richly rewarding
if you will	running start
in-depth study	sadder but wiser
in the final analysis	strong as an ox
in the wink of an eye	tip of the iceberg
in view of the fact that	ways and means

MISUSES

Unfortunately, many individuals use words they think they understand, without going to the trouble of making sure that they do. If explanations offered here are inadequate, reference to any good dictionary should clarify the point. Following are a few examples I have encountered:

Anxious when the right word is *eager, avid,* or any of its synonyms.

Assignation when the writer meant *assignment*. This is more than humorous; it is embarrassing if an error of this type finds print.

Convince when the right word to use is *persuade*. This is a most common and distressing error found in newspapers especially (but not exclusively). A good dictionary should straighten this out. You do not "convince" people to *do* anything (except to *believe* something. You *persuade* others to *do* something, *convince* them *of* something.

Duplicity when the right word is *duplication*. No comment required here.

Hopefully, for which there is no single right word that comes to mind, but which is used to mean "I hope that . . ." It is now a fairly well accepted colloquialism but still incorrect in the view of many authorities.

Interface when the right term is *intercommunicate* or *match*. *Interface* is a noun, not a verb, a term of technical origin to define the point or points at which two equipments (that is an accepted plural in the technical world!) or systems are matched to each other and can intercommunicate.

Irregardless when the right word is *regardless*. The word is of uncertain authenticity and certainly an unnecessary redundancy of the correct word.

It's when the right word is *its*. *It's* is a contraction of *it is*; *its* is the possessive of *it*.

Reiterate when the right word is iterate. To iterate is to repeat something; to reiterate is to repeat yet again. Most of the time we iterate; only rarely do we reiterate.

Who's when the right word is *whose*. *Who's* is a contraction of *who is*; *whose* is the possessive case of *who*, of course.

Xerox a copy when the right expression is *make a copy*. *Xerox* is a proper noun (a name) and not a verb. It is also a registered trademark, which means that the owner of that trademark has the obligation to protect that ownership and trademark status by protesting your misuse of the noun as a generic verb because that threatens the owner's rights to the trademark. (The law requires the owners of trademarks to protect their trademarks by making immediate and direct protests of all misuses or risk loss of trademark rights of ownership.)

Infer when the right word is *imply*. To suggest or hint broadly at a meaning is to imply; to infer is to conclude or to draw a meaning from something. For example, you imply that my philosophy is a reactionary one or I infer, from your remark, that you believe my philosophy to be a reactionary one.

Continuous when the right word is *continual*, and vice versa. Anything that is continuous is constant, without end, as the continuous flow of a river; but anything continual is repetitive, such as continual floods.

Affect when the right word is *effect*, and vice versa. To affect something is to influence it in some manner, whereas to effect something is to cause it to happen. But *effect* is also a noun meaning result, as when the net effect of an effort is rather slight. (Affect is also a noun but rarely used as such.)

Principle when the right word is *principal,* and vice versa. "He was the principal instigator, but I was opposed to the principle on which he based the program."

Less when the right word is *fewer*. Less money but fewer dollars. Fewer when referring to discrete units, less when referring to a collective mass.

Amount when the right word is *number*. "There was a greater amount of downtime as result of a greater number of breakdowns." Same principle as less-fewer.

Much when the right word is *many*. "Many of the changes came about as the result of much effort by the engineer." Same principle as less-fewer again.

Consensus of opinion when the right word is *consensus*, which means agreement or unanimity.

Point in time when the right word is *point*, which means the same thing.

Concur in when the right expression is *concur with*, and vice versa. You concur in an idea but you concur with others.

It when the right word is *they* or *them*. Corporations are artificial entities, and are thus properly referred to as it. Companies, on the other hand, are *people* and are thus properly referred to as *they* and *them*.

Maximize when the right word is *increase*, and *minimize* when the right word is *reduce*. To maximize sales, for example, is illogical because the maximum is the greatest number or amount possible, and logically you can never reach that in sales. If you minimize errors, however, you reduced them to zero, and then the right word is probably *eliminate* or its equivalent.

Optimum when the right word is (probably) *best* or something similar, because optimum is much more often an idealistic goal than a fact or attainable actuality.

I.e. (*id est*, which means *that is*) when the right abbreviation is *e.g.* (*exempli gratia*, which means *for example*). Preferably, avoid those Latin abbreviations entirely and use English language equivalents.

PURPLE PROSE

The poetic term *purple prose* is admirably apt in describing much of what is wrong in writing. A great many writers deliberately imitate and attempt to emulate what they believe to be the grand style of historians and classicists or—even worse, Hollywood scriptwriters—and thus manage to achieve the nadir of prose style. Among the expressions favored by such misguided poseurs is *nation* when the less-pretentious term would be *United States, country,* or *government*. But there are many such words and phrases—euphemisms, designed to gild the lily, even at the cost of accurate communication and clear understanding. For example, a onetime neighbor earned his family's bread by driving a truck for an area supermarket chain. His wife was a little embarrassed to confess to strangers that her husband drove a truck, so to lend a little more dignity and importance to his work, she always responded, when asked what her husband did, that he was "in food distribution!"

Many people resort to similar devices in writing, apparently in the belief that their writing is more professional, more impressive, or a better reflection of their images when they find sufficiently portentous words in which to present their thoughts, rather than simpler, everyday words and phrases. In any case, following are a number of words and phrases that are less than crystal clear or are, at least, quite a bit more pretentious than they need to be. After each such word there is then listed one of several possible simpler and clearer, if less purple, alternatives.

banking facility: bank
retail facility: store
financial resources: money
transportation equipment: trucks
human resources: employees
support staff: clerks
secretarial station: desk
human relations skills: tact
repudiated: rejected
in order to: to
dimensions: size
utilize: use
mortician: undertaker
conceptualize: conceive
fabricate: make
by means of: by
possess: have
transmit: send
so as to be able to: to
terminate: end
effectuate: cause
in the event: if
for the purpose of: to
on those occasions in which: when
integral element: part
home environment: house
audio output device: loudspeaker

OVERSTATEMENT

Most redundancies are illogical and even humorous, and all are embarrassing when pointed out by readers. *Point in time*, a redundant phrase made infamous during the Watergate hearings and investigations, is one such case. But there are many others. Following is a list of examples, in which a redundant term or overstatement is followed by a suggested correct one.

repeat again: repeat
refer back: refer
past history: past or history

past experience: experience
entirely complete: complete
true facts: truth or facts
midway between: midway or between
present status: status
unknown stranger: stranger
tangible enough to be felt: tangible or felt
consensus of opinion: consensus
completely dedicated: dedicated
utterly rejected: rejected
perfectly clear: clear
quite precise: precise
quite innovative: innovative
radically new: new

A FEW SPECIAL CASES

Perhaps some of the following are my own "pet peeves," as is the constant misuse of *convince* for *persuade* (referred to earlier). (I find that a particular irritant, even more so than awkwardly split infinitives, to which I do not object in principle.) However, while I make no pretensions to scholarliness, I do revere the language and do what I can to oppose whatever I consider to be assaults on it. Following, therefore, are a few cases I think worthy of entering the lists for.

Stemwinder

Our language is rich in idiom and figures of speech generally, many of unknown origin. (In fact, a great many thousands of words have been written, many of them highly speculative, on the origins of many common, but old, expressions.) Many of them have become clichés and platitudes, and should be shunned for that reason alone. However, any figurative language you use, even clichés and platitudes, should be used correctly or not at all.

One of my favorites is *stemwinder*, a long speech. It's origin is unknown, although one writer, William Safire, speculates that it is derived from the word *spellbinder*. I doubt that; I believe it derives from the practice of many bored victims of lengthy harangues, in which they drew their watches from their pockets, listened for the ticking, and, unbelieving that time could really be moving so slowly, wound them impatiently. In any case, the word refers to a long speech, with overtones of interminable boredom.

Bottom Line

Bottom Line is a more recent coinage, although, again, of uncertain parentage. I first heard it used in connection with the lengthy and fairly intricate cost forms the government requires of its aspirants for government contracts. There, the bottom line—literally—is the final cost to the government, and again and again I encountered government contracting officials who were not interested, for the moment at least, in our overhead rates, profit margins, or other cost factors, but wanted to know immediately and only what the "bottom line"—cost to the government—was.

On the other hand, the bottom line of many financial reports is the final, net (after taxes) profit or loss figure, and—understandably—that is the line of primary interest to many executives, officials, and stockholders.

The phrase then refers to whatever is the final essence or principal interest of the matter. Take-home pay is the bottom line for the wage earner, as title and influence may be for the high-paid executive, sales figures for the marketing director, press coverage for the PR specialist, perquisites for the public official, votes for the politician, and rank for the military officer. It is always different for each of us, according to what concerns us most and what constitutes our major goals.

That Modifier *Only*

A general rule for using adjectives and adverbs is to place them as close as possible to the nouns and verbs they modify and, quite often, it is necessary to place the modifier before the word it modifies, rather than after it. Otherwise, it is often difficult to be sure which nouns or verbs it is your intention to modify. One of the most common misuses is that of the word *only*. Compare these two sentences:

I only hoped to win a promotion.

I hoped to win only a promotion. (Or: I hoped to win a promotion only.)

The question is, of course, whether *only* is intended to modify *hoped* or *promotion*. The second sentence makes the intended meaning clear enough.

There are other cases, as severe and as serious in their consequences. Here is another example:

The report just lists the casualties of the last year.
The report lists the casualties of just the last year.

And here is still another case where carelessness in placing the modifier can cause confusion as to meaning:

Managers who "lay down the law" often inhibit productivity.
Managers who often "lay down the law" inhibit productivity.

CHAPTER FOURTEEN

Marketing the Newsletter

WHAT ARE YOU SELLING?

It has been said (and I am one of those who has said it often enough) that far too few businesspeople really *know* what business they are in—that is, they do not know what they are selling. Or, perhaps to put a finer point on it, they may know what they are selling (or wish to sell) but too often they do not know what customers are buying (or wish to buy). And that simple truth sums up the difference between successful and unsuccessful marketing: Everyone knows what they are selling, but the most successful marketers are those who know what the customers are buying. And if that is a bit cryptic, hang on; it will all become clearer eventually.

My dear wife patronized a baker who made a type of cookie she favors. But he was not consistent, and he did not always make it the way she wanted it made—sometimes he baked them too long, and they became hard and dry. When she protested that sometimes these expensive cookies were inedible, he bristled and said that he was the baker, these were his cookies, and he would make them the way he wanted to make them. And she responded that she was the customer, this was her money, and she would spend it anywhere she wanted to spend it, which exchange ended the relationship permanently.

You can't sell a customer what you want, but only what the customer wants. That is so painfully obvious that you wonder now why I bother to point this out. That surly baker was unquestionably an exception: Most businesspeople—including independent consultants—are glad to give the customer what he or she wants, once it becomes apparent what that is. But that is where the problem lies: So often we do not know what the customer wants, even when we think that we do.

Let's take the simple case of a woman in a drugstore who asks the pharmacist for a bottle of aspirin. She knows what she wants—aspirin—does she not? But suppose the pharmacist says, "Have you tried this new headache remedy, Nopane? It doesn't upset your stomach and it works much faster than aspirin."

The pharmacist has surmised, reasonably enough, that the woman really wants relief from headaches, not aspirin per se, but asks for aspirin out of habit, as almost reflex action because she has come to associate aspirin with headache relief.

No Place for Subtlety

This is a simple case. It is easy to infer that anyone ordering aspirin probably really wants headache relief. Unfortunately, that kind of inference is not as easy to draw in other cases. My offer to teach people how to write better proposals through one of my newsletters brought some response—subscriptions—but not nearly enough of them nor from the prospects I thought I should be reaching and selling. My subsequent offer to help people win contracts through better proposal writing produced the results I was seeking. The difference? The first approach requires the prospect to translate the offer into what he or she really wants—in this case, for "better proposals" read "win more contracts." But not enough prospects do that. They are busy and they are distracted by dozens of other things competing with you for their attention, and so they do not make the connection to see that what you offer is the bridge to what they really want—they do not sell themselves. You must make that connection for them—sell them—and be as plain as possible in specifying the benefit—the end result the prospect wants—and promising to deliver it.

Maxwell Sackheim, often acclaimed as the dean of mail-order advertising copy, was making exactly that point when he related how changing the title of the book *Five Acres* to *Five Acres and Independence* brought a decisive increase in sales of that book. Ted Nicholas put this same idea to work when he titled a book (and used the title as his highly successful advertising headline): *How to Form Your Own Corporation without a Lawyer for under $50.00.* Dale Carnegie did it many years ago with his classic *How to Win*

Friends and Influence People, and Napoleon Hill followed suit with *How to Think and Grow Rich*.

For practice in mastering this all-important idea, consider the following 10 headlines and decide which ones are most likely to be appealing to true needs or wants:

1. You can laugh at money worries if you follow this simple plan.
2. AT&T, the Right Choice.
3. Share the Wealth.
4. The Lazy Man's Way to Riches.
5. Richman's Elixir for a Better Future.
6. How I Made a Fortune with a "Fool Idea."
7. If You're Looking for Who Builds Them Best, Look at Who Backs Them Best.
8. No Computer is an Island Entire of Itself.
9. Attention, Teachers: Free Classroom Guide.
10. Cordon Rubie. Clearly an Outstanding Cognac.

I am most tempted to withhold my own choices, in the hope that you will be thereby compelled to think harder about your choices, but you are entitled to whatever will pass here for a "school solution." My nominees for the advertising arguments that probably appeal directly to basic needs and wants are numbers 1, 4, and 6. All the others are simply claims of superiority or gimmicks to arouse curiosity in the hopes that the reader will be intrigued enough to pause and read further or even send for more information. And some, notably 3 and 8, are simply cryptic, based on what theory of advertising copy I know not. Number 7 is really based on the hope that because the now well-known and highly respected Mr. Lee Iacocca is depicted as the spokesman making that statement, it will bear much weight with prospects, even if the rationale is a bit strained. Number 9 is one exception because this type of advertisement is pure inquiry advertising, designed to draw requests from teachers for the advertised free classroom guide, which will be accompanied by a suitable direct mail package.

Reasons to Buy

What it comes down to, finally, is that the prospect must be given a reason to buy, and that reason must be made painfully obvious:

It must not require the prospect to think through some chain of logic or rationale to find the reason. It must not require logical thought at all, in fact, but should provoke an emotional reaction, for that—emotional reaction—is the principal motivator in all sales.

When last I bought a new automobile I sought economy, as I always do. Or think I do. But I didn't seek true economy; I have been corrupted beyond redemption by power windows and power door locks, digital dashboards, stereo players (that I never use), and other such gadgets. I wanted economy that included all of these. And so I happily paid about twice what I had decided I would pay—absolute maximum!—when I started my quest. But I became convinced that I had found a good buy because no one else included all those shiny toys in the base price!

I study the tactics of salespeople when I buy things. I note the difference between the salesperson who questions me to find out what I think I want and the salesperson who patiently probes to find out what I really want and perhaps have not yet articulated even to myself—*who may even help me discover what I really want.* For example, the first time I bought a new car (I had had years of driving the worn out clunkers of former owners!) I was truly "just looking." I really did not believe that I could yet afford a new one and so I was "not ready yet" for a new one. But a shrewd salesman perceived my intense desire for a new car, which I was suppressing because of my fear of taking on what I thought was a formidable new debt. He shrewdly showed me what the cost would be and turned my thinking around with effective emotional appeals. (The principal and most effective one was that I had already driven my old clunker for the last time, if I would sign here, because I could take possession of the new one immediately!)

The irony here is that although I fully understand my own frailties as a buyer yielding to emotion rather than to reason, I cannot help myself: I will continue to be ruled by my emotion, as are all buyers. Even those tough customers who always furnish elaborate rationales for resistance to buying are probably using the rationales to mask their emotional biases against buying. (Yes, we have emotional biases con as well as pro, and it is often ourselves we must first convince, one way or the other!)

The appeal to emotion is not a secret. It does not need to be, for we all base most of our decisions on the influences of our emotions even as we strive so hard to convince ourselves that others may act for the wrong reasons—emotionally—but we are completely rational; we operate only and entirely on reason alone. And that explains the second of the two sides of advertising and selling.

PROOF AND PROMISE

There is a mountain of literature on the arts of marketing and selling and, in fact, many people consider the two terms synonomous. Much of that literature is philosophical and even profound, dealing with marketing in almost an abstract sense. However, here we will discuss the subject on as simplified and as practical a basis as possible, since the purpose is not to turn you into a master marketer or salesperson, but to guide you in the successful marketing of your newsletter, no more.

"Proof and promise" sums up the philosophy of this approach. Chronologically they are applied in the reverse order—promise first—but the expression is more alliterative and trips off the tongue more easily, I believe, as "proof and promise." But on to the basic idea: Effective selling relies on an appeal to the emotions—the promise of a benefit the prospect wants very much emotionally, although he or she may want it on rational grounds also—followed by "proof" that you (the seller) can and will deliver what you promise.

In short, we—all of us—permit powerful emotional desires to overcome our rationales. Perhaps it would have been more prudent for me to have resisted the salesman and gone on driving that creaky—but totally paid for—old clunker. But I wanted to be convinced that it was time to enjoy a new car and that in the end it was more of an economy than driving that bucket of bolts that always needed repairs. Having the wish to believe that, I needed only someone to help by somehow assuring me that my wish made good sense and represented sound judgment. I had to believe that latter. I needed only a little help to do so.

Everyday, advertisers make claims that we, the prospects, find hard to believe, unless we are remarkably unsophisticated. An entire "buy American" campaign is currently being waged on TV by celebrities who exhibit a "made in the USA" label and loudly proclaim the superiority of U.S.-made goods. That is the promise, that when you buy domestic goods you get better products. There is no real proof of this claim offered, of course, because no proof is possible. In fact, there is a good deal of evidence to the contrary. But emotional factors help viewers to believe because they *want* to believe on general grounds of pride (who does not want to believe that we and what we do are the best in the world?) and because we are assured that this is right by celebrated people whose names, faces, and voices we know so well.

In this case there is not even evidence, let alone proof. And yet there is. There is because the proof is *whatever the customer will accept as proof.* And that points out an important relationship between proof and promise: The amount or weight of the evidence necessary to constitute proof to a customer is in inverse proportion to the believability of the promise. It is affected also by the intensity with which the customer wants to believe the promise. Once it was probably true that many, if not most, American-made products were superior, and so the claim that this is still true is fairly believable on its own merits, but is made far more so by national pride.

Kinds of Promises

All effective promises are emotional ones. Here are a few current advertising headlines that illustrate the point, along with comments:

● *Why more people shop at K mart than any other store in America.* The claim made here may or may not be absolute truth. (I suspect that it is not, but that may depend on who is counting and how they are counting!) But that is not relevant. The headline appeals to the herd instinct in us, the sense of security or rightness of doing what most other people do. If so many others do it—and why should the statement not be true?—it must be right and in my best interests. (Nevertheless, it is a weak headline because it asks the reader to make this rationalization instead of making a direct and specific promise of some benefit. There are no points for subtlety in selling, where you must be as specific as possible.)

● *SPEAKERS! Want More Bookings?* The promise of more business is implied here by the question, of course, and the copy following promises to help the patron to more success by creating a powerful promotional package. The proof offered is a series of testimonial letters. This should be effective—if the reader can be persuaded to stay with the full-page copy until he or she gets to the testimonial letters. But it would probably be more effective if it steered the reader directly to those testimonials or at least to the lead testimonial by a headline that said something along the lines of "Let _____ _____ tell you how _____ _____ can multiply your speaking income," and then went directly to the first testimonial.

● *You're invited to discover how BUSINESS TRAVELER'S REPORT can make business travel less expensive, easier, and more enjoyable.* This somewhat less than sparkling copy is promoting a newsletter, and the appeal is based primarily on the promise of cutting travel costs, which is probably the strongest appeal that can be made for this subject. Unfortunately, the headline features the name of the newsletter, not the cost-cutting promise, most prominently, which is the first mistake. Even more serious, however, is the dilution of the message with other, secondary and less appealing benefits, so that the whole thing simply does not come off well.

● *The secrets of successful selling* . . . introduces another newsletter, *Master Salesmanship®*. It is addressed to management as a journal to be purchased in quantity for distribution to the sales force. Although more powerful than the copy for *Business Traveler's Report*, it still fails to define its main promise early enough. It should use a headline that addresses managers of salespersons along the lines of "How to help your staff sell more." Busy sales managers are likely to discard this before they realize that it is addressed to them.

● *CAD and Mouse* . . . is a headline promoting a computer "mouse" for engineering work (CAD stands for "computer aided design"). It has the virtue of identifying immediately what it is all about. It has the faults of failing to make a promise at all and of surrendering to that often fatal disease of cleverness. This copywriter, like so many others, could not resist being oh-so-clever with the painfully trite and tasteless pun device so many unimaginative copywriters resort to. It was far more important to be clever than to make the promise necessary to arouse serious interest.

The Major Sins

We could go on looking at many more examples, but it would be simply more of the same. The cardinal sins of copywriters fall into certain clear categories:

1. Unsupported claims of superiority. The reader is asked to accept the claim because it is the loudest, most vociferous, most prominently displayed, most unabashedly strident, most outrageous, most extravagant, most artfully expressed, most artistically illustrated, or most something or other. The very fact that the advertiser demands to be believed simply because he says so in large print is what is truly outrageous.

2. Klever Kopy (with "Ks" because the Klever Kopywriters love to resort to such shopworn devices almost as much as they like to use puns to demonstrate how klever they are). The kleverness kould possibly be forgiven if they managed to also sell effectively while they are being so klever.

3. The attention-grabber headline that has little or nothing to do with the copy. A TV commercial depicts two teenagers discussing the unhappiness of one at his parents' constant quarreling. What this has to do with selling yet another brand of designer jeans is remarkably unclear. (Nor is it really very effective as an attention grabber, unfortunately.)

All these types of copy usually fail to even suggest a promise, much less actually make one. Thus, the customer—who is more properly still a prospect and who may never become a customer if the copy doesn't improve—is not given a reason to buy, but is expected to furnish his or her own reason. Unfortunately, that is not likely to happen. Most customers will go on to someone else, someone who will give them not only a reason to buy but a compelling reason to do so.

And thus the heart of the matter: a *compelling reason to buy*. But that reason is always the customer's self-interest. That is the only reason that motivates a customer. But that raises still another question: What is the customer's self-interest?

Self-Interest: Two Kinds of Buyer Motivation

Self-interest is a general concept that is easy to understand, especially in our modern society, which is characterized by certain outstanding characteristics that most of us understand, although not necessarily in these terms:

1. It (our society) is highly competitive; you must compete at every turn, even for mere survival.

2. It includes a large number of predators, individuals who survive and prosper by preying on the less-savage members of our society.
3. It offers a potpourri of opportunities for the fleet of mind and bold of heart.
4. But it offers also a forest of hazards for the unwary, sand traps, booby traps, deadfalls, and other dangers.

This can be summed up by pointing out that our self-interests are represented by the instinct for self-preservation and the desire for gain. Or, to put it another way, customers are motivated by fear and greed—by the fear of and desire to avoid a calamitous consequence and the desire to gain a direct benefit of some sort. The Howard Ruff book *How to Prosper During the Coming Bad Years* was a direct appeal to both instincts, which may have had a great deal to do with its achieving the best-seller status it enjoyed for so many months. But most sales depend on one or the other of the two general kinds of buyer motivation, not on both. It is rare that both can be combined effectively.

MOTIVATIONS

Except for those rare occasions and situations where both major motivations—fear and desire for gain—can be combined effectively in a single campaign (that is, when the two happen by fortunate circumstance to fit together), trying to force-fit both motivations into a campaign only weakens the offer overall. In most cases, even if you can find the means for using both motivations and wish to do so, to use both effectively you must conduct two separate campaigns as though they had absolutely nothing to do with each other.

The Fear Motivation

Insurance, burglar alarms, fire alarms, locks, and many other items are sold on the basis of fear—the promise of protection from disasters of one sort or another. Those are principal among the products that obviously (more or less) must be sold via fear motivation; which is inherent in the nature of the products. But there are other products—even some kinds of newsletters—that fit this model. And principal among these are newsletters aimed at some kinds of businesspeople and investors.

Investment newsletters are rather obvious candidates for marketing via fear motivation because investors are driven by the desire for gain but always conscious of the potential for loss. They are never disinterested in promises to steer them away from the shoals and sandbars of unsound investments and into the deeper, safer channels of the stock market. But because the most basic motivation of investors is gain, the astute publisher of a newsletter for investors often makes both appeals. That same Howard Ruff who fared so well with his first book (and not badly with his second book, *How to Make Money*), for years challenged prospective subscribers to his investment newsletter with the large-type, boldfaced query asking whether they thought they could afford to be without his advice, a definite (and apparently successful) appeal to fear.

The implication of that direct mail challenge was plain enough: Proceeding without the benefit of Howard Ruff's advice in his newsletter was risking disaster. Was it a successful strategy? Evidently it was, for it went on for some years—perhaps is still in use. That is itself an indicator of success.

More than one insurance company has depicted the poor victim of a fire or other disaster as either the sad-faced victim of his own foolishness of having failed to have adequate insurance, or the happy, wiser individual who was farsighted enough to have had ample coverage. The first alternative is probably the more commonly used and the more successful ploy, since the average person tends to some insecurity to begin with and is usually more concerned with disaster prevention than with gain.

Even those whose message is geared primarily to gain, as in the case of those purveyors of little books that allegedly contain the secrets of instant riches, play on the fears of readers that they, too, may be faced with financial ruin if they fail to take advantage of the great opportunity being offered. Almost without exception, they cite a claimed desperate personal situation—unemployment, pregnancy, repossession of their automobiles, eviction from their apartments—before (and often as the cause of) the sudden revelation that catapulted them into great wealth in a short time. (They have remarkably similar tales to tell, all closely resembling that of the late Joe Karbo, who pioneered this field.)

The Gain Motivation

The gain motivation is a strong one in our society, albeit possibly not as great as that of fear. We are a nation of aggressive doers, builders of businesses and whole industries, and we are success oriented. But we tend to measure success strictly in material terms, and so even those who are already comfortably situated economically are usually interested in adding more to their resources.

The natural result is that many people respond to the promise of gain if they "identify" with the appeal—if, that is, they see themselves as those who are being addressed and to whom the appeal has relevance. For example, someone who is having great difficulty merely paying his or her rent each month is not likely to identify with someone being addressed with an appeal to invest $5,000 in even the most attractive opportunity. No matter what blandishments you offer, you will not "reach" someone in such unfortunate circumstances.

Even in mail order you must qualify your prospects. You may sell insurance in personal property to those who rent, but you cannot sell insurance coverage of real property to anyone who does not own real property. That seems rather obvious, of course, and yet mailers apparently overlook this constantly. Some rather large proportion of all direct mail—it is nearly impossible to do more than guess at how much of it—is totally wasted by such misguided effort. At today's costs of $200 to $400 per 1,000 pieces mailed (the lower figure for the most frugal of campaigns) it is increasingly impossible to accept the waste of addressing unqualified prospects. Profit margins are simply not large enough to accommodate the waste of mail-order dollars.

Gain motivation need not be in terms of money or its equivalent. It can be almost any kind of benefit from better career opportunities to a more slender figure, better health, greater self-esteem, more popularity, or any of many, many other possible gain benefits, as some of the earlier examples illustrated.

In short, the sound principles of marketing generally apply to newsletter marketing as much as they do to other marketing challenges. People subscribe to newsletters for the same reasons. Still, there is some conventional wisdom concerning newsletter marketing.

NEWSLETTER MARKETING

Admittedly there are exceptions to every rule, and what I shall advocate here is based on conventional wisdom, which is simply the most widely accepted practices, based on the experience of many who have gone before you. That is, many newsletter publishers have passed on to others what has and has not worked for them in building up their own successful newsletters. Methods for soliciting subscriptions—advertising, that is—are the subject of much of that conventional wisdom.

Advertising Methods

It is rather widely accepted today that direct mail is by far the most effective method for advertising a newsletter and soliciting orders. This is based on experience and observation, rather than on any formal theory. Yet it has its exceptions. One exception is that of a certain well-known and highly successful investors' newsletter, *Value Line*, which advertises widely in many of the print media. Nevertheless, that is an exception; by far the majority turn to the many direct mail options.

Sample Copies

Many newsletter publishers offer sample copies to anyone interested. At least one study indicated that this is not an effective strategy in most cases. The research indicated that those receiving sample copies were more often than not disappointed, finding that the newsletter did not live up to their expectations, whether those high expectations were justified or not. (The study did not suggest directly that the newsletters in these test cases had been oversold, but that seemed to be a logical inference.)

This is not an unvarying truth, however. Sending sample copies to prospective subscribers does work out successfully for many newsletter publishers, especially when the "sample" is really the first issue of a subscription represented as a trial subscription with a free sample issue (a method that will be explained in greater detail presently). But there are some other approaches to sending out free sample copies, sometimes as part of or in connection with a direct mail campaign, but also in connection with other types of advertising or sales promotion. We'll have a look at each of these.

DIRECT MAIL BASICS

There are three terms of interest involved in discussing direct mail marketing. In addition to the term *direct mail*, there are *mail-order* and *direct response* marketing, also referred to more simply sometimes as *direct marketing*.

These terms are related to each other and are used almost interchangeably, although there are differences, and many marketers insist on discriminating accordingly in using the terms. Technically, it is all direct marketing or direct response marketing, with mail order a subset of that and direct mail a subset of mail order. However, direct mail is by far the most dominant and most widely practiced method of direct response marketing, and we will stick with that term in our discussions here.

Direct mail is a simple enough proposition in principle. It involves mailing solicitations—advertising matter that constitutes a sales appeal—to prospects. Orders are received via mail, usually, although there is no reason that telephone orders should not be invited also, and they usually are. Orders may be filled via mail also, and normally are in the case of newsletters.

There are two critical factors. One is the appeal itself—the effectiveness of the offer and its presentation. The other is the correctness of the prospects—the mailing list. And there is a pitfall, too: Again and again I find that many direct mail experts tend strongly to assume that when a campaign is unsuccessful, the cause is usually that of using the wrong mailing lists. Admittedly, the best offer and finest presentation are seeds on barren ground when the mailing list is all wrong—when the offer and presentation are made to those who are not suitable prospects for the newsletter—but when a campaign fails to produce satisfactory results it is necessary to examine and consider all elements, especially the offer itself.

THE OFFER

Most marketers attach a different meaning to that term *the offer* than I do. (I plead guilty to being something of a maverick.) To most an offer represents the description of the item and the terms and conditions of its sale, as in the following examples:

> Send only $9.95 for 13 monthly issues (an extra month FREE!) of *Making Extra Money* and receive also, as a BONUS for prompt action, a FREE copy of our best-selling book, *How I Earn $500 a Day, Every Day.*

> Send no money! We'll bill you $14.75 later, and you can pay in installments, if you wish, and you can even charge all payments to your Visa or MasterCard. But act now, before the price rise!

It is my philosophy that an offer is a statement of what I promise to do in response to the questions I *assume* are in the prospect's mind, to wit: "Why should I buy what you are trying to sell me? What's in it for me? What are you going to do for me?" An offer is that *promise* I said so much about in earlier pages. It must include the "proof" also, but in its strictest sense the offer is that promise. Here are examples of what an offer is, according to that philosophy:

> Now you can learn how to begin earning $500 a day doing whatever it is that you know best how to do—finding the best tax strategies, designing quality control systems, specifying security systems, training plant personnel, or other specialty. The success secrets of successful consultants and other specialists are reported every month in *Inside Consulting.*

> You can stop paying that 10–12 percent overpayment in taxes that you and other small businesses pay because until now you couldn't afford high-priced tax lawyers and other tax specialists. But that is changed now. *Inside Tax Tips for Small Business* now makes the advice of those high-powered tax specialists YOURS for only a few pennies a day.

> Lose as much weight as you want to as fast as you want to and keep it off with the sensible guidance of *Slim and Trim,* 12 pages of sound advice each and every month from the professionals—doctors, dieticians, and nutritionists.

The offer in each of these cases is the direct benefit promised: help in making money, reducing taxes, and losing weight—what you promise to *do* for the prospect. Or, more exactly perhaps, what (you promise) buying what you are selling will do for the prospect.

(That which is often pointed out and defined as the offer, as in the two earlier examples, I define as the *proposition,* about which much more will be said shortly.)

My experience has been that while the right mailing lists are important, much more often than others appear to think it is the offer that is somehow deficient. To keep things simple in an area that can easily become quite complex, I deliberately made a misstatement a few paragraphs ago. I said that there are two critical factors, the appeal, which I equated with the offer or presentation, and the mailing list. In fact, there are four, for the offer is not synonymous with the appeal or the presentation. To get everything into proper and accurate perspective—and this is absolutely essential if the marketing campaign is to be successful—what I referred to as the appeal is actually made up of three elements: (1) the offer; (2) the proposition; and (3) the presentation. And each of those is as important to marketing success as is the mailing list.

THE OTHER ELEMENTS

In terms of relative importance, I consider the offer to be by far the most important, for it is the basic motivating factor and it is probably the weakest link in far too many marketing campaigns. Nothing truly compensates for an ineffective offer, although a powerful offer can compensate for many other weaknesses in a marketing campaign. (The "power" of an offer is the degree to which it makes prospects *want* to believe the promise; prospects who want to believe the offer will themselves help you sell it to them.)

The proof is necessarily part of the offer, and yet there are so many variants possible here that it is necessary to discuss it as a separate element, which I must rank as second in importance. Some offers require little proof because they embody proof automatically, somehow (we'll have a look at this idea shortly) or because most prospects will accept the promise without much in the way of specific evidence to back it up. (Study the second set of examples, those I identify as offers, and see if you can determine which need lots more backup evidence than that already stated and which do not.)

The mailing list is third in importance in this hierarchy, in my opinion. In fact, mailing lists are rarely ideal; most are compromises. Some of the names are those of excellent prospects, some are of poor prospects, and some are of prospects qualifying between these extremes. A truly effective offer will sell many of those mid-grade prospects who would not respond to a less-effective offer.

I consider the proposition to be next in importance. An attractive proposition is certainly a factor, especially in nudging undecided prospects. The proposition is the set of terms and conditions, which includes specifications of the item or service and of the price, mode of payment, and any other items that are properly a part of terms and conditions. Many propositions include special inducements—discounts, bonuses, rebates, gifts, and other blandishments to help the undecided become subscribers.

Finally, there is the presentation itself—the printed matter, ranging widely in size, diversity, type, and sophistication. There is a certain amount of mystique about this, too, with much conventional wisdom that I have found to be at odds with my own experience.

We'll discuss these one by one, starting with the proof—I think we have now covered the basic offer (promise of benefit) adequately—and proceeding through all the other elements.

PROOF

For our purposes, "proof" is not what might be required in a court of law, a hearing, a scientific conference, or other formal proceeding. Quite the contrary, what passes for proof in marketing campaigns might be rejected out of hand in formal investigations and discussions. In fact, we might find it more convenient to use the term *evidence* in referring to that which we must have to support and validate the promise in our offers, but proof is more definitive for our purposes, so we'll continue to use that term. In any case, proof is whatever the buyer will accept as proof.

That is a key point in all marketing. It refers to *perception*, the buyer's perception. It gives us the definition of proof as whatever the buyer perceives as proof.

Perceptions

Philosophers have sometimes pointed out that there is no such thing as absolute Truth, but that Truth exists only in the individual's perception of what is true. Most of us accept certain things as truth without verifying those things personally or, in most cases, without being able to verify those things personally. This morning's *Washington Post* carries a statement by a spokesman for the Flat Earth Society that disputes current stories about a special aircraft now completing a nonstop, unrefueled around-the-world flight. That aircraft, says this spokesman (in all seriousness, I presume) has merely described a circle around the flat Earth. The spokesman also says that the sun is about 32 miles wide and 3,000 feet above the Earth. Those are truths to the members of that society, no matter how the rest of us may regard such beliefs.

Credibility

Of course, the case of the Flat Earth Society is an extreme one. Some might even call those belonging to that organization and believing such things the lunatic fringe, because few normal people dispute the basic knowledge of mankind. But the principle that individual truth is based on individual perception applies in marketing. Most of us believe what we wish to believe. A popular president, such as the one currently occupying the White House, is forgiven by the public what an unpopular president is not forgiven, simply because the public likes the individual too well to believe that he is capable of doing wrong or of not doing the job very well—they may like him too well, that is, to be willing to believe that. They manage to persuade themselves otherwise, even in the face of rather good evidence to the contrary.

And so, because most people will work hard at trying to believe what they want to believe, "proof" depends largely on understanding what people will want to believe. Here are a few factors bearing on what most people want to believe, in the probable order (descending) of credibility:

> They want to believe anything that is a direct benefit.
> They want to believe the words—opinions—of popular public figures.
> They want to believe those who represent respectable and respected authority.
> They want to believe what neighbors, friends, and relatives believe.
> They want to believe what they think most people believe.
> They want to believe whatever a likable individual says.
> They want to believe whatever they see in print.

You can see each and every one of these principles applied daily in marketing: in print advertising, radio and TV commercials, and sales presentations by individuals. We'll look at each one individually.

Benefits and Credibility. The basic principle here is that the more attractive the benefit is, the greater is the desire of the individual to believe the promise, and thus the less demanding the individual is of proof. However, that is balanced by another principle: The more extreme (and thus incredible) the promised benefit is, the more proof the buyer requires to make it credible.

There are, for example, numerous print advertisements today promising to reveal the secrets of overnight wealth for a small sum, ranging from $10 to $20, in most cases. The usual proof offered is the advertiser's claim of miraculous good fortune resulting from a revelation, after years of desperation and despair, supported by a statement from a CPA attesting to the advertiser's great wealth. This proves sufficient for many readers, who then gamble their 10 or more dollars.

Less extreme but equally indicative of how powerful is the desire to believe are the many best-seller books on dieting, finding love, playing the stock market successfully, becoming happy, and all the other blessings that can flow from the inspired and inspirational formulas for a better life.

Oddly enough, it is sometimes necessary to restrain promises that are probably so extreme, despite being true, that prospects may find them difficult to accept. But it is also essential that you understand the class of prospects to whom you address your offer and appeal. A certain class of prospect may accept as truth a promise to reveal the secrets of great wealth for a mere $10, whereas a more sophisticated prospect will snort at it and go on to other matters. In dealing with such a prospect you must temper your promise in terms of what you think will be credible to that prospect, even if that means being more modest in your claims than you believe you are justified—*unless you can produce unusually powerful proof.*

You must remember that you have three factors to balance in offering proofs:

1. What the prospect (probably) wants to believe.
2. What the prospect is likely to believe or accept.
3. The "power" of the proof you can offer.

The art lies, then, in estimating these factors and balancing them effectively.

Public Figure Testimonials.   A favorite tactic of large-scale national advertisers is to pay public figures, stars of sports and the entertainment world especially, to endorse their products and services by providing testimonials. One movie star is currently on TV plugging AT&T long-distance service, while another is assuring us that a competitor is superior. Brewers, razor-blade manufacturers, and others selling products associated primarily with men tend to turn more to well-known male sports figures to assure us that their beer, razor blades, and other products are better than those of their competitors. Of course, manufacturers of cosmetics and other products for whom women are the chief buyers turn to female public figures—usually glamorous actresses—to help persuade us to buy their products.

Public figures are heroes and heroines, and we like to think of them as infallible, honest, and trustworthy. That makes them automatically believable, even authorities. We ascribe great wisdom to obviously outstandingly successful individuals, and we can't believe that such individuals would ever mislead us, deliberately or otherwise. So their assurances become proof for many.

Authority Figures and Credibility.   As an alternative to a well-known public figure as an authority, many advertisers create a generic authority figure, an unknown or little-known actor or model made to represent authority. An individual in a white jacket might represent medical authority—a doctor, pharmacist, or scientist—and assure viewers that the product is a superior one. Or someone in a police officer's uniform might help sell a burglar alarm. Or an actor wearing an automobile mechanic's smock might verify that a certain brand of gasoline is by far the best one. Despite knowing that the individual is an actor, the testimonial is somehow impressive, and it tends to persuade the prospects to find the claims credible.

On the other hand, Chrysler Corporation has found its chief executive officer to be the best instrument of credibility in its commercials, as has the advertising agency for a now very well-known brand of chicken. So Lee Iaccoca has now become a celebrated public figure as a result of representing his company on TV and, subsequently, in other media. He was not totally unknown previously, since he had been the company's president at Ford and a center of attention when he was fired by Henry Ford. Still, the average person did not know who he was until he began to do the commercials for Chrysler.

Even less known before he spoke in behalf of his own chickens was Frank Perdue, now known perhaps even more widely than Iaccoca. He has become a well-known public figure, too.

These are not isolated cases. They are matched by others, such as that of Victor Kiam, who has been the advertising spokesman for his company, selling Remington electric shavers and, more recently, other products of his company.

That means coming full circle, ironically. The executive, although important, is an unknown and offers a quite special kind of believability. But in the process he or she becomes a public figure and now has the presumed authority and believability that accompanies that new status.

What Friends, Neighbors, and Relatives Believe.   Many salespeople learn of the persuasive effectiveness of citing other sales to prospects. A door-to-door salesperson learns, for example, that being able to remark that Mrs. Beatific, several doors away, is now the happy owner of a Beautiful Baby Makeup Set, helps persuade Mrs. Reluctant that she ought to own one, too. The remark about Mrs. Beatific is practically an endorsement and testimonial, and lends the product validity.

Most of us tend to resist going it alone, and especially bucking the tide. We tend to "go along," believing and accepting what others believe and accept, especially if those others are friends, neighbors, or relatives. And the more we see or hear of others accepting the item, the more we want it. That's the stuff of which fads are made. We are all basically imitators of whatever seems to be in vogue, from fast foods to clothing and hairstyles. It's what creates overnight fortunes for the fortunate inventors and/or promoters of hula hoops, pet rocks, blue jeans, and all the other crazes that periodically overwhelm us.

What We Think Most People Believe.   That latter example of a fad—and we have those quite frequently—illustrates that we do not even have to know or know of the people who appear to endorse the item. The mere fact that a large number of people endorse a product or service is good enough for most of us. Reading a long list of testimonials from unknown or anonymous people sways many prospects.

What We Believe When a Likable Individual Speaks. Many people, especially political observers and commentators, are a bit puzzled by the enduring popularity of and admiration for our current "Teflon" president, who makes numerous gaffes and is well known for overdelegating, to state it generously. He is perhaps even more popular than was Franklin Delano Roosevelt, who was elected an unprecedented four times and who managed to generate enormous hostility in certain quarters while remaining enormously popular with the voting public.

As at least one columnist has finally deduced, the answer is simple. People find him likable, as they did Roosevelt, although the latter had a certain charisma, too. It's an emotional issue: Few want to believe that this likable man is not the public hero and the wise leader he purports to be.

A salesperson can fill that role, too, if he or she manages to be likable enough. Your credibility—the believability of what you promise and the proof you offer—is in some proportion to your likability.

This applies also to written copy. Friendly, informal copy that manages to achieve that aura of likability by projecting a likable personality behind it is normally far more effective than are those stiff, formal declarations of superiority. It is possible to achieve that tone in written copy and worth the effort necessary to do so.

The Credibility of "Black and White" Print. Sometimes in a dispute or heated discussion one of the parties will launch the intended crushing blow: "I saw it in black and white in the newspaper." Even among the most sophisticated people there is an almost automatic tendency to accept immediately anything found in print, and to dispute it only reluctantly and hesitantly.

THE PROPOSITION

The importance of the proposition is secondary to that of the offer because the proposition is not a serious factor until and unless the prospect is seriously interested in the offer. But then the proposition is often all-important, bearing the major burden for converting that interest into a buying decision. That is when the terms and conditions—the proposition—can make the difference between winning and losing the sale.

The Four Elements of a Proposition

To the average consumer, the proposition is an extremely simple matter: An item, product, or service, is offered for a price. But to a marketer, planning a sales campaign for greatest impact and appeal to prospective buyers, it is (or should be) a carefully orchestrated ensemble of four major elements:

1. The item specified.
2. The price.
3. The payment plan or method.
4. The inducement(s).

These elements are not always totally independent of each other, but may be closely related. The price, for example, may be a variable, depending on how the buyer chooses to pay, and that may in turn involve some kind of discount or rebate (that latter has become increasingly popular with marketers), which is offered as an inducement, of course. But the item specified may be a variable, also, and that can affect one or more of the other factors, so all may become closely linked. Examples to be shown will illustrate this rather clearly. However, for purposes of analyzing and thoroughly understanding the subject it is convenient to segregate the factors as though they were, indeed, separate and independent of each other.

The Basic Item Specified

Some direct mail pieces focus on and specify a single item, but a great many offer the prospect a choice. The basic item in marketing your newsletter is a subscription, of course. And the item you specify in your proposition can be as simple as a single, one-year subscription, or it can present a variety of choices, from a "lifetime" subscription, to a multiyear subscription, to a trial subscription. A subscription invitation now on my desk from *Business Traveler's*

Report, for example, offers me a 6- or 12-month subscription, as does *Executive Productivity.* But another, *Daily Action Stock Charts,* invites me to try it for only eight weeks on a trial-subscription basis, while *Desktop Graphics* offers me a simple and straightforward one-year subscription with no alternative suggestions or choices offered. On the other hand, the publisher of *Penny Stock Market Newsletter,* a brokerage firm, offers a free subscription to anyone interested. At the moment I do not have any literature proposing a lifetime subscription, but many such propositions have crossed my desk in the past and no doubt will again. But the offer of a lifetime subscription raises the question of *whose* lifetime is being referred to. The qualification often made clearly by the publisher offering a lifetime subscription defines what that "lifetime" is by specifying, "My lifetime, not yours," although I have also seen such qualifications of lifetime subscriptions as, "Your lifetime or mine, whichever comes first!"

Some newsletter publishers will furnish a free sample copy on request, but a great many ask for payment, presumably to discourage idle curiosity seekers, children, and others who are not serious prospects, of whom there are many. And some charge but will credit the cost if a subscription follows.

Pricing Your Newsletter

The price of newsletter subscriptions is almost infinitely variable. Here are just a few examples to illustrate that:

Publication	Frequency	Subscription Fee
Aerospace Daily	Daily	$520
Job Prospector	Monthly	88
The Corporate Examiner	Monthly	25
Speechwriter's Newsletter	Twice monthly	82
UM Communicator	10 times/year	10
Data Channels	Biweekly	147
Living Free	Bimonthly	6
Chartcraft Options	Weekly	180
Action Report	Twice monthly	3
Johnson Redbook Service	Weekly	450
Brainstorms	Monthly	29
Stockholders & Creditors News Service	Twice monthly	900

That works out to a range of from \$0.125 to \$37.50 per issue, and that is why it is impossible to project anything remotely resembling an average or typical price; there simply is no typical price.

Even if you attempt to find typical prices for newsletters of any given category, such as computers, for example, you find wide ranges:

Publication	Frequency	Subscription Fee
The Anderson Report	Monthly	\$ 75
Datacomm Advisor	Monthly	125
Focus	Monthly	10
EDP Japan Report	Bimonthly	150
Small Business Computing	18 times/year	39
EDP Industry Report	Bimonthly	245

Even that more limited range works out to from approximately \$0.83 to \$25 per issue, which makes it quite obvious that the subscription prices are based on something other than the costs of creating the newsletter and publishing each issue. There must be some other basis than marked-up costs for establishing the selling price.

Finding a Basis for Pricing. It is easy to see that the main problem is not pricing per se but finding some rational basis for pricing subscriptions. In fact, the price must necessarily be based on perceived value, as the publisher (you) perceives it and can persuade enough subscribers to perceive it—to agree with the price set. Perhaps this method of pricing can be characterized as charging whatever the market will bear, cynical as that may sound, and yet in a larger sense it is not cynical at all: There is no other practical way of setting a value on a newsletter, for the value has nothing to do with the labor and production costs, any more than the selling price of a diamond has to do with the cost of getting it out of the ground. It has to do, rather, with such intangibles as perceived value, just as consulting service itself does. It has to do with those factors that make it possible for one consultant to command \$5,000 a day, while another has difficulty getting \$500 a day.

It does not even have to do with the cosmetics—the physical appearance of the newsletter—for simple typewriter-composed newsletters that are printed on inexpensive white sulphite paper often fetch much greater prices than "slick" newsletters set formally and printed in two or more colors on fancy and costly paper.

Such intangibles responsible for perceived values are especially in evidence in the case of certain types of newsletters: those that provide information not easily available elsewhere; and/or those that offer specialized advice that would cost considerably more if rendered under the classical consulting arrangement, a description that ought to fit your own newsletter. It comes down, finally, to putting a value on the information you provide and especially on your expert advice. For in the end your newsletter is very much a part of "the advice business." It is a method of delivering that advice at a fraction of the cost that the reader would have to accept if he or she were to retain you directly as consultant.

What Is Your Advice Worth?   To get a proper perspective on the value of your newsletter, you must consider it as an integral part of your practice, a consulting service in itself. (And, of course, you must conduct it as a consulting service.) You must not consider your readers to be merely subscribers; they are clients. In your newsletter you are serving them with information and advice, as you would and do serve any client, although here you are consulting on a group basis, as it were. All these rather special clients are thus sharing the cost of your service among them, as in group therapy, group insurance, group hospitalization, and so on. This changes the perspective: You must now attempt to judge what your *consulting* service is worth when it is delivered in this mode! That is, do not charge your subscribers a subscription fee for your newsletter; charge them a group consulting fee.

Perhaps those who publish investment newsletters are in the best position to set a price because they can estimate what their advice has been or should have been worth directly in dollars and cents. But that should not change the basic fact that your newsletter is a consulting service and must be priced as such, albeit on a group basis. If you can put a fair value on your personal services by the day or hour, you should be able to do as much with regard to valuing your newsletter.

In short, the price is based on the content of the newsletter— what that content is worth to the reader. If several thousand people are willing to pay as much as $10 to $37.50 per issue for a dozen or so pages of text, they must find something of great value in those few pages.

The Payment Plan

In earlier years, even in my own lifetime, relatively few small purchases were made on credit—at least not on long-term credit. When cash did not change hands immediately in consummating the transaction, there were perhaps "terms," usually meaning that the buyer undertook to pay the bill within 30 days. But long-term credit then was usually applied to only major purchases.

Of course, that is no longer the case. Hardly any of us today are without a credit card or two, and newsletter publishers have learned, as have all merchants, that making credit easily available induces sales from many who might otherwise procrastinate and perhaps never buy at all. Most newsletter publishers therefore offer credit via Visa and MasterCard, the "bank cards," and many also honor other credit cards. Moreover, almost all offer to extend credit spontaneously, agreeing to bill you later.

It is not difficult to arrange authorization to accept credit card charges. Your banker can guide you. You will find that credit card charge slips are better than checks, for you can verify the standing of the account and get authorization (or rejection) immediately via telephone. Moreover, once authorized, the credit card slip may be deposited in the bank like cash; it does not have to "clear," as a check does, but is immediately available.

All but one of those newsletter solicitations on my desk at this moment agree to accept credit card payment, and all include that "bill me later" proviso, also. That has become almost obligatory in selling subscriptions, and the rationale is quite simple: The possible out-of-pocket loss, an issue or two, is negligible, so there is no risk worth mentioning in sending out the first issue without having been paid in advance.

The typical trial subscription that many offer is generally for six months (although I found it helpful in launching a new newsletter to offer three-month trial subscriptions).

Not surprisingly, most offer extended subscriptions of two or three years also, usually with a price that reduces the per copy cost significantly, as well as provides a hedge against price rises during that period.

Recognizing that in some cases an individual will order a newsletter for personal reasons, while in other cases the individual may be acting for an organization, many newsletter order forms provide a choice of "bill me" or "bill my company."

Figure 14–1 illustrates these kinds of features. Note the provision of a toll-free telephone number to facilitate orders. The form illustrated is a "business reply" postcard—the advertiser will pay the postage—so that the customer need do little but write in the information and check off the appropriate boxes. Note that a variety of different payment plans are offered: Check or money order with subscription, billing individual or company, and three different credit cards.

This publisher offers only a single year's subscription at $72. Another, who publishes *Executive Productivity,* offers one year at $39, which he says is a special $38 reduction from the regular $77 subscription rate, and six months at $20.

Inducements

A newsletter publisher I know, finding himself in an awkward cash flow situation, made a special offer to raise money that year. He offered a two-year subscription at the one-year price plus one cent. He offered to apply that to new subscriptions, renewals, and extensions of existing subscriptions.

The results were gratifying, he reported; a great many people hastened to take advantage of his offer, and he enjoyed an un-

FIGURE 14–1: Typical Order Form

Subscribe today to:

DeskTop Graphics

The How-To Newsletter
for Desktop Graphic Designers

FILL OUT AND MAIL
ATTACHED CARD OR

CALL TOLL FREE

800-255-8800
Continental U.S., Hawaii, Puerto Rico
& Virgin Islands

800-533-8800
Illinois

800-628-9094
Canada

VISA, MasterCard & AMERICAN EXPRESS cards accepted

**Prepay your subscription
and receive a FREE ($6.95 value)
File Binder for your issues**

☐ **YES,** I want to subscribe to *DeskTop Graphics* at the Special Introductory price of $72 for one year, 12 issues (outside USA add $6.00 postage and handling, payable in U.S. funds).

Please check one
☐ Check or money order enclosed
☐ Bill my company (terms net 10 days)
☐ Bill me (terms are net 10 days)
☐ Charge to my credit card
☐ ☐ VISA ☐ MasterCard ☐ AMERICAN EXPRESS
ACCOUNT NUMBER (include all raised numbers on your card)

Please give us your expiration date so we can process your order
Expiration date ____/____ month year

ATTENTION TITLE
COMPANY (if applicable) PURCHASE ORDER NO (if required)
STREET
CITY STATE ZIP
TYPE OF BUSINESS BUSINESS PHONE If evening only check here
SIGNATURE & TITLE

FOR OFFICE USE 10FP-87000

Reproduced by permission of Dynamic Graphics, Inc

precedented high renewal rate that year. (The bad news came the following year, when his renewal rate suffered badly as a result of the eagerness with which so many of his regular subscribers hastened to take advantage of the great bargain he had offered.)

Typical Inducements. It is a rather rare subscription campaign that does not include one or more inducements in the proposition. The inclusion of special inducements to subscribe are such common practice now as to be almost obligatory; prospects have come to expect some kind of bribe to sign up. Like banks, magazines have been giving away telephones, clocks, watches, pocket encyclopedias, books, and a variety of other inducements to sign on the dotted line. However, what evidence there is suggests rather strongly that saving in money—discounts, special sales, rebates, and similar cost-related inducements—is the most appealing and thus the most effective inducement. Still, newsletter publishers offer a variety of inducements. The following, for example, are the inducements offered by several of those newsletter publishers whose offers are currently resting on my desk.

● *Executive Productivity* offers a $38 discount from its regular price, as mentioned a few paragraphs ago. Also offered is the privilege of cancellation and refund, prorated, of the unused portion of the subscription fee. This, however, is almost universal; it would be a rare case where the subscriber would not have this privilege. And it's a quite "safe" offer to make: Few subscribers ever demand refunds; those not satisfied simply do not renew.

● *The Kiplinger Tax Letter* offers a "special introductory price" of $30, a claimed $12 saving, or one half that price—$15 with a $6 saving—for a six-month subscription. If you pay up front—with your order—you are promised a "free bonus 'Tax Action' Report."

● *Trendline* promises their "OTC Chart Manual" and a booklet, "How Charts Can Help You Spot Buy and Sell Signals in the Stock Market," without specifying that these are conditional on paying in advance.

● *Desktop Graphics* will give you a 3-ring binder to hold your copies of their newsletter if you pay for a year's subscription in advance.

● *Bottom Line Personal*, to whose blandishments I yielded some time ago, now wants me to extend my subscription for up to five years, which would save me $46.80. They promise me six months of *Tax Hotline* free and advise me that the whole bill is a deductible expense for this year. (It is near year-end now.)

An Inducement with a Catch.   These (not including the special one-cent sale!) are all rather typical inducements. Another quite common one, one that does not happen to be among those solicitations I have at hand at the moment, offers a "free" issue, with this "catch," not apparent until you read past the bold promise: You will be billed for a regular subscription, which you agree to when you accept the invitation to request a free copy. If you don't like that first issue, simply write "cancel" across the face of the invoice when it arrives. That initial copy is yours to keep without charge; it is the free, sample copy promised. Undoubtedly, many busy people sign without being fully aware that they have ordered a subscription!

Original and Novel Inducements.   In marketing one newsletter, *Buyer's & Seller's Exchange*, I experimented with special inducements, one of which was the quite successful "BSE Associates" described in Chapter 2. But there was another rather successful inducement I tried earlier, during the introductory phase of marketing it as a new newsletter: I offered to add a free subscription period to all new subscriptions, renewals, and extensions equal to one half the paid-for period. That is, a subscriber who paid for a six-month subscription would get three additional months free, a one-year subscription would be elevated to a one and one-half years, and so forth.

A cost-saving offer helped greatly in marketing *Government Marketing News* also. Offering the newsletter together with two reports at $100, a saving of $42, brought good results. However, the respondent had the option of ordering only parts of that package, and that also brought in many orders for subscriptions and reports from individuals who wanted parts of, but not all of, the package. I have found that multipart offers with several options available to the prospect are often quite effective.

A Misleading No-No.   While not exactly an inducement, the following is an example of a dishonest device used in the past to swell circulation. It is, of course, not recommended, but it is something you should know about.

Until a federal law was passed banning the practice, some unscrupulous newsletter publishers began unsolicited subscriptions to companies and sent invoices to those new "subscribers." In a great many cases the companies simply passed the invoices to their accounting department and the accountants paid the invoices as a matter of routine.

The law now requires that unless it is a legitimate invoice, any form resembling an invoice must be plainly marked "This is not an invoice," and the law specifies the minimum-sized type that may be used for this. Still, many order forms for newsletters closely resemble invoices, and the lettering denying that the form is an invoice is not always very prominent.

Obviously, it is not necessary to resort to such dishonest means to sell subscriptions, as the success of so many newsletter publishers reveals.

The Advantage of Being Different.　I have the suspicion that while the several "different" kinds of inducements described here are each in themselves worthwhile marketing strategies, the fact that they are different from the tiresome, run-of-the-mill offers is itself responsible in large part for their success. "Me too" is never especially effective, particularly when you are a small fish imitating much larger fish who have much larger marketing budgets. The reader who sees no difference between what you offer and what others offer hardly notes your offer, much less is especially attracted by it. Still, there is a hazard in the energetic and enthusiastic promotion of special inducements that should be noted.

Remember What You Are Selling.　In the enthusiasm of promoting subscriptions through some imaginative and highly attractive inducement, some publishers lose sight of the fact that their objective is to sell subscriptions to a worthwhile newsletter. Instead, they allow themselves to be lured into selling the inducement or premium, instead of the newsletter and the benefits of reading it. Be watchful to keep things in their proper places: Sell the newsletter and use the inducement to help the procrastinators and the undecided come to a decision.

THE PRESENTATION

The successful writing of fiction calls for the creation of an illusion. The reader must somehow begin to view the characters and events as real, while well aware rationally that they are not. Unfortunately, some direct response marketers appear to perform the same feat of illusion and self-deception about their campaigns and about direct mail marketing in general. They seem to become confused between the offer or proposition itself and the presentation. They either manage to convince themselves that the presentation *is* the offer or proposition or they somehow convey an impression of that belief to those new to the field. That is, to put it more bluntly, they often suggest, intentionally or not, that the success of the campaign depends primarily on the skill with which you create the presentation—the impact and persuasiveness of the words, the visuals, the color, the gimmicks, and whatever other influences are included in the package. That is the inescapable impression you must get from the great importance some marketers attach to incidental factors and elements of the presentation.

But before embarking on an extended discussion of all these matters, we must first examine what the term *presentation* means according to the philosophy offered here.

What Is a Presentation?

The presentation is two things: (1) it is the combination of words and graphics in which the offer and proposition are explained— presented—to the prospect—that is, the manner and strategy of that explanation; but (2) it is also the physical embodiment of that explanation—the package of paper, metal, plastic, letters, brochures, envelopes, typefaces, colors, and other tangible elements that implement the manner and strategy of the explanation and persuasive devices.

For example, more than a few of those newsletter solicitations used as examples here were presented physically as simple postcards, while others were complete packages of letters, brochures, order forms, and other physical elements, bundled thickly in large envelopes covered generously on the outside with sales messages in colored inks. In most cases, the postcards made presentations quite similar to those made in the thick bundles of literature, as far as the basic explanations, offers, and propositions are concerned. But the bundles of literature went into great detail—largely iterations of the main messages—and stressed certain features.

I should explain, if it is not already clear, that the postcard presentations were not individually addressed, but were included in "card decks," packs of 50 or more such cards mailed out by professional mailers who serve direct marketers' needs in this manner. However, the presentations made up of bundles of literature arrived (via bulk mail) in individual envelopes, some addressed to me personally, some addressed to me under one of several business designations, and some addressed to "recipient" or "resident." (The latter are admittedly relatively rare.)

Few professional mailers of such literature attempt today to deceive recipients into believing that the envelope bears personal mail. For example, the outside of one envelope bearing such a pack of literature is dominated by red lettering 5/8-inch high shouting the message "NO-RISK TRIAL!" Above and below this scream for attention is a message in smaller (but bold) black ink that makes it clear enough that what is being offered is a newsletter titled *Who's Selling What,* that it offers valuable information every month, and that the offer is addressed specifically to "Direct Marketers." The content is the classic and completely typical direct mail package:

A salesletter.
A brochure.
An order form.
A discount certificate.
A postage-paid return envelope.

Still another mailing piece, falling between the extremes, is represented by a single piece mailed by *Business Opportunities Digest.* This presentation packs a great deal into a single 8½- x 11-inch sheet of paper, in which are combined typewriter and formal type composition soliciting new subscriptions for this long-successful newsletter based on perhaps the simplest of newsletter propositions. Consultant/publisher/entrepreneur Jim Straw lists hundreds of both wanted-to-buy and wanted-to-sell types of items each month in his *BOD.* His simple presentation merely points out the types of information offered—no charge for inserting notices, which will be run if they appear to be legitimate propositions—in a message signed by Straw. Fifteen impressive testimonials are also listed.

How Important Is the Presentation?

This *Business Opportunities Digest* presentation does not include all those obligatory order forms, brochures, return envelopes, and other such items (although I knew that Straw has included such items in other mailings), but that does not seem to handicap it in any way, since it goes on year after year with apparent success. I believe that this supports the idea that while flashy presentations may help close sales, the offer (the promise *and* the proof) is really where the sale is made or lost. Straw believes—and my own experience supports his belief—that while it does no harm to learn all the conventional wisdom, you must take it all with a grain of salt and discover for yourself what works for you. Direct mail is as much an art as is all marketing. There are no infallible rules or guidelines; there are only reports of what has worked for someone else in certain specific circumstances. Emulation may or may not work for you in your circumstances.

Are There Any True Rules?

It is probably a human foible that compels those with experience to formulate what they consider to be rules for success in whatever the field is. Here, for example, are just a few of the "rules" of direct mail that have been and are still propagated as inviolable principles by individuals who purport to be experts:

- The summer months—June, July, August—are no good for direct mail, and the wise marketer does nothing during these months but coast and wait for the fall.
- Direct mail business picks up sharply immediately after Labor day, peaks in January, slows down after March.
- A "BRE"—business response envelope (that's the one with the postal permit indicia that says no postage is necessary)—is a must.
- A "response device"—euphemism for an order form, usually, although sometimes applied to special gimmicks used to involve the recipient, such as in those multimillion dollar magazine con-

tests—is a must. The order form should be a separate item, easily mailed.

- Printing in two or more color inks and/or on colored paper increases the response (percentage of people sending orders).
- Using better quality paper for literature increases the response.
- "The more you tell, the more you sell."
- Follow-up mailings to the same lists produce better results than the first mailing.
- Accepting credit cards is a must.

As far as my experience and that of others with whom I have exchanged information is concerned, most of these alleged rules are true in some cases and totally untrue in others. Let's examine these a bit more closely in the light of experience:

Seasonal Fluctuations. Obviously, certain items have their special seasons. Sales of gift items begin to peak as Christmas approaches, for example. Otherwise, seasonal fluctuations are almost always unpredictable. Many of us have found the summer months excellent for sales in some years, poor in others. And the same may be said for the other months of the year. Sometimes, after a depressingly slow fall and early winter, sales have picked up sharply for me in January—but not always.

BREs, Colored Inks, Paper, and Other Such Matters. There are many claims of studies showing differences, but these increases and alleged increases are usually on the order of tiny fractions of a percent, such as 0.02 percent improvement. That assumes some significance when it is applied to a mailing of millions of pieces, perhaps, but has little practical value for the mailer of a few thousand pieces. In fact, the added cost of the refinements in the presentation often exceed the value of the extra orders (if extra orders do actually materialize). I suspect that bias and emotion—and perhaps self-interest, when the expert is in a position to prosper from the use of the refinements—not evidence, motivates many experts to insist that these factors are important. In any case, my personal experience, including actual experiments I have conducted, and that which a few others have reported to me, indicates that these are not decisive factors at all. Still, a BRE may help produce a more rapid response from a consumer who does not have an envelope and postage stamp readily available, but that would not be the case if the respondent is a businessperson. Ergo, BREs and other devices may or may not be of help, depending on surrounding circumstances, and you must take this into account. And, oddly enough, there are numerous cases where the least costly paper looks to be expensive and vice versa. The average customer has no idea of what the cost of the presentation is.

The More You Tell, the More You Sell.   I agree with this because my experience bears it out. This says that the postcard presentations will not produce the response rate—percentage of mailouts bringing back orders—that the full direct mail packages will. This appears to be true enough, as a general principle. But that does not mean that it is unfailingly true. It means that it is probably true for any offer that the prospects find attractive. That qualification is important.

Follow-up Mailings.   Follow-up mailings to the same mailing list do tend strongly to produce increasingly better results. The mailings have a cumulative effect, so that each has a somewhat greater impact than the previous one. (The first mailing may be considered to be a kind of introduction only.) Quite often, this improvement will hold for as many as five or six repetitive mailings before the response peaks.

Credit cards.   This was mentioned earlier, and my experience is that as much as 25 percent of your sales may come in this way. Presumably, you would not have been favored with most of these had you not offered to honor credit cards.

Is It a Guessing Game, Then?

What has been said here may sound rather negative and suggest that direct mail is all a wild guessing game. Not so; the risks are far too great to permit your success to depend on the chance that you might make the right guesses. In fact, the key to success was given rather subtly a few paragraphs back in suggesting that you must make your own rules, although that is probably better expressed as *discover* your own rules. And even then you do not uncover immutable rules, but only rules that are in force at the moment, under whatever happen to be the circumstances of the moment. But it is not—does not have to be—a matter of chance; there is a way to discover what those rules are. It is called *testing*, and that is, in my opinion, the single most important rule: Test before every campaign, even a repeat of a recent campaign, and monitor results constantly to measure the response and thus guide your efforts. That is the only way you can truly know what you are doing—how good the elements of your program are for the present circumstances and conditions—and can free yourself from the bias of wishful thinking or blind faith in conventional wisdom and hunches. (It is quite incredible how much money is gambled on hunches—"gut feelings"—by otherwise responsible executives.) We will discuss testing in Chapter 15, but first, let us talk seriously about mailing lists.

Mailing Lists

The direct marketing industry is quite large, representing probably a minimum of $10 billion annually in sales. Not surprisingly, a large and vigorous support industry has grown up over the years, with the vendors of mailing lists certainly not the least of the support industry players. There are dozens of sizable firms whose main business revolves around supplying mailing lists, and there are more dozens of organizations, large and small, who rent mailing lists as a by-product or adjunct to their main enterprises.

There is probably no adult in the United States and Canada who is not on several mailing lists, and probably not many children of high school age escape getting on a few mailing lists. And once on any mailing list, one's name and address increasingly appear on other mailing lists. Subscribing to any periodical or buying anything by mail tends to produce an unending stream of what some call "junk mail" from people you never heard of.

Generally speaking, owners of mailing lists own the names and do not sell the lists. The usual arrangement is to rent the list, and the rental is for a single use. The list must be rerented for additional uses, although some vendors of mailing lists offer multiuse propositions of various kinds, and some even rent lists for unlimited use for some given time period, such as one year. (However, anyone who responds to your mailing becomes your name, of course, and those names and addresses go on your own customer list.)

Where Mailing Lists Come From

The basic sources for most mailing lists are organizations doing a great deal of business by mail, although many lists also come from people who compile lists for one reason or another. For example, every publisher of a periodical builds lists of subscribers and former subscribers and every mail-order dealer builds lists of customers and inquirers. But so do associations and other nonprofit organizations, as well as firms who report credit information, statistics (demographic information), or other data on people and organizations and publish directories of various kinds for various uses.

Here, for example, are listed a few of the many organizations whose mailing lists are being managed by their owners or by list brokers and are available to users in the various categories for which they have been coded:

> American Management Associations
> *Ladies' Home Journal*
> New Generation Shampoo and Conditioner
> American Crafts, Inc.
> *High Technology*
> *Video Review*
> *Digital Audio*
> Shopsmith, Inc.
> Stationery House
> Citibank
> Trend Magazines
> Reliable Corporation
> Donnelley Marketing (Dun & Bradstreet Company)
> Dun's Marketing Services (Dun & Bradstreet Company)
> The Drawing Board
> City and Regional Magazine Association

All these organizations discovered, sooner or later, that they had a tangible asset with cash value in their steadily growing lists of names and addresses, especially when the lists are those of customers. (Names of people and organizations with known characteristics, such as mail order buyers, buyers of specific items, spenders of given sums of money, of known economic status, education, career, etc., tend to be more valuable than "cold" names; and names of customers—known spenders—are more valuable than those of inquirers.)

There are some other means and circumstances through which mailing lists are born, and we'll cover these too, as we proceed.

The Marketing of the Mailing Lists

Some of the organizations whose work generates the mailing lists referred to—a minority—choose to keep their mailing lists and customer lists (they are not necessarily the same) completely private and reserved for their own use; some (again, a minority) choose to market—rent—their lists themselves. The majority turn to list brokers—the brokers tend to designate and think of themselves as "list managers" when making their appeals to list owners to commission the list—to market their lists on a commission basis, typically 20 percent of the proceeds, but obviously negotiable in many cases.

The mailing list manager will computerize the client's lists, if they are not already computerized. (Even if they are, it is often necessary to convert them to the list manager's system.) That means setting the list up as a database of names and addresses from which a variety of lists may be drawn, according to the way in which the names and addresses have been coded. And the codes are established to facilitate compiling the kinds of lists users are most likely to want. For example, one user may want only men on the list, while another wants only known mail-order buyers, and still another wants only professionals. With the names properly organized and coded, the computer can compile all these and other kinds of lists from the database of names, and the list manager prepares descriptive catalogs for customers explaining the various categories in which names are available.

Costs vary considerably. Some of the list vendors are relatively large and prominent organizations or branches of large corporations, while others are quite small. The smaller ones tend to offer smaller selections and lower prices, so the range is rather wide, from a low of $15–$20 per 1,000 names (the typical unit) to $75 and more per 1,000 names. Moreover, many, especially the larger firms, set a minimum order of 3,000 to 5,000 names.

Lists are made available in various forms, such as on self-stick labels for those doing their own mailing, and in other forms, including computer tape, for those who turn the mailing over to professional mailers. In fact, if you have a mailing house do your mailings, the mailing house can arrange to rent lists for you or may have their own lists. (Some professional mailers are also list brokers and, vice versa, some list brokers offer mailing services. In fact, the diversity goes even further than that, as you will soon see.)

Other Sources

The conventional wisdom in direct marketing is that using the right mailing lists is all important and that compiled mailing lists—mailing lists built up by consulting a variety of directories, such as the membership lists of associations—are inferior.

That may very well be true in the experience of others, especially in the experience of the big mailers—those who mail on the scale of hundreds of thousands and even millions of direct mail pieces—but it is not necessarily true for all mailers and/or all situations. It was certainly not true for me. I had disappointing results with rented lists and much better results with lists I compiled myself, and I believe that the rationale I shall shortly present for that explains the apparent anomaly and serves as useful information for your own applications. But first a little personal history that is relevant.

In mailing solicitations for a newsletter addressed to those who do or aspire to do marketing to federal government agencies, I soon found that no list broker had lists oriented to such prospects. I was obviously in a unique or at least unusual situation and market. I tried those lists that appeared to be suitable—training developers and engineering firms, for example—but the results of mailing to these were not encouraging.

I tried using lists I was able to get from federal agencies, such as the Small Business Administration's published lists of "8a" (minority-owned contractors certified as such by the SBA) firms, a list of contractors and suppliers to the U.S. Navy, and membership lists of various organizations. I got somewhat better results, but results that still left something to be desired. I decided then that rented lists and others furnished ready-made might be helpful, but were not enough in themselves for my needs. I therefore then turned to compiling my own lists.

I used several sources in compiling lists of my own (to be added to those ready-made lists already cited). The first and, as it turned out, by far the best, was that which I compiled from help-wanted advertisements in the *Washington Post, New York Times* (Sunday editions), *Wall Street Journal* (Tuesday and Wednesday editions), and others heavy with classified and display classified advertising by defense contractors. (Today I would use several relatively new publications that are devoted exclusively to such advertising, with undoubtedly greater efficiency.)

That the results of my independent compilation of names and addresses were superior is due solely, in my opinion, to the fact that I knew far better than any list broker the types of prospects that were right for me. In compiling my own mailing lists I hand-picked my prospects. As a veteran of government contracting I recognized many of the firms who were "right" for my purposes, and could easily judge which others were also good prospects. Probably no list manager/broker, in coding lists, can anticipate my (or your) individual needs as well as I (you) can, nor should we expect it. On the other hand—and consider this seriously—I (and you) cannot compile truly large lists ourselves. So the question of where and how to get your mailing lists must depend to at least some extent on the size of the lists you require. I freely confess that had I required 50,000 or 100,000 names, I would have had no choice but to turn to commercial list brokers. Compiling your own mailing lists is a highly practical project if you are out to compile only a few thousand names, but not if you plan to launch a major campaign with heavy mailing.

Building Lists via Inquiry Advertising

One fruitful avenue for building mailing lists is inquiry advertising. If you want an instant education in what this is, consult the classified columns of any periodical and seek out those notices that invite readers to send for more information. Sometimes the advertisers even offer a free gift, such as a sample newsletter, a special report or brochure, a calendar, or other item. Note, too, how many of these ask for a "SASE"—a self-addressed stamped envelope.

The purpose of such advertisements is to build mailing lists, and the offer of something free is primarily to encourage and induce response. Inquiry advertising, skillfully done so as to attract the right kinds of respondents, is an excellent and inexpensive way to build your mailing lists rapidly. Requiring a SASE helps with the postage bill, but it may reduce response somewhat because it asks the respondent to go to some special trouble. However, in one case where my inquiry invitation produced about 3,000 inquiries, I was happy that I had asked for a SASE with each inquiry—the postage bill alone to respond to those would have been at least $600, added to about $1,000 for printing and many late hours of labor required to respond to all those inquiries.

Using Publicity to Elicit Inquiries

Although inquiry advertising—usually via the classified sections—is relatively inexpensive, it is also possible to solicit inquiries via PR—publicity—efforts. Sending out suitable releases to editors and to columnists often produces abundant inquiries. In more than one case, I found such efforts even more productive than paid advertising, not to mention that they were far less expensive! (Even classified advertising in major media today has become quite costly, with rates of $5–$6 per word not at all unusual.)

Mailing Services

You may or may not wish to undertake the labor of your own mailings—and it is labor. But there are many professional mailers who will gladly undertake your mailings if you wish. Most large mailing houses will, in fact, handle your entire campaign, supplying all services needed. The largest ones often have internal printing plants and sometimes even copywriting and related capabilities to serve you. Or you may retain the services of a professional direct mail consultant, who can and will gladly attend to all the details for you. There is no shortage of support services in the direct marketing industry.

Expanding Your House Lists

The lists that are yours—your own clients, for example, as distinct from those lists you rent—are known as "house lists." You can do as you wish with them, including renting them to others, either on your own or via the services of a list manager. But that is usually viable only when your lists have reached some large size—at least 25,000–50,000 names and addresses. Still, there is at least one other profitable use you can make of your lists almost immediately: You can trade lists with others, enriching both parties in each such trade. In my own case, for example, by the time I had compiled between 5,000 and 10,000 names of my own, I began to inquire of others whose lists were compatible with my needs but not directly competitive whether they were interested in trading lists. Of course, many were, and it was not long before my own house lists were approaching the 50,000 mark.

Of course, there will be some duplication of names when you do this, although that is a problem in any process of building mailing lists. Fortunately, today you can put even a little desktop computer to work in ferreting out the duplicates and purging the lists of them. In fact, "merge and purge" operations are standard in today's computer programs, and you can accomplish those with standard, off-the-shelf programs. You can also code your entries so as to retrieve items selectively.

Different Lists

You will want to have at least three lists: a subscriber list, a customer list, and a general list. The general list will be a list of prospects, individuals and/or organizations who have not yet bought anything from you. The subscriber list will be that of current subscribers, of course. And the customer list will be of those who have subscribed in the past or bought something from you. However, as time passes, it is likely that you will want to have even more lists, including a client list, an about-to-expire list, a former-subscriber list, and possibly different customer lists, according to what they have bought from you.

You do not necessarily have to have physically separate lists, although it will probably be convenient to do so. You can use merge and purge processing to withdraw from your general mailing list the names of those who have become subscribers and transfer those names to your customer list, and otherwise manipulate the separate, individual lists as necessary. But you can also keep all names in a single list and code them suitably so you can withdraw names from any of the lists as though they were separate.

Card Decks and Other Piggyback Mailing

One way to minimize the complications and struggle of mailing is to turn the entire job over to a professional mailer, who will handle any part or all of the job for you. But there are even less complicated (and usually less expensive) ways of doing your mailing, using the "piggyback" mailing technique, which means having others' mailings carry your advertising messages and solicitations. One of these ways that has become quite popular is the card deck, mentioned earlier.

Perhaps you have yourself received such packs of solicitations. Typically, such cards are the size of an index card—approximately 3 × 5 inches—and are sent out in a pack or deck of 50 cards, more or less, by a mailing house. The card has advertising on one side and a postage-paid indicia on the other side, usually, but some advertisers will use both sides for advertising messages and some will require the respondent to furnish a postage stamp.

Frequently, the cards are all related to a single subject—that is, of potential interest to a single, specialized group of prospects, such as investors or computer professionals—but they may also be addressed to a more general group. You pay for the service either directly or on a "PI" or "PO" basis—that is, a fee for each inquiry or each order received. In the latter arrangement the inquiries or orders must come to the mailer, to be forwarded to you with a bill for payment of the fees.

This is a rather specialized form of piggyback mailing—including your advertising solicitation in a general mailing on a kind of group basis. However, piggyback mailings are carried out in other ways. The principal way is by enclosing your advertising material—cards, circulars, order forms, or whatever you choose to use—in someone else's mailings. Credit card companies, for example, often enclose others' brochures with their bills and magazine publishers do likewise in enclosing cards and circulars with their publications. And in my own case, I piggybacked advertising material for my newsletter and manuals with my seminar solicitations. (Once you reach a certain level of circulation—number of readers—you may be able to piggyback others' advertising to produce a little additional revenue for yourself.)

CHAPTER FIFTEEN

Testing, Monitoring, and Final Admonitions

THE NEED TO TEST

All the conventional wisdom in the world, and even all the personal and direct experience of the past, is not equal in reliability to the immediate experience of proper testing and monitoring—of the knowledge gained by testing, that is. It's a case of the best laid plans, perhaps more popularly expressed today as "Murphy's Law," but the things that you least expect to go wrong do so anyway, and they go wrong at the worst possible times, perversely enough. Again and again, beginners in direct mail—and even some who are not exactly beginners—"roll out" (launch full-scale) the campaign with nothing more than a naive guess or last year's experience to guide them, and find the results fail to bring back even the postage costs.

There is no question among professionals and those properly experienced in direct mail that testing is an absolute requirement before rolling out a campaign. It is necessary to know that all things are favorable before making the major investment of a mass mailing. Ergo, the need to test is not in dispute; it is an accepted premise. But what is apparently not accepted or agreed upon is what to test.

WHAT TO TEST

Unfortunately, far too often marketers start out by testing the wrong thing: the presentation—that is, the items in the presentation. For example, they may test the difference between sales literature printed in black ink on white paper and the literature printed with colored ink on colored papers; or they test the pulling power of a package including a BRE (business response envelope) as compared with one lacking a BRE; or of using one of the more recent gimmicks, a little folder with a message saying something along the lines of "Please do not open this unless you have decided not to buy." (Presumably the premise here is that curiosity will compel the prospect to open and read the folder, thus giving the marketer an opportunity to deliver one more sales message.)

Perhaps all of these and other factors have some significance. Perhaps each can make a tiny fractional difference in the response rate, and perhaps if a dozen or so features are tested and maximized the result may be a total of as much as a full percentage point difference in the response. And perhaps, to pursue the hypothesis further, that can make a substantial difference in a multimillion-piece roll out, and so be quite worthwhile. Even so, unfortunately, the cost of testing a dozen features would be prohibitive for a small publisher—perhaps even for a large publisher—so that the gains would be hypothetical but the losses real.

The time for that kind of testing, if it is to be carried out at all, is after the campaign has proved to be successful. Then such testing may help maximize the success and the profits. But if the success of a direct mail campaign rests on fractional differences in response rates and small differences in the presentation, the campaign is a loser— much too marginal a proposition—to begin with. But aside from that, the real mistake is in wasting time and money testing such trivia when the real issue revolves around those major features we have been discussing: the *offer*, the number one and most critical item to test, and the *proposition*, far less critical but still worthy of the time and effort of testing as a follow-up, when the offer has proved to be viable. Only when those items have both proved their worth as the basis for a successful campaign does it even begin to make sense to think seriously about the various items in the presentation.

In short, what difference do all the items in the presentation make if the prospects do not find the *offer* attractive? Even the proposition counts for nothing if the prospect is not interested in your offer.

THE BASIC PRINCIPLE

The basic method of direct mail testing is to send out split mailings, trying to keep everything but the item being tested identical in each mailing so that the difference in responses is likely to be a measure of the effectiveness of what is being tested. For example, in testing the offer in *Government Marketing News*, one part of the mailing promised a continuing series of articles on proposal writing, while the other mailing promised help in winning contracts. The results demonstrated quite clearly that the promise of articles on proposal writing was not nearly so appealing as was the promise of help in winning contracts, despite the fact that the help was in the form of guidance in writing winning proposals. But that was part of the sales argument—part of the proof, not the promise. (The promise is not *how* but *what*.)

Of course, you can split the mailing into three, four, or even more sections, testing a different offer in each. However, you must be careful that the difference in the offer or promise made is the only thing that is different in each test mailing. If you have more than one difference between or among the test mailings you can never be sure just what it is that is responsible for differences in response.

This means that you must make a separate mailing for each item you wish to test. (That is why it is impractical to test a dozen or more of the relatively minor items.) You must also address each mailing to identical kinds of prospects. The way most marketers achieve this is by dividing a given mailing list, preferably on a random basis, keying the mailing in some way so you can tell to which offer each order responds. To achieve as random a distribution as possible and so make the results as reliable as possible, the best way is to simply mix the different sets of literature physically, rather than dividing the list. Otherwise, because mailing lists are usually in either alphabetical or zip code order, you do not get true randomness.

KEYING

You can key your literature in several ways. Here are just a few suggestions:

- By minor differences in your address. One order form might address "Dept MO.1" at your address, while another might read "Dept MO.2," and so on. Or you might add a letter to your address—9234-A Rodeway Blvd.

- By differences in your name. One might read A. G. Greene & Associates, another Arthur Green & Associates, another A. Green Co., and so on.
- By supplying an order form with an inconspicuous number on it.
- By serially numbering your order forms, each number group representing a different mailing.

SIZE OF TEST MAILINGS

Obviously, a test mailing is by its very nature a fraction of the intended roll-out mailing in size. Those planning huge campaigns are likely to make test mailings of 5,000 or more pieces in each mailing. That is a bit impractical for someone who is going to mail not more than 5,000 or 10,000 pieces at a time. Probably for such cases as those we are discussing here, test mailings of 500 to 1,000 pieces are adequate. (I have gotten definitive and reliable results from test mailings as small as 300, in fact.)

FOLLOW-UP TESTS

Once you have tested the offers and chosen the one that brings the greatest response, you can test the proposition in the same way, testing payment plans, bonus plans, discount plans, or whatever variations in the proposition you think worth trying out. And once you have found the offer and proposition that brings the best results, you can then launch—roll out—your campaign and, if you wish, start testing the various presentation items for maximum benefits. That way you are rolling along successfully, and the tests of the presentation items do not cost you either time or money.

RECORDING AND MONITORING

The results of mailings trickle in for many months, sometimes even for years, strangely enough. But the bulk of the response should arrive within three to four weeks, so it is usually not necessary to continue measuring results beyond that period before making final decisions.

Monitoring and recording the results accurately is essential, of course, but quite simple. A form such as that shown in Figure 15–1

FIGURE 15–1: Form for Monitoring and Recording Test Results

Test mailing _____   No. pieces mailed _____   Date of mailing _____

Total no. subscriptions received _____   Response rate _____%

Date	No. subscriptions received	Date	No. subscriptions received
	Subtotal: _____		Subtotal: _____

is usually adequate. One such form is used for each test mailing, which is suitably identified as the first item in the head data. Each day the number of subscriptions is recorded, and when it is apparent that the bulk of the response has been received, probably in 3–4 weeks, the columns are totaled and the grand total recorded in the head data. The response rate—number of orders received divided by the total number mailed out and multiplied by 100—is calculated. A mailing of 1,000 pieces that brings back 15 orders has a response rate of 1.5 percent, for example.

RESPONSE RATES

A great deal is made of response rates by some in direct mail, It is not difficult to get the impression that 3 to 4 percent is an average acceptable rate and even a minimum acceptable rate, and that more than 5 to 7 percent is a vain hope generally, except under certain special circumstances, such as mailing to an especially good list.

Simple mathematics will demonstrate that any such standards are nonsense because circumstances are almost infinitely variable, and what is an excellent response in one case is quite unacceptable in another. First, look at some basic costs. There are generally three base costs in direct mail: Printing, postage, and mailing lists. (Even if you compile your own lists it costs you money to do so.)

A typical direct mail package mailed out will probably cost you about $300 per 1,000 pieces mailed if you are reasonably careful. A 5 percent response rate would have to show you $6 net profit per order merely to break even—to recover your out-of-pocket costs—leaving you nothing to compensate you for your time and risk. A 3 percent response would have to produce a net of $10 per subscription to achieve the same thing.

On the other hand, I did very well in several campaigns that produced orders at 1 to 1.5 percent responses. But the average order size was about $67, and that made quite a difference.

The response rate per se is therefore a matter of interest and useful in comparing campaigns or test mailings where conditions are similar, but its utility stops there. The simple fact is that even aside from all other factors that can and do affect rates of response, the size of the order you are asking for will certainly have an effect on how many recipients respond with an order. You can hardly expect as many $100 orders from a mailing as you might $10 orders.

ROI

What really counts is not response rates but what entrepreneurs refer to as "ROI"—return on investment. The rate that is important is the earnings rate—the percentage rates of returns—profit—received. If you have invested $3,000 in mailing and perhaps another $7,000 in your time and other costs, the response rate of interest is in dollars returned by your total investment.

But even that is not the whole story, for there are spin-offs. Many direct mail campaigns bring back fewer dollars in orders than they cost and yet are profitable. They can be profitable in at least two ways:

1. Some campaigns are conducted to create customers, rather than sales. It is almost certain that large direct mail merchants—

catalog vendors such as consumer-goods Spiegel and stationer/ office-supplies Quill Corporation—lose money on the first order they get from a new customer. Winning new customers is always costly and especially costly in direct mail, and the cost of winning each new customer is almost always greater than the profit on the first order from that new customer. But the repeat sales to that customer cost little or nothing to win, and the new customer eventually becomes a profitable asset.

2. There is also what is known in direct mail parlance as the "bounce-back" order. That's the new order you get from the customer as a result of the sales literature you enclose when you fill the original order. That may produce profit you didn't get from the original order. In fact, one prominent mail-order firm constantly and deliberately features in their advertising a loss leader, personal name and address stickers to put on letterheads and envelopes, because the new names are worth the cost of acquiring them.

A FEW FINAL WORDS OF COMFORT

But even that is not the whole story. As a newsletter publisher, and (I sincerely hope) as a publisher of a continuing series of other information products (reports, books, training manuals, etc.), you have the enormous advantage of control and large markup. You manufacture the product, first of all, and that, plus the fact that the physical product is paper, gives you certain enormous advantages:

1. Your products are exclusive; they are available only from you.
2. You have a highly favorable markup; the paper is cheap.
3. You have the potential for bounce-back orders and repeat business.
4. Your products are easy (and inexpensive) to package and ship.

If you have prepared yourself to try for bounce-back orders and repeat business from customers, response rates and even direct profits on response to your mailings may be of purely academic interest.

The remaining pages will be given over to reference materials that should help you achieve your goals.

APPENDIXES

Modern Desktop Publishing: What Is It?

THE MAJOR INFLUENCES IN PUBLISHING

Historically, the greatest influence in publishing has long been regarded as the invention of movable type by Johann Gutenberg of Mainz, Germany in 1440. That was the invention of movable *letterpress* or *relief* type.

Many improvements in printing and publishing were made over the next four centuries, including the linotype machines of modern times. But even those finally gave way to more modern methods, especially one that changed the very nature of the typesetting and printing processes: lithographic—offset—printing, which was developed over the past few decades and does not require a raised surface for printing, as letterpress does. This has simplified the printing process and made printing available readily, swiftly—even while-you-wait printing—and inexpensively to everyone.

The swift success of offset printing also spelled the beginning of the end for letterpress typesetting—raised metal type—since in the offset process anything that could be photographed could be made into an offset press plate of metal, plastic, or paper and printed quickly and easily. That gave rise to a variety of new composition—typesetting—methods.

The earliest new composition methods were based on photo-composition, using conventional photographic methods, but these soon progressed to strike-on composition available in ordinary office environments—electric typewriters and other typewriterlike machines, including computer printers.

The latest technological breakthrough, microcircuit technology (e.g., computer chips) soon brought the desktop computer to even the smallest offices. It soon became plainly apparent that the most popular application of the desktop computer was for word processing, a process that began to idle the electric typewriters in many offices.

In the meanwhile, another new technology was proliferating with unprecedented speed. The xerographic copying process came along, circa 1960, and crude as it was in the beginning, it caught on swiftly because despite the poor quality of the copies made by the early systems, the process was still far superior to any copying method that preceded it. Finally, however, in recent years, the xerographic process has progressed to where it rivals printing for speed, convenience, and quality for small printing jobs. Together with the swift and inexpensive offset-lithographic method of printing, it birthed the neighborhood copy/print shop that is now so plainly in abundance.

The new revolution in publishing is now at hand. It is the outgrowth of the computer revolution of this decade, the marriage of the personal computer, word processing, and the laser/xerographic printer, a printer that paints the words and drawings on the xerographic drum or master instead of photographically copying them as the office copier does. (In fact, some laser printers can do double duty by serving also as office copiers.)

Despite this, the laser printer is not a must for desktop publishing. Good-quality dot matrix printers, especially the newer 24-pin types, do an excellent job of printing out the copy. (See Figure A–1 for a sample of 9-pin dot matrix printing with desktop publishing software.)

WHAT IS NEEDED TO RUN DESKTOP PUBLISHING PROGRAMS

A first requisite for desktop publishing is a good word processor. Those programs that are designed specifically for desktop publishing usually include a capability for word processing, but few are quite as convenient to use or as efficient as are the standard word processors, and most full-featured desktop publishing programs include provision for importing text composed via a word processor.

The hardware may be either one of the Apple Computer Inc.'s

FIGURE A–1: Newsletter Page Created with Fontasy Software Using a 9-Pin Dot Matrix Printer

PROSOFT
818-765-4444
Fontasy

NEWSLETTERS

On The
PC

Personal Publishing

If you want to produce occasional newsletters on your dot matrix printer, but don't want to spend several hundred dollars on software, FONTASY may be just what you need. It brings affordable desktop publishing to the IBM PC, lets you combine typefaces with illustrations, and even reserve room for photos. The program shows you an on-screen, "what you see is what you get" image. Page size is limited only by memory, not by screen size.

FONTASY accepts text and commands directly from the keyboard and from disk files. The keyboard approach is best for single pages such as signs, overhead foils, certificates, and banners; and is the only approach for drawings. When preparing a lot of text, particularly for fancy page layouts like this one, it's best to use a word processor, save the result to disk in ASCII (non-document) form, and then let FONTASY format the text on-screen.

How Fontasy Works

To create a page of text and illustration with FONTASY, select any available typeface from a full-screen menu, then just start typing. Your words will appear on-screen, in the font you've selected, *as you type them*. You can change fonts at any time, even in mid-line. FONTASY takes care of proportional spacing, kerning (letters can overlap like this: "AVA"), word wrap, and right justification. You can center a line by pressing "ALT-C", and magnify your text as you type or when you print.

You can draw from the keyboard or with a mouse, or select professionally drawn pictures from our optional ART FOLDERS collection. FONTASY helps you make straight lines, boxes, and ovals; then lets you fill-in any enclosed area from a palette of 95 patterns. You can move things around, turn them sideways or upside down, and print them in black/white reversal.

Highlights

* On-screen fonts & drawing
* Multi-column Templates
* Read text from disk and keyboard
* Select and position Clip Art

$69.95

Includes templates, 28 fonts, 60 small pictures

Templates

Composing a multi-page or multi-column newsletter like this one is a three step process. First, use FONTASY to design the "fixed" parts of each page: drawings, the masthead, and any reserved areas. You can also set the margins and columns. Second, write the text with a word processor or other "ASCII" editor (we used SIDEKICK), and save the text to disk (you probably will want to revise your text after you see the early results). Finally, tell FONTASY to format that text onto the template you designed in step one. You can use several templates for different pages, and you can save each page to disk as well as print it out ... automatically.

All this, and more, for only **$69.95.** To order FONTASY, just give us a call:

818 - 765 - 4444

P.S. We prepared this page with FONTASY and printed it on an Epson FX-85.

3

Macintosh™ computers, acclaimed by many as peerless for the purpose, or the IBM XT™, AT™, or equivalent—one of the many XT and AT "clones."

In general, your machine usually requires a minimum of 256K RAM (random access memory) and two floppy disk drives or a hard disk. (Some programs require a hard disk.) A mouse is a useful addition but is usually not required. However, it is usually necessary to have a computer equipped with a graphics card, and in some cases a color graphics card ("CGA," in the jargon) is required. However, in these cases, it is possible to use a mono-graphics card together with a program that simulates the color graphics card and deceives the software! (I have done this successfully.)

Following is a brief listing, description, and—in some cases—comments on word processing and desktop publishing programs.

Word Processors

Today WordPerfect™, product of SSI Software, is reported as by far the best-selling word processor, having elbowed aside the venerable WordStar®, which had ruled the roost and has been the word processing standard for years. Critics say that MicroPro®, creators of WordStar, refused to improve their product and so were finally edged out of their commanding position. On the other hand, the very sophistication of WordPerfect makes it somewhat complex, and some of its critics find that a problem for the average user, despite its popularity and current best-seller status.

Emigrés from the MicroPro staff created a vastly improved WordStar called NewWord, but never reached the big leagues with it somehow. However, MicroPro bought out NewWord and presumably will soon upgrade WordStar accordingly. (MicroPro did create a WordStar 2000 some time ago, but it never succeeded in seriously challenging the original WordStar or any other word processor.)

There are many other word processors available today, most of them quite good and well regarded, in fact, such as Microsoft Word®, product of Microsoft Corporation, PC-Write, product of Quicksoft, and others. The differences are probably more of personal preference than of anything else.

List prices vary considerably for these, but list prices are of little significance because discounting is universal in the computer business.

DESKTOP PUBLISHING PROGRAMS

Those programs that bill themselves as desktop publishing programs tend to stress their application to publishing newsletters in an ordinary office environment and to tend quite heavily to graphics features, including clip art, multiple type fonts, headlining, and page makeup capabilities. Following are brief descriptions of several that are prominent in the field.

Fontasy (ProSoft). Fontasy offers a wide variety of type fonts and graphics—clip art of many kinds of figures and charts, including pie charts. And, like several other programs of similar type, it enables the user to change the shape, position, size, and orientation of figures, including rotating the figures and creating their mirror images. The instruction manual is quite easy to follow, if just a bit too painstaking a primer for those already experienced in such programs. (But the manual does make some provision to skip over the more basic details, if desired.) Figure A–1 illustrates a newsletter page composed with Fontasy, and Figure A–2 illustrates some of the program's capabilities. The text of Figure A–1 reveals that the copy was printed with an Epson FX-85, which is a 9-pin dot matrix printer. This is a good example of the type quality that is available with today's dot matrix printers. If the recent history of technology is any kind of guide, that quality will improve steadily and probably swiftly over the next few years.

FormWorx (Analytx International, Inc.). FormWorx is not exactly a desktop publishing program in the same sense that Fontasy and others are, but it is nevertheless quite useful as an asset in newsletter publishing. It is designed to enable the user to create forms and charts of many kinds, and the program furnishes many basic formats to seed the process (the forms furnished can be easily modified to suit your own needs), with a quite functional manual to guide the user. Samples of the charts and diagrams are illustrated in Figure A–3.

NewsRoomPro™ (Springboard). NewsRoomPro is oriented specifically to newsletter production, as its name suggests rather clearly. It's a rather sophisticated program, also offering a wide variety of type styles and clip art. The program uses many icons, in the style

FIGURE A–2:   Using Word-Processor Copy with Desktop Publishing Software

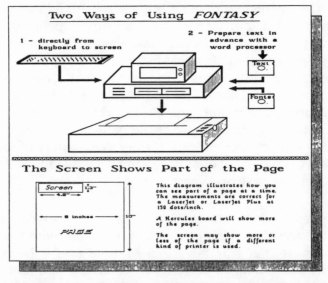

of Apple's Macintosh computers, and is newspaper oriented, with a pictorial opening screen that includes a "Photo Lab" for clip art, a "Banner" option for the creation of headlines, a "Copy Desk"

FIGURE A–3. Computer Generation of Charts and Diagrams by FormWorx

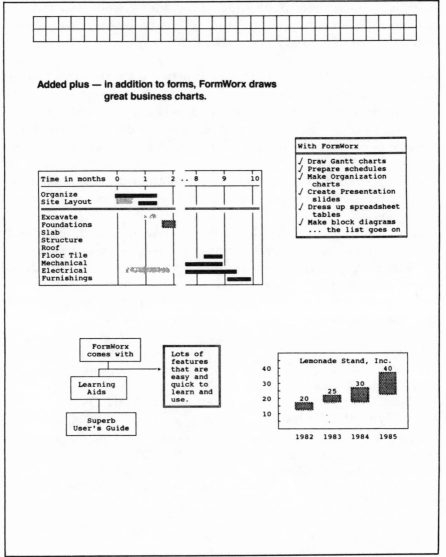

Added plus — in addition to forms, FormWorx draws great business charts.

for layout, "Press" for printing, and "Wire Service" for communicating with remote computers using the same software. The program requires a color graphics card, but will work in monochrome with a monochrome graphics card and a CGA simulator.

ClickArt Personal Publisher (Software Publishing Corporation).
ClickArt Personal Publisher is another desktop publishing program oriented to newsletter publishing. It includes a well-designed and easy to follow instruction manual, with step-by-step instructions and software that has typical menus.

Harvard Presentation Graphics™ (Software Publishing Corporation). Harvard Presentation Graphics, while designed with the development of presentations in mind, is heavily oriented to charts and graphs of various kinds, and includes an unusually large and well-detailed instruction manual that guides the user in the selection and design of charts generally, as well as in the operation of the program. In fact, the manual is itself an education in charting techniques. Like other programs of this type, it uses many menus and icons.

Most software "ages" rather quickly; new, modified, improved, and/or otherwise updated versions of most successful programs are issued frequently. Addresses of the manufacturers of the desktop publishing programs referred to here are furnished below so you can write to them for more information about whatever are the latest versions and/or new programs available.

Fontasy
ProSoft
7248 Bellaire Avenue
Box 560
No. Hollywood, CA 91603

FormWorx
Analytx International, Inc.
1365 Massachusetts Avenue
Arlington, MA 02174

The NewsroomPro
Springboard Software, Inc.
7808 Creekridge Circle
Minneapolis, MN 55435

ClickArt Personal Publisher
Software Publishing Corporation
P.O. Box 7210
1901 Landings Drive
Mountain View, CA 94039

Bibliography and Recommended References

A number of sources for more information and guidance are listed here, along with names and addresses in those cases where the publications are not readily available through bookstores and newsstands but must be ordered directly from the publishers.

BOOKS

ARTH, MARVIN, and HELEN ASHMORE. *The Newsletter Editor's Desk Book*, 3rd ed. Shawnee Mission, KS: Parkway Press, Box 8158, 1984.

BOVE, TONY; CHERYL RHODES; and WES THOMAS. *The Art of Desktop Publishing*. New York: Bantam Books, 1986.

BROHAUGH, WILLIAM, ed. *The Writer's Resource Guide*. Cincinnati, OH: Writer's Digest Books, 1979.

GOSDEN, FREEMAN F., JR. *Direct Marketing Success*. New York: John Wiley & Sons, 1985.

HOLTZ, HERMAN. *Advice, a High Profit Business*. Englewood Cliffs, NJ: Prentice-Hall, 1986.

HOLTZ, HERMAN. *The Direct Marketer's Workbook*. New York: John Wiley & Sons, 1986.

HOLTZ, HERMAN. *Marketing with Seminars and Newsletters*. Westport, CT: Quorum Books, 1986.

HOLTZ, HERMAN. *Word Processing for Business Publications*. New York: McGraw-Hill, 1985.

HUDSON, HOWARD PENN, ed. *Hudson's Newsletter Directory*. P.O. Box 311, Rhinebeck, NY 12572: The Newsletter Clearinghouse.

JONES, GERRE, *Newsletters, Hot Marketing Tool.* P.O. Box 32387, Washington, DC 20007: Glyph Publishing Company, 1982.

KUSWA, WEBSTER. *Sell Copy.* Cincinnati, OH: Writer's Digest Books.

LEWIS, HERSCHELL GORDON. *Direct Mail Copy That Sells!* Englewood Cliffs, NJ: Prentice-Hall, 1984.

MAKUTA, DANIEL J., and WILLIAM F. LAWRENCE. *The Complete Desktop Publisher.* Greensboro, NC: Compute! Publications, Inc., 1986.

SPARKS, HOWARD. *The Amazing Mail Order Business and How to Succeed in It.* New York: Frederick Fell Publishers, 1966.

Style Manual. Washington, DC: U.S. Government Printing Office, 1976.

PERIODICALS

Consulting Intelligence. 2030 Clarendon Blvd., Arlington, VA 22201: American Consultants League.

Consulting Opportunities Journal. J. Stephen Lanning, pub./ed. Gapland, MD 21736.

Desktop Graphics. 6000 N. Forest Park Drive, Peoria, IL 61614: Dynamic Graphics, Inc.

DM News. Stony Brook, NY 11790: DM News.

Pages (fillers, clip art, other editorial material each month). 300 N. State Street, Chicago, IL 60610: Berry Publishing.

Publish! San Francisco, CA: PCW Communications, Inc.

Target Marketing, Philadelphia, PA: North American Publishing Co.

Writer's Digest. Cincinnati, OH: F&W Publications, Inc.

Writer's Market (annual, editors: various). Cincinnati, OH: Writer's Digest Books.

Writer, The. Boston, MA: The Writer, Inc.

Writer's Yearbook (annual). Cincinnati, OH: Writer's Digest Publications.

Glossary

The world of in-office business publications has its own jargon, some of it indigenous to offset publications generally and some of it peculiar to technical manuals, newsletter, and similar publications work. Much of it is also a reflection of desktop computers and word processing equipment and practices. In any case, you will run across these terms, at least occasionally, and will want to know what they refer to. Words in the definitions that are set in italic are themselves defined in this glossary.

address block/box.   Block of white space used for name and address on self-mailer.

annotate.   Practice of placing notes at bottom of page or elsewhere (such as appendix) to explain or elaborate on text passages.

archive.   Storage or backup copy of data.

automatic pagination.   Word processor function of recognizing each new page and placing folio (page number) there without special command.

backup.   "Insurance" copy on separate disk or tape.

baud, baud rate.   In practical terms, rate at which data bits are sent/received in bits per second; used especially with reference to communications via modem and telephone.

bidirectional (printing).   Ability/action of printers to print in both directions.

bird-dog.   To monitor, administer, and generally "stay on top" of all details of publications project.

bleed.   Printing that runs to edge of page and "bleeds off" the page when the edge of the paper is trimmed on the press, usually a solid ink block or illustration; both noun and verb.

block.   Section of text, treated as unit, for word processing functions.

block move. Word processor function of moving entire block of text.

blowup. Photographic enlargement or enlarging process (both noun and verb).

boilerplate. Standard or stock information, which may be pasted up in more than one document, physically or electronically.

boldface. Heavy typeface, available as separate font of most type families.

buffer. Storage device, usually for temporary storage of data to free up computer for other work while printing.

burn. Process of making metal printing plate from negative by exposing plate, through negative, to strong light in "plate burner"; also colloquial for making xerographic copies.

byte. Group of digital bits processed as a group, currently 8 bits, representing one alphanumeric character.

camera-ready. Any materials in final condition and ready to be photographed for plate-making or fitted with other copy as part of master copy, ready for platemaking.

cathode ray tube (CRT). Tube with screen for displaying data of all types with phosphorescent illumination, similar to TV picture tube.

center head. Centered headline or caption.

character. Individual letter, numeral, symbol, or diacritical mark; one byte in word processors.

chip. Functional electronic element consisting of entire circuit or set of circuits etched into tiny sliver or wafer of silicon.

coated paper. Paper for masters, made with coatings such as clay, to make it dense and extra smooth, for sharp, well-defined printing.

cold type. Type set by strike-on (impact) or phototypesetting methods.

color registration. Process of aligning plates to print different colors in correct positions or "registration" with each other.

color separation. Process of preparing camera-ready copy for printing in more than one color by providing separated copy for each color ink.

composite negative. Negative that includes both line and screened material, either spliced or mounted together.

comprehensive. Short form of *comprehensive layout*, a detailed diagram of precisely where each bit of copy and other elements will fit in final mechanical.

contributor. A free-lancer who sells original material to a publication.

copy. Material for publication.

copy fitting. Process of editing copy to fit space.

crop marks. Marks on board bearing mounted photograph to show photographer/platemaker what is to be printed.

cropping. Marking photo or other illustration to show printer which portion is to be printed.

cps. Characters per second, measure of rate at which printer operates.

daisywheel. Printing element used in many letter-quality printers.

database. Bank of related information.

database manager. Computer program used to manage, manipulate, process filed/stored data.

dele. Mark, comment to order deletion.

disk. Metal or plastic disk coated with magnetic oxide and serving as storage medium. See also *floppy*.

dot matrix. Method of printing wherein characters are formed by series of dots.

download. Receive files from another computer via modem and telephone connection.

dropout. Tendency of some copy to fade in photography or platemaking, especially large areas of solid blacks and fine details.

dummy. Mock-up of final product, used for study and evaluation or to guide someone, as in *printer's dummy*.

editor, text editor. Portion of word processor program responsible for entering, correcting, manipulating text.

em, em dash. An em is the width of the capital M of any type font, and an em dash is of the same width. For typewriters and most printers, use a double hyphen for em dash.

en. One half an em.

ENTER/RETURN. Both are used to enter commands and, usually, to start a new paragraph.

file. Set of related records in storage or in work, identified by unique name.

floppy. Colloquial for floppy disk or diskette, a flexible plastic disk, encased in a paper sleeve, 3, 3½, 5¼, or 8 inches in diameter, used to store data on its magnetic coating.

folio. Page number; also report or other brief document.

follow copy. Editorial instruction to reproduce copy exactly as shown, despite apparent misspellings or other errors.

font. Entire set of type characters, including numerals and symbols. Sometimes applied to entire "type family," which includes italic, boldface, small capitals, and special symbols.

foot, footing. Special copy appearing at bottom of page, such as *running foot*, a notice, title, or slogan appearing at foot of each page.

form. Paper form used to facilitate pasteup and layout. Usually represents a single page or two-page spread. Completed form is then camera-ready—mechanical—final copy, ready for platemaking.

format. Design of publication, including type style, layout, other characteristics.

global search (and replace). Refers to ability of word processors to find any/all references/uses of a word or term and, if ordered, to replace that word/term with another.

goldenrod. Yellow paper forms used in print shops for mounting negatives for making metal plates.

graphics. Drawings, other illustrations (although printing is itself one of the graphics arts); in word processing refers to ability of computer systems and programs to generate drawings of many kinds.

gutter. White space between columns of type in two- or three-column copy; (inside margins between pages in single-column copy).

halftone. Photograph or other continuous-tone material converted to dot pattern for printing; also applied to screen used to convert copy to dot or halftone pattern and to resulting negative and plate.

hard copy. Printed copy, as distinct from screen display or "soft copy."

head, heading. Abbreviation for headline as in *sidehead* and *center head*. Also title, notice, slogan appearing at top of page, as in *running head* (when it appears on every page).

headnote. Note appearing at top of page, usually used only with tabular data.

imprinting. Printing over surface already printed or printing in space reserved for purpose during prior printing; see also *overprinting* and *surprinting*.

indicia, mailing. Printed block on envelope, wrapper, or mailing label that carries permit number for bulk mailing and serves as notice of postage paid.

insert. Editorial meaning: copy to be added by insertion in text (done electronically in word processors). In direct mail: items added to basic letter in direct mail package.

justification. Condition of left- and/or right-hand edges of lines in alignment, resulting in absolutely even margins; generally accomplished by adjusting spacing between words, letters, or both. Most word processors can justify automatically. Also called right justification and justified right because left justification is taken for granted.

kilobyte (Kb). 1024 bytes; each byte equals one alphanumeric character; standard page of double-spaced typed copy equals approximately 2Kb or (more commonly) 2K.

layout. Plan for organizing copy and illustrations; actual design sketch or plan for doing so; design itself; can be preliminary (rough layout) or final (comprehensive layout).

line copy. Any copy that does not require halftone screening; usually includes all text, tables, and line drawings, such as graphs, charts, and engineering sketches.

line drawing. Drawing that consists of lines and other black and white contrast, without shades between the two (see also *tone.*)

line negative. Negative of line copy.

logo. Abbreviation for logotype. A distinctive symbol, stylized letter or word, or other unique designation of identity; usually a registered trademark.

makeready. Installation of printing plate and adjustment of press to begin printing; a specific item charged by most printers as a separate item.

makeup. Assembling and preparing all camera-ready material to create the mechanicals from which printing will be done.

mask. Rectangle of black or red paper/plastic pasted on camera-ready copy where photo will appear to create *window* in negative for making composite negative.

masthead. Column of type, in most periodicals, listing ownership and key editorial staff.

mechanical. Complete final page or multipage spread ready for platemaking and printing.

memory. Internal circuits of computer that store information, generally on a temporary basis, referred to as RAM (random access memory).

modem. Term derived from *mo*dulator-*dem*odulator, a device that enables computers to communicate (exchange data) with other computers over telephone lines.

monitor. Usually refers to "soft copy" or "soft display," represented by CRT (cathode ray tube) screen, liquid crystal display, or other such presentation, as distinct from "hard copy" printed output.

nameplate. Headline/title block of newsletter, other periodical, usually at top of front page.

offset. Colloquialism for modern offset printing processes and related items, such as "offset plates," "offset presses," "offset paper," and so on; also refers to undesired transfer of ink from freshly printed surface to another surface, such as the back of another sheet.

on-line. Refers to database/information services available via modem-telephone connection and communication and to intercomputer communication.

overprinting. Printing one character on top of another; printing on top of already printed surface; also called *surprinting; imprinting;* also used to create special characters, such as those used in foreign language fonts.

page display. Word processing term for displaying entire page on screen.

pasteup. Act of pasting up copy; also copy that has been pasted up.

photocomposition. Copy composed by phototypesetting.

photo-direct. Platemaking by xerographic and other devices that create printing plates (usually paper or plastic, rather than metal) without a negative.

pitch. Number of characters and spaces per linear inch—for example, 10 pitch = 10 characters per inch.

pixel. Contraction of *picture element,* and measure of resolution or ability to present detail on computer screen.

plotter. Device for making hard copy graphics from computer output.

printer. Typewriterlike machine for making hard copy printouts of computer data.

printer's dummy. Mock-up of publication to guide printer in making up small publications, such as brochure; for larger publications, a *running sheet* is used.

process color. Color printing of continuous-tone material, such as color photos.

proportional spacing. Allotting horizontal space for each type element according to width of the element.

ragged right. Opposite of right-justified.

RAM. Random access memory.

reduction. Opposite of blowup: reduction in size by photographic means.

registration. Alignment of elements on a page, especially of pages that must go through the press more than once for successive printings.

registration marks. Guides on copy to help printer in aligning plates for proper match of printed material.

roman, roman types. Whole class of typefaces, with serifs and other characteristics.

rough. Refers to preliminary—rough—layout and, also, to preliminary sketch.

rub-downs, rub-down type. Colloquialisms for decalcomania type.

runaround. Type/text set to permit space, usually of irregular shape or different than normal column width, for tables or illustrations.

running foot. See *foot.*

running head. See *head.*

running sheet. Form instructing printer how to print the publication.

sans serif. Without serifs, as in gothic types.

screened negative. Negative of photo made through screen; also referred to as halftone negative.

search and replace. Same as *global search (and replace).*

self-mailer. Mailing piece—brochure, newsletter, or other—that has address box on outside and does not require envelope or wrapper to be mailed.

sidehead. Headline that begins flush left.

spelling checker. Program that includes dictionary and reviews words for spelling; many are designed to permit additions by user.

spooler. Buffer device, used to store information temporarily to permit computer to do other work while printer is operating; see also *buffer.*

stet. Editorial direction to "let it stand" as it was originally (before editorial change).

strip. Splicing line and halftone negatives together to form composite negative.

sulphite bond. Paper made of wood pulp, but resembling rag bond paper.

surprinting. Printing over already printed surface; *overprinting; imprinting.*

T/C. Common abbreviation for table of contents.

tint block. Technique of printing block of light color, usually by "screening back," and overprinting in other color.

tone. Material used by illustrators to create special effects, such as shading, somewhat resembling effects of screening back.

upload. Opposite of download; to send file to another computer via modem and telephone connection.

window. Transparent area in negative created by using *mask* in camera-ready copy, so that *composite negative* can be made up with splicing negatives.

Sources of Support Services

Services to support you in your publishing venture are abundantly available. You can get support in both the publishing of your newsletter—editorial and production services, that is—and in the distribution—marketing—of the newsletter and any ancillary products you decide to offer your subscribers and clients. One of the first kinds of support you should be aware of is the Newsletter Association.

THE NEWSLETTER ASSOCIATION

The Newsletter Association was organized a relatively few years ago with its headquarters in Washington, DC, a not unreasonable choice considering how many newsletters originate there. It is, of course, an association of newsletter publishers, and that association holds meetings and annual conferences where you can meet other newsletter publishers, many of them "old timers" and experts in the field. Many association members are vendors of supplies and services you need also, and meeting them in the environment of the association is a great asset. You can gather up a great deal of valuable information and relevant materials, too, at the meetings and conferences.

Typically, such subjects as the following are covered at meetings and conferences:

Financing operations.   Using PR to sell newsletters.
Strategic planning   Information sources.
Electronic publishing.   Alternative marketing methods.
Increasing renewals.·   Direct mail methods.
Postal rates.   Marketing strategies.

The association offers a variety of helpful instruction manuals and holds seminars to help members to greater success. For more detailed information—a thick, direct mail package, in fact—write the headquarters office directly:

The Newsletter Association
The Colorado Building, Suite 700
1341 G Street, N.W.
Washington, DC 20005
(202) 347-5220

MAILING LIST SOURCES

There are a great many list brokers. They are to be found throughout the United States, although it is not necessary to be in proximity, for they deal largely by mail, naturally enough. Following is a list, not a complete one by any means, but representative of list managers and brokers who are well known and well established. Most will supply you literature and catalogs on request, explaining in detail what they have available.

American List Counsel, Inc.
88 Orchard Road
Princeton, NJ 08540
(201) 874-4300
(800) 526-3973

Association for Computing
  Machinery
11 West 42nd Street
New York, NY 10036
(212) 869-7440

Boardroom Lists
330 West 42nd Street
New York, NY 10036
(212) 239-9000

Cahners Direct Marketing Service
1350 East Touhy Avenue
Des Plaines, IL 60018
(312) 635-8800

Compilers Plus
2 Penn Place
Pelham Manor, NY 10803
(914) 738-1520
(800) 431-2914

Dependable List Management
33 Irving Place, NY 10003
(212) 677-6760
1825 K Street, N.W.
Washington, DC 20006
(202) 452-1092

Direct Media List Management
Group, Inc.
70 Riverdale Avenue
Greenwich, CT 06830
(203) 531-1091

D-J Associates
Box 2048
445 Main Street
Ridgefield, CT 06877
(203) 431-0452

Ed Burnett Consultants, Inc.
2 Park Avenue
New York, NY 10016
(212) 679-0630
(800) 223-7777

Hayden Direct Marketing Services
10 Mulholland Drive
Hasbrouck Heights, NJ 07604
(201) 393-6384

ICO List Rental Services
9000 Keystone Crossing
P.O. Box 40946
Indianapolis, IN 46240
(317) 844-7461

The Kleid Company, Inc.
200 Park Avenue
New York, NY 10166
(212) 599-4140

List Services Corporation
890 Ethan Allen Hwy
P.O. Box 2014
Ridgefield, CT 06877
(203) 436-0327

Phillips List Management
7315 Wisconsin Avenue, Suite
1200N
Bethesda, MD 20814
(301) 986-0666

PCS Mailing List Company
125 Main Street
Peabody, MA 01960
(617) 532-1600

Qualified Lists Corp.
135 Bedford Road
Armonk, NY 10504
(212) 409-6200
(914) 273-6700

Roman Managed Lists, Inc.
101 West 31st Street
New York, NY 10001
(212) 695-3838
(800) 223-2195

Steve Millard, Inc.
Spring Hill Road
Peterborough, NH 03458
(603) 924-9421

Woodruff-Stevens & Associates,
Inc.
345 Park Avenue South
New York, NY 10010
(212) 685-4600

ADVERTISING SERVICES AND MAILERS

Among the many support services are consultants and specialists
of many kinds—individuals and organizations who will write copy,
plan campaigns, mail your literature on a custom basis or via one

of the several piggyback mailing arrangements explained earlier, and otherwise serve your needs. Following is a small representative listing, with notations of their principal, but not necessarily only, services offered.

DialAmerica Marketing, Inc.
125 Galway Place
Teaneck, NJ 07666
(201) 837-7800
Telemarketing

Fala Direct Marketing, Inc.
70 Marcus Drive
Melville, NY 11747
(516) 694-1919
Mailing, fulfillment, printing, data
  processing, telemarketing

Hahn, Crane, Inc., Advertising
114 West Illinois
Chicago, IL 60610
(312) 787-8435
Advertising, consulting

Hughes Communications, Inc.
211 West State Street
P.O. Box 197
Rockford, IL 61105
(815) 963-7771
(800) 435-2937
Card deck mailings

Mar-Tel Communications, Inc.
375 S. Washington Avenue
Bergen, NJ 07621
(201) 385-7171
Telemarketing

Progressive Marketing Services
3649 W. 183rd Street
Hazel Crest, IL 60429
(312) 957-5200
Telemarketing

Solar Press
5 South 550 Frontenac
Naperville, IL 60566
(312) 357-0100
Card deck mailings

Tele America, Inc.
1955 Raymond Drive, Suite 112
Northbrook, IL 60062
(312) 480-1560
Telemarketing

WorldBook Telemarketing
799 Roosevelt Road, #3
Glen Ellyn, IL 60137
(312) 858-4703

INFORMATION SOURCES AND SERVICES

The popularity of the desktop computer has inspired the rise of many public databases, services available to anyone with a computer, a modem, and a telephone. Again, the complete list is too long for inclusion here, but the following listing is a representative sampling of a number of the most prominent and most useful such services, along with notations of·the principal kinds of information each offers.

ADP Network Services, Inc.
175 Jackson Plaza
Ann Arbor, MI 48106
(313) 769-6800

Business information—forecasts and projections.

Boeing Computer Services, Inc.
7990 Gallows Court
Vienna, VA 22180
(703) 827-4603

Economic and financial data (securities/stock-market).

Bolt Beranek and Newman, Inc.
50 Moulton Street
Cambridge, MA 02238
(617) 497-3505

Timesharing, electronic mail, data/text processing.

Brodart Co.
500 Arch Street
Williamsport, PA 17705
(800) 233-8467
(800) 692-6211 (in PA)

Database, library support services. References over 1 million monographs. Book orders accepted on-line.

Broker Services, Inc.
8745 E. Orchard Rd., #518
Englewood, CO 80111
(303) 779-8930

Over 100 stock-analysis/investment programs.

BRS/Bibliographic Retrieval
    Services & BRS After Dark
1200 Route 7
Latham, NY 12110
(518) 783-1161
(800) 833-4707

Over 80 databases in medicine, education, engineering, science business, finance.

BRS/Executive Information
    Service
John Wiley & Sons, Inc.
One Wiley Drive
Somerset, NJ 08873
(201) 469-4400

Summaries of recent major business articles from 600 periodicals; abstracts of other business articles/information.

Chase Econometrics/Interactive
    Data
486 Totten Pond Road
Waltham, MA 02154
(617) 890-1234

Historical data and forecasts, all countries, all U.S. counties on labor, energy, savings, insurance, related topics.

Chemical Abstracts Service
2540 Olentangy River Road
POB 3012
Columbus, OH 43210
(614) 421-3600

On-line search service; accesses Registry File of structural information of over 6 million substances, related data.

Citishare Corporation
850 Third Avenue
New York, NY 10043
(212) 572-10043
(212) 572-9600

Computer support, economic/financial/securities databases, stock quotations, other financial data and services.

Commodity Information Services
327 S. LaSalle, Suite 800
Chicago, IL 60604
(312) 922-3661

Financial, agricultural, other futures, updated daily, library of programs for analysis, trading models.

CompuServe
5000 Arlington Centre Blvd.
Columbus, OH 43220
(614) 457-8600
(800) 848-8990

Data and various services for the general consumer—news, stock market reports, schedules, banking and travel services, electronic mail, games, business news, other data services.

The Computer Company
POB 6987
1905 Westmoreland Street
Richmond, VA 23230
(804) 358-2171

Timesharing, access to various business databases in banking, energy, and transportation industries.

Computer Directions Advisors, Inc.
11501 Georgia Avenue
Silver Spring, MD 20902
(301) 942-1700

Profiles of 6,000-plus public companies, updated daily as filed with SEC; covers institutions, other organizations.

Comshare, Inc.
3001 S. State Street
Ann Arbor, MI 48104
(313) 994-4800

Decision support systems for financial planning, marketing, personnel applications. Also demographic data.

Connexions
55 Wheeler Street
Cambridge, MA 02138
(617) 938-9307

Employment positions on-line; on-line résumé services; electronic mail.

Control Data Corp.
Business Information Services
500 West Putnam Avenue
POB 7100
Greenwich, CT 06836
(203) 622-2000

Marketing, financial, other business databases on variety of business topics; profiles of companies, industries, consumers, markets.

Cornell Computer Services
G-02 Uris Hall
Ithaca, NY 14853
(607) 256-4981

Database featuring 1,000 time series on various economic factors, including car sales, consumer buying and forecasts, financial indicators, and help-wanted advertising.

Customer Service Bureau
Box 36
Riverton, WY 82501
(800) 446-6255
(800) 442-0982 (in WY)

A network that offers subscribers gateways (access) to a variety of other networks and databases.

Data Resources, Inc.
1750 K Street, 9th floor
Washington, DC 20006
(202) 862-3700

Business and investment data, data on various companies, business patterns, and financial information.

Delphi
3 Blackstone Street
Cambridge, MA 02139
(617) 491-3393
(800) 544-4005

Databases on travel, finances, stock quotes, investments, commodities, and securities. Also on-line brokerage games, conferencing services, buying and selling via on-line connection.

Dialog Information Services, Inc.
3460 Hillview Avenue
Palo Alto, CA 94304
(800) 227-1927
(415) 858-3785

Contains hundreds of databases, including CBD On-line, business, advertising, economics, politics, government, medicine, other topics.

Dow Jones News/Retrieval
Service
POB 300
Princeton, NJ 08540
(800) 257-5114

Twenty-seven databases business/economic and financial/investment services.

Dun & Bradstreet Corporation
299 Park Avenue
New York, NY 10171
(212) 593-6800

Timesharing and such business services/information as D&B is already well known for.

General Electric Information
Services Co.
401 N. Washington Street
Rockville, MD 20850
(301) 340-4000

Teleprocessing and data processing services, access in 700 cities and 20 countries, hundreds of software programs available.

GTE Telenet
8229 Boone Blvd.
Vienna, VA 22180
1 (800) TELENET

Electronic mail, intercomputer communications/network service, medical, pharmaceutical, clinical practice information; stock quotes.

GML Information Services
594 Marrett Road
Lexington, MA 02173
(617) 861-0515

Technical databases on computers and related technologies.

InnerLine
95 W. Algonquin Road
Arlington Heights, IL 60005
(800) 323-1321

News and other information for bankers: banking news, money market funds, related databases.

Interactive Market Systems, Inc.
19 West 44th Street
New York, NY 10036
(212) 869-8810
(800) 223-7942

Access to media and marketing related services, timesharing services, legal-research services.

ITT Dialcom, Inc.
1109 Spring Street
Silver Spring, MD 20910
(301) 588-1572

Databases for Fortune 100 companies, government agencies, other large organizations; electronic mail, airlines schedules, other.

Mead Data Central
POB 933
Dayton, OH 45401
(513) 865-6800

LEXIS for legal research; LEXPAT for patent information; NEXIS for general news service.

NewsNet
945 Haverford Road
Bryn Mawr, PA 19010
(215) 527-8030 (in PA)
(800) 345-1301

Business information utility distributing variety of on-line business newsletters and wire services and providing search services.

The Source
1616 Anderson Road
McLean, VA 22102
(800) 336-3366

One of the, if not the, oldest on-line database service, for general consumers: news; schedules, TV listings, stock quotes, and so on.

TRW Information Services, Div.
Business Credit Services and
   Credit Data Service
500 City Parkway West, Suite 200
Orange, CA 92668
(714) 937-2000

Provides both business and individual consumer credit as names reveal, plus related business information.

United Communications Group
8701 Georgia Avenue, Suite 800
Silver Spring, MD 20910
(301) 589-9975

CBD On-Line (government contract bids and proposals), other general data.

Westlaw
West Publishing Co.
50 West Kellogg Blvd.
POB 43526
St. Paul, MN 55164
(800) 328-9352

Legal research and related information, plus news and index coverage of several financial and general newspapers.

Starter Ideas

EVERY EDITOR GOES DRY NOW AND THEN AND NEEDS A BOOST

In newsletter publication, as in the newspaper business, it is either feast or famine most months: One month your biggest problem is what to choose from among a superabundance of good material, then in another month you are scratching desperately for something worthy. It's a common enough problem, and experienced editors soon learn that they can't afford to sit idly and wait for stories to come to them; they have to go out and dig up the stories. Often as not, the problem is simply one of going stale—being out of ideas for stories as a result of fatigue or for any of many possible reasons. But "going out after stories" does not necessarily mean physically leaving your snug and dry office to plod the streets; even telephone calls can start things going, once your adrenaline is stirred up a bit. What you really need is an idea or two. (Or perhaps three or four!)

That is what this section is all about: getting that idea or two to get you stirred up and chasing after the stories that are always out there waiting for you. What follows is a list of starter ideas for you to call on when the well appears to have run dry. Some of them pulled me out of the hole more than once. (Of course, some of these may not fit well into your newsletter, but most of them will start your gray cells stirring if you concentrate on them.)

News Items. Mergers, divestitures, new starts, joint ventures, buy-outs. Changes in key personnel anywhere in your industry. Reviews of recent conventions and conferences. News/notices of upcoming major events such as seminars, conventions, conferences, meetings. New associations formed. Other association news. New legislation. Awards dinners. Business club affairs. Local people honored.

Useful Ideas.   Tax tips, keeping healthy, cutting costs, marketing ideas, reducing stress, increasing profit margins, smart new investments, adding profit centers. New products. New trends in the industry. New ideas from government sources.

Columns.   Editorials by publisher, guest editorials, answers to readers' queries, solving common problems, best buys, personnel news. Letters from readers. Projections: What does the future appear to promise us? How does this year compare with last year?

Interviews.   Talk with prominent figure in industry on his or her retirement. Ask personnel managers what companies are looking for today in new hires, what are major recruitment problems, hardest jobs to fill; do telephone surveys of marketing directors, ask key questions.

History.   What are this month's milestones, anniversaries of important events? What companies became or will become 100 years old this year? Fifty years old? How did they start? Which had the most modest beginning? Which has had the greatest growth? Important anniversaries of your community. (How old is your town, for example? Who is the oldest resident? What historical events— e.g., Civil War battles, great public works projects, pioneering breakthroughs—are connected with your community?)

Novelty Items.   Who/where is oldest individual in industry still working actively? Which company is in entirely different business than the one it started in; why and how is that? What about special gimmicks, such as puzzles and contests: Isn't it time to think about these?

Marketing.   Interviews with clients, what are they looking for in a consultant? What are their pet peeves? What do they consider their outstanding good and bad experiences with consultants or vendors? What kind of message would they like to send consultants and vendors?

Book Reviews. What was/is outstanding (most useful) book (relevant to your field) of year? Which the worst (least useful)? Check with others: what do they think? What books do you/others recommend? Are any of the new books by local authors? Can you interview them? Have them do a guest column or guest editorial?

Computers. How have they affected your industry? Horror stories? Good and bad experiences? Reviews of hardware and software. Best and worst (most and least useful) programs. Tips on using computers effectively. Case histories. Ideas for using personal computers to improve things. Interviews with local computer professionals. (Guest columns, editorials by the local experts?)

Tech Talk. Technical developments, insights, explanations, how it works, why it works, what's good about it, what's bad about it, what's new, R&D news, new technologies developing, breakthroughs, history of new products.

Quality Control. New ideas, new methods for QC. New literature about QC. Local QC experts: interviews with; public statements of; awards. Local QC experts? If so, guest columns? Interviews? Guest editorials?

Competitors. What are the other fellows doing? Do they have a few good ideas? Let's look at their latest marketing ploys: What are they offering customers? Are there any new trends in the industry? Different marketing methods? New products? New services?

Seasonal. What's the special event this month? Lincoln's birthday? Washington's birthday? Memorial Day? First day of summer? Christmas? Fourth of July? Veteran's Day? Labor Day? Halloween? There is not a month that does not have some holiday or special day of some sort, and every one merits a special piece covering it.

INDEX